NEW HORIZONS IN CRIMINOLOGY

TRANSNATIONAL CRIMINOLOGY

Trafficking and Global Criminal Markets

Simon Mackenzie

New Horizons in Criminology series

Series editor: **Andrew Millie**,
Edge Hill University, UK

New Horizons in Criminology series provides concise, authoritative texts which reflect cutting-edge thought and theoretical development with an international scope. Written by leading authors in their fields, the series has become essential reading for all academics and students interested in where criminology is heading.

Forthcoming in the series:

A Criminology of Narrative Fiction
Rafe McGregor, January 2021

Visual Criminology
Bill McClanahan, June 2021

Out now in the series:

Wildlife Criminology
Angus Nurse and **Tanya Wyatt**, April 2020

Imaginative Criminology
Of Spaces Past, Present and Future
Maggie O'Neill and **Lizzie Seal**, July 2019

A Criminology of War?
Ross McGarry and **Sandra Walklate**, July 2019

A Criminology of Policing and Security Frontiers
Randy Lippert and **Kevin Walby**, February 2019

Find out more at

bristoluniversitypress.co.uk/new-horizons-in-criminology

For s, for ever s.
And for a, l, h:

A lookout high above lakes held arrested
lonesome hearts and lost hopes.
All low heat and leaking hours.
Altered lately, hallowed and lifted heavenward.
A life healed, a life halved.
At last here all longing has arrived, lowered heads, arrhythmic leaps.
Hallways alive, luminous, happy. A loud house.
Always love, health and laughter.
Home.

First published in Great Britain in 2022 by

Bristol University Press
University of Bristol
1-9 Old Park Hill
Bristol
BS2 8BB
UK
t: +44 (0)117 954 5940
e: bup-info@bristol.ac.uk

Details of international sales and distribution partners are available at bristoluniversitypress.co.uk

British Library Cataloguing in Publication Data
A catalogue record for this book is available from the British Library

ISBN 978-1-5292-0378-3 hardcover
ISBN 978-1-5292-0380-6 paperback
ISBN 978-1-5292-0384-4 ePub
ISBN 978-1-5292-0385-1 ePdf

Cover design: Dave Worth
Front cover image: shutterstock_378057229

Bristol University Press uses environmentally responsible print partners.

Printed in Great Britain by CMP, Poole

All the wise guys have rackets, and they see little difference between their rackets and the rackets of those who look down on them

(Haller 1990: 229)

Nothing personal, it's just business

(attributed to Otto 'Abbadabba' Berman, mob accountant)

Contents

Preface by Professor Andrew Millie ix

1 Introduction: Trafficking as Transnational Crime 1

2 Drug Trafficking 21

3 Human Trafficking 37

4 Wildlife Trafficking 55

5 Diamond Trafficking 71

6 Arms Trafficking 89

7 Antiquities Trafficking 105

8 Conclusion: A Social Theory of Transnational Criminal Markets 121

References 137

Index 165

NEW HORIZONS IN CRIMINOLOGY

Series editor: Professor Andrew Millie, Department of Law and Criminology, Edge Hill University, UK

Preface

Simon Mackenzie is an expert on global trafficking. *Transnational Criminology* is the eleventh title in the *New Horizons in Criminology* book series. All books are high quality and authoritative texts which reflect cutting edge thought and theoretical development in criminology, have an international scope and are also accessible and concise. Simon's knowledge of the various overlapping and discrete forms and structures of transnational crime is unparalleled. And his writing takes the reader with him, explaining ideas and developments with clarity before going deeper into the subject. Simon's research focus in previous books has been the global trafficking of antiquities with titles including *Trafficking Culture* (2019), *Criminology and Archaeology* (2009), and the award-winning *Going, Going, Gone* (2005). The current book builds on this earlier work in a natural progression, broadening out to illicit transnational trade in other areas such as drugs, wildlife, and human trafficking.

A lot of criminology is naturally focused within national boundaries limited by a country's legislation, policy and criminal justice practices. Yet criminal activities cross borders. It is a cliché to say that we are all affected by globalization; but behind the cliché is a truth that expands opportunities for criminal exploitation. This is reflected in the activities of organized crime groups, white-collar criminals and the broader field of illicit trade. In the introduction to this book Simon sets out the intellectual framework required to understand such 'international trafficking and global criminal markets'. A key argument made in the book is that the divide between licit and illicit trade is not always distinct and, alongside this, that 'illegal business dances to very much the same tune as legal business, using similar methods, having similar aims, and achieving similar ends'. As the text goes on to illustrate, trafficking is big business and traffickers adopt 'the norms and values of globalized neoliberal capitalist markets: profit and power first, ask questions later'. Those involved in trafficking and global criminal markets do not always *feel* their acts are straightforwardly illegal or wrong; the experience of participation in trafficking is more complex than that. In some cases that is because legal and illegal markets are so closely intertwined. In others it is because in focusing on the business routines of commodification and trade the harm caused by this type of criminal behaviour can be 'compartmentalized', and ignored.

The book includes separate chapters on the trafficking of drugs, humans, wildlife, diamonds, arms and antiquities. Each chapter explores the nature, extent and structures of the trafficking, along with its international regulation and control. And each type of trafficking is viewed as a form of business or enterprise. These chapters can be read as standalone contributions to the literature; however, there is greater benefit in reading the book as a whole, which is brought together in a concluding chapter where Simon proposes a social theory of transnational criminal markets.

There are many highlights to this book. It recognizes that traffickers can act as both legitimate and illegitimate business people, and that in the context of global capitalism, transnational crime is, for some, simply another business opportunity. As Simon has put it, 'criminal trafficking is just another form of morally indifferent capitalism'. Laws of supply and demand are generative, business risks are calculated, and things (or people) are constructed as commodities to be transported to a market destination and sold for maximum gain.

The book is novel in that it considers a broad range of trafficking enterprises. It is essential reading and likely to become the go-to book for criminologists and others interested in transnational criminality and the business of crime. It complements other titles in the New Horizons in Criminology series, especially *Wildlife Criminology* by Angus Nurse and Tanya Wyatt (2020). I am delighted to see *Transnational Criminology* come to fruition. It is a vitally important text that merits a wide readership.

References

Mackenzie, S. (2005) *Going, Going, Gone: Regulating the Market in Illicit Antiquities*, Leicester: Institute of Art & Law.

Mackenzie, S., Brodie, N., Yates, D. and Tsirogiannis, C. (2019) *Trafficking Culture: New Directions in Researching the Global Market in Illicit Antiquities*, Abingdon: Routledge.

Mackenzie, S. and Green, P. (eds) (2009) *Criminology and Archaeology: Studies in Looted Antiquities*, Oxford: Hart.

Nurse, A. and Wyatt, T. (2020) *Wildlife Criminology*, Bristol: Bristol University Press.

1

Introduction: Trafficking as Transnational Crime

Taking the illicit economy out of the shadows

Transnational crime crosses borders and is a term that has come to be applied to a variety of crimes that affect more than one country (Marmo and Chazal 2016; Natarajan 2019c). Transnational crime can be thought of as distinct from international crime, a term that has developed into an academic and legal reference to genocide, war crimes and other crimes against humanity that offend the basic common normative understanding of peace, security and wellbeing in the world order (Reichel and Albanese 2016). Neither is transnational crime a term synonymous with global crime, since global crime has come to mean either looking at crime in different places around the world, often comparatively (Galeotti 2005; Roth 2017), or a general focus on globalization as the context for developments in crime and justice (Findlay 2003; Aas 2007; Friedrichs 2007).

Some writers on transnational crime, in keeping with the United Nations discourse (United Nations 2000; UNODC 2010), address transnational *organized* crime (Albanese 2015; Albanese and Reichel 2014). However, in addition to the globalization of the interests and activities of organized crime groups, which we might call the 'narrow' interpretation of transnational organized crime, quite a lot of networked forms of criminal activity across state borders might reasonably be considered to be organized crime even though they may not fit a traditional understanding of that term (Edwards and Gill 2003; Beare 2003). This gives a 'wider' interpretation of the idea of transnational organized crime. In this wider context, which includes and goes beyond the study of the international reach of organized crime in the narrow sense, my take on transnational criminology approaches the topic from the perspective of illicit trade. My approach to transnational crime and transnational criminology is to seek to understand international trafficking and global criminal markets.

Market-oriented crimes 'constitute the great majority of all serious crimes in advanced capitalist societies, [and] are committed in response to consumer demands for the goods or services criminals provide' (Rosenfeld and Messner 2013: 104). Globalization has increased the speed and amount of international travel and communication and as such brought people around the world 'closer together' in a process that has been called time–space distanciation (Giddens 1990). Using these communication and transport networks, in some cases new, in others simply rapidly expanded, business has globalized. And so has illegal business. The process of globalization described in the political, social and economic textbooks on the subject, and treated so often in these as an expansion and step-change in legal business, has in fact been the globalization of everything – including illegal business. The major argument running throughout this book is that illegal business dances to very much the same tune as legal business, using similar methods, having similar aims and achieving similar ends. So, of course, the opportunity structures of a world getting smaller have been exploited by illegal enterprises just as much as by legal ones.

It has not infrequently been pointed out that illegal transnational commerce is not a new phenomenon. Piracy and smuggling have a long history. Now, however, trafficking can happen more quickly than ever before, can reach more end consumers and consists of opportunities that can be exploited by a greater number of people. Crime control has also globalized, but not to the extent that international commerce has, so the somewhat anachronistic nation state-based structures of crime control are not best placed to engage with crime that by definition crosses jurisdictions. International organizations, treaties and other arrangements go some way towards mitigating this problem, but as we will see the fundamental contemporary challenge of trafficking is the way that the globalization of legal international trade has been of such a scale that it allows a variety of globalized illegal trades to interlace with it.

Neoliberalism incorporates at least two basic ideas: first, that people act as rational maximizers, pursuing self-interest as cost–benefit calculating profit-seekers, and second, that the conceptual field in which this self-interest is realized is the market (Harvey 2005). Neoliberal globalization has been based on a platform of free market ideology that includes fundamental commitments to laissez-faire policies, so the state recedes as privatization of business increases and deregulation is normalized in the face of an attitude to government controls that sees them as barriers to trade. Spaces open up around the world which in multi-jurisdictional trade flows exist 'between the laws' (Michalowski and Kramer 1987), fully captured by the legal regulatory and control apparatus of neither the countries where the harm occurs nor the countries where the 'harm agents' (Presser 2013) are based. Jurisdictions where banking secrecy is high present opportunities for legal and illegal globalized business actors to hide their wealth, from taxes on the one hand and from law enforcement on the other. As regulation is portrayed by business lobbies and conservative politicians as inimical to trade, the international barriers to commercial exchange of goods are synchronized to facilitate rather than unduly impede trade flows, as much as possible.

Globalization, therefore, signifies an intensification of the processes which facilitate the geographical expansion of businesses: 'the formation of networks of interdependencies forging a new world-system, the corrosion of borders and the increasing "placelessness" of the economy' (Ruggiero 2009: 118). The geographical base of a multinational conventional business organization is now largely irrelevant to its global reach and influence, and companies can now choose to establish their headquarters in jurisdictions congenial to their overall profitability, such as US corporations like Apple being headquartered in Ireland despite doing comparatively little business there. Comparably, the influence of Colombian drug cartels, Ukrainian arms traffickers, Bangkok art dealers or Asian wildlife traffickers, for just a few examples, is hardly geographically constrained now other than through the choices these actors may make in identifying places where the weakness or corruptibility of state agents provides the conducive environment to the building of illegal enterprise. The globalization of criminal enterprise has in some cases been seen as facilitated directly by the globalization of legitimate enterprise: 'for example, as Japan's large corporations globalized their business, the criminals moved with them, extorting from the corporations' foreign affiliates' (Shelley 2019: 226; Kaplan and Dubro 2003).

Globalization of trade has benefitted from, and in turn supported the growth of, technical and infrastructural developments such as the containerization of commodity shipment and improved transport links especially in developing countries. Such developments have lowered the cost and the time for international transit of export commodities to global markets and allowed trade to become practically more anonymous through the use of shipping agents and corporate trading entities that can obscure the people behind shipments. The massive increase in the volume of financial flows around the world has made it easier to launder criminal proceeds, hiding these suspicious transactions like needles in the electronic haystack of world financial systems.

So-called informal economies occur outside the purview of the state: they are defined as economic activities that avoid state regulation

(Portes et al 1989). They are usually local, untaxed, responses to a need to earn a living on the one hand and on the other a consumer need for goods and services which the state is not providing. Illicit economies often overlap with informal economies but the distinction is in the criminal nature of the goods being traded. The markets examined in this book are illicit insofar as they deal in prohibited goods, or in prohibited ways, and they are at points informal while at other points their flows form part of the formal global economy. The distinction might perhaps best be constructed in the observation that informal economies are not necessarily harmful, whereas all of the global criminal markets discussed in this book are.

It has been observed that informal economies do not feel illegal to those participating in them. They become a normalized part of daily economic life for those who trade in them and are considered a grey area by participants 'in actual practice as everyday people not only attempt to make a living, but strive to justify and legitimate that living to themselves and others' (Galemba 2008: 21). An illustration of living with this kind of 'grey area' approach to informal economies is given by Galemba, where she quotes a resident of the clandestine passage on the Mexico–Guatemala border in her ethnographic study. The resident says: 'The flow of corn (over the border) is not really *legal* legal. But it isn't really illegal either… It is a bit legal, a bit illegal' (Galemba 2008: 19). The kinds of prohibited goods and services we address in this book are considerably less benign than corn, but a similar attitude is seen among market participants: discursive work to blur the moral and legal binary distinctions (good/bad; legal/illegal) creating a greying of the social meaning of these illegal markets.

It has often been argued that in making sense of the relationship between the informal/formal and the illegal/legal, and perhaps going some way to breaking down those binaries in the process, we should think about the metaphor of 'shadow' economies. The 'shadow' in question is the metaphorical silhouette cast by neoliberal globalization. This shadow is sometimes referred to as the 'dark side' of globalization, or its 'underbelly', or in the literature of organized crime scholars, the 'underworld' (Ruggiero 2009). As with some other researchers, my interpretation of these so-called shadow economies largely rejects the upperworld–underworld version of events (Edwards and Gill 2002; Ruggiero 2001), which conjures images of the gleaming edifice of clean neoliberal trade, a towering monolith of progressive enlightenment and industry. This skyscraper of legitimate endeavour and harmless profit-generation casts a shadow in which, outside the building on the streets, the disenfranchised and the left-behind go about their informal and sometimes illegal business. Surely not.

A better metaphor is the story of neoliberal globalization as business that is done in shades of grey: a story in which we are all players, tied together through worldwide systems of licit and illicit consumption and supply. This late modern juggernaut (Giddens 1990) comes with a series of implicitly understood instructions on how the world *really* works that we internalize and act upon. This is not, therefore, a world of legal business outside of which exists a shadow economy; this is a global business world that accommodates upright and shadow entrepreneurs alike.

If the legal/illegal is a political distinction, and the licit/illicit a social one (van Schendel and Abraham 2005), so that, for example, some formally prohibited (illegal) conduct can be socially normative and accepted (licit) (Beckert and Wehinger 2013; Beckert and Dewey 2017), then both of these political and social meanings are situated in a larger discourse comprised of narratives that allow these meanings to exist. We shall explore some aspects of those meta-narratives in this book, to consider how thinking of crime as business can resolve some of the persistent tensions that exist at present in the literature around trafficking and global criminal markets.

Globalization has increased the polarities in wealth between rich and poor, or 'developing', countries, and looking within countries we can see that it has also assisted some sectors of society internal to both rich and poor countries to accumulate wealth hugely disproportionate to, and at the expense of, poorer citizens. So the wealth and income inequality divide is growing both on a global level (that is, between countries) and on a national level (that is, within countries). Shelley considers that this context generates a pattern she thinks is observable in global illicit trade:

> What all these transnational crimes have in common is that they are conducted primarily by actors based in developing countries who cannot compete in the legitimate economies of the world, which are dominated by multinational corporations based in the most affluent countries. Therefore, the criminals have exploited and developed the demand for illicit commodities such as drugs, people, arms, and endangered species. (Shelley 2019: 224)

This is only to focus on the supply end of the chain of international criminal trade, though. The demand end of many of these transnational criminal markets reaches into affluent world trade centres and hotspots of global consumption. So while it is certainly true that people exploit the resources they have at their disposal, this is only part of the story of trafficking as a transnational crime. In market countries for trafficked goods, 'illicit business conducted by "aliens" needs a receptive environment, along with a range of indigenous partners and agents, in the countries in which it operates' (Ruggiero 2009: 118). While Ruggiero is talking in terms that refer to the 'alien conspiracy' theory of organized crime – the partial view of crime markets that has historically considered organized illegal enterprise not to be a home-grown problem in countries such as the US but to be imported with immigration by overseas mafias – the point stands for global illicit commerce generally. Global illicit market enterprise is a systemic economy that connects actors in both rich and poor countries, developed and driven not exclusively by one side of a 'supply' or 'demand' equation but both.

The spectrum of enterprise

'Americans have traditionally treated white-collar crime and organized crime as if they were two independent phenomena', observed Dwight Smith Jr (1980: 358), but they are not. In his 'spectrum-based theory of enterprise', he suggested a move away from the dichotomy of an organized crime problem explained by an alien conspiracy theory and a white-collar crime problem explained by a differential association theory. Among the assumptions underpinning the exclusion of organized crime activity from the study of the infractions of business and therefore precluding the development of a more general category of enterprise crimes were that 'business and crime are distinct, and totally separate, categories of behaviour; [and] that business is most appropriately understood in terms that encompass legitimate and legal products and services'. Even when the mafia investigations in the US in the 1960s identified business-like structures characterized by stability and longevity, structural formality, profit motives and rationality, Smith considered that business framework to have been used as 'merely an overlay':

> Under it, the operating style and objectives of organised crime were those of a conspiracy, motivated by alien forces intent upon subverting legitimate society with techniques previously unknown to (or at least not practiced by) legal businesses. Resources that could have supplied operating

> analogies were left generally untapped. Clues that businesses sometimes operate in questionable ways were ignored or downplayed. (Smith Jr 1980: 368)

Smith replaces the previous assumptions about the severability of illicit from conventional enterprise. Instead he proposes 'that enterprise takes place across a spectrum that includes both business and certain kinds of crime; [and] that behavioural theory regarding organisations in general and business in particular can be applied to the entire spectrum' (Smith Jr 1980: 370). Despite quite wide acceptance of many of the premises of the spectrum approach in the years since its introduction to the discipline of criminology, many of the problems it identifies persist. The white-collar criminal is still considered a businessman or woman who has erred but is not a committed wrongdoer, while the organized criminal is still conceptualized in many areas of the criminological discourse – perhaps especially policy and policing – as a class apart, with criminality as a master trait. The proposition that both positions on the spectrum may conform to common behavioural rules has been somewhat lost.

Trafficking, as we shall see, exists on the spectrum that runs between legitimate and illegitimate business, encompassing white-collar and organized crimes and being structured according to the common behavioural rules of economic activity to which Smith refers. Trafficking is business, and big business at that. All of the markets we discuss in this book bear the classic hallmarks of free market business activity, among these: developing or sourcing a quality product to trade; competition from other traders and the imperative to grow a client base; buying low, selling high, in other words focusing on making profits and avoiding losses; collection/making of regular payments; dispute resolution mechanisms; employing or partnering with people to help grow the enterprise; managing the risks in the operating environment; negotiating the trade-off between the number of personnel required and the distribution of the shares in the overall profit; and so on.

In that respect, as trafficking is essentially a business enterprise, the really interesting questions for criminologists are how traffickers negotiate two of their metaphysical relationships: first, with the law, and second, with morality. These are the two signal differences between legitimate and illegitimate business, and as we have seen they do not necessarily both apply. So for markets where certain types of illegal behaviour are morally grey and socially normative, it may only be the relationship with the law that is hard to explain, just as where legal business transgresses moral norms it will be the latter that is most in need of analysis.

The compartmentalization of crime

In developing his spectrum-based theory of enterprise, Smith considers that 'the metaphors of business serve to reinforce the conceptual distinction between business and crime' (Smith Jr 1980: 364). He means that the way the business community talks about its activities precludes consideration of illicit economic activity as being on the same spectrum as legitimate business. The metaphors of business can, however, be implicated in illicit economic activity like trafficking to a degree that is constitutive. That is, while it is clear that business metaphors can be used (and surely are, as Smith rightly points out) to create a conceptual distance between legitimate and criminal trade, the metaphorical language games of business can equally be used by those plying illegal trades to conceptually draw what they are doing closer to the habitual norms and routines of a legitimate business.

How do people become indifferent to the suffering of others? Quite a considerable literature has considered this question, often from the perspective of international crimes such as war crimes and genocide. One of the answers proposed is the concept of 'compartmentalization'. This is an idea that stems from psychology (Showers 1992; Amiot et al 2007) and admits of various interpretations. One version of the proposition is that (a) people are constantly working to create a stable and unified concept of the self, (b) acts and thoughts which diverge from this picture of ourselves that we have created can generate cognitive dissonance and therefore (c) one way to reduce or eliminate that dissonance is to 'compartmentalize'. In this psychological sense, compartmentalization means hiving off certain actions into areas of our social lives that are deemed subsidiary to our main conception of our master identity. Severe cases of the compartmentalized mind may lead to a diagnosis of mental illness, as patients with more than one identity might be considered to be suffering from schizophrenia. Other social psychologists are more comfortable with an interpretation that is less focused on a master narrative of the self and allows for people that move between identities (Goulding et al 2010), dropping one as they move into another depending on the context (Gregory-Smith and Manika 2017), perhaps deliberately constructing different compartmentalized selves in order to fit in with the perceived norms of different groups (Cantor et al 1986 – a proposition sociologists will find chimes familiar alongside both Sutherland's differential association theory and Goffman's presentation of the self), and overall constructing identity as comprised of both positive and negative aspects (Bowlby 1980).

Beyond this strongly psychological interpretation of compartmentalization, however, a more sociological reworking of the idea has begun to emerge which recognizes that we are all leading compartmentalized lives to some extent, that the fragmentary (Bauman 1995) or 'liquid' (Bauman 2000) aspects of late modern existence support and may seem to necessitate compartmentalization and that living with the kind of contradiction implied by a compartmentalized sense of self is universal, therefore being empirically surely a condition of mundane normality and necessary survival in our highly complex social world, rather than a symptom of madness.

The argument throughout this book is that trafficking is an illegal form of enterprise. In other words, it is most appropriately considered as proscribed business rather than as a practice defined by an inherent criminality that is pathological, inconceivable or in some other way fundamentally different from the usual routines of the global neoliberal economy. It is just business, albeit very bad business (legally, morally and in terms of harm, if not in terms of relative profitability). Following the spectrum of enterprise approach outlined above, we should ask: if trafficking is 'just business', in what ways do the organizers of and participants in harmful business enterprises come to choose to carry out the socially harmful practices that they do? As Smith observed at the outset of his spectrum-based theory of enterprise, this is not just a question of organized crime or only of white-collar crime but of both: an approach is needed that can capture both ends of the spectrum of enterprise, and all points in between.

Clearly there are many perspectives that would be important to consider in working towards such a universal synthetic theory of enterprise harm. Here, I only want to pick what appears to me to be both the low-hanging fruit and among the more powerful explanations: low-hanging because it is implied by the observation that trafficking is business, and is considered so by organizers and participants, and powerful because it draws the causal line between the micro-level choices made by traffickers, the meso-level dynamics of organizational deviance and differential association (Vaughan 1999; Sutherland et al 1995), with their emphasis on group-based cultural norms, and the macro-level structures of the global economy. This is the idea of the realm of business as being a compartmentalization.

Conventional business organizations are structured into roles. Roles provide the framework through which the tasks of the business are allocated and performed. People, the humans behind the roles, step into the role and perform as the role-player. This can have significant and observable effects on their sense of moral judgement. It can lead to them performing harmful acts because they see these as being part of the demands of the role and because the role provides moral distance: it is not the person causing harm, it is 'the manager', or 'the salesperson'. The mechanisms by which the role can diminish personal or group moral judgement are several (Duster 1971). The individual may use the role and its situation among the many other roles in the business to consider themselves only a cog in the machine of the overall enterprise, diluting their sense of responsibility. The role demands obedience to authority, respecting the chain of command, and as such so-called 'crimes of obedience' have been identified in the military and corporate worlds alike. Crimes of obedience are set up by processes of authorization, routinization and dehumanization: the perpetrator feels authorized in their harmful action by a higher power, the harmful action is part of a process that has been performed regularly enough to have become routinized and the victims are dehumanized, stripped of their value as rights-bearing human beings (Kelman and Hamilton 1989). A role can become a mask, behind which the true face of the person hides, destroying the human connection between people which is necessary to nurture emotional concerns like sympathy, empathy and moral care (Levinas 1981). Roles can support the destructive forces of 'anonymity, deindividuation and dehumanisation' (Zimbardo 1970). Some of these examples refer to studies of serious international crimes and human rights abuses, but the criminogenic mechanisms of 'role' have been observed equally in studies of white-collar crimes, as in Shover and colleagues' research on boiler room share sales scams (Shover et al 2003, 2004). And they have been observed in relation to organized crime, as in studies of role modelling in mafia neighbourhoods and the differential association that supports the process of stepping into a role (Firestone 1993; Kemp et al 2019).

The matter of compartmentalization has been observed in business settings: that 'our mindsets have accepted that "business is business" and leaves no place for something else' (Rozuel 2011: 685). This has been theorized as a 'moral threat' to the self and an explanation of how organizational actors in conventional business settings come to see harmful consequences of their choices as mere externalities. Such externalities are then considered either outcomes for which the individual is not fully responsible, since they are incidental to the main goal of serving the organization's interests, or where there is a sense of responsibility the outcome is not something that the individual needs to worry about. In this latter sense, demonstrable outcomes drop off people's moral radar. This analysis has not extended to illegal business enterprise. Yet if we accept the 'spectrum' argument that there is no intrinsic difference between legal and illegal business then there is no defensible reason to assume that arguments about the effect of a 'this is just business' approach to moral compartmentalization should not also apply equally to traffickers. Indeed, the wealth of empirical evidence suggests that it does.

The role of someone who is carrying on business can be thought of as a certain type of performance which, like other social performances, involves the playing of a frontstage character while the backstage of the inner conversations we have about our personal identity develops behind the scenes but in correspondence with the roles we take (Goffman 1959; Baumeister 1986). In this way, business-like behaviour and thinking has become one of the 'multiple selves' (Elster 1986) that individuals construct. Some professional roles that we take on may indeed increase or highlight ethical ways of thinking. For example, academics reading this book will be familiar with the role of the institutional ethics review board, which calls on members to bring the ethics of research to front of mind. Some business ethics may be similar, for example perhaps the current trend for discussions of corporate social responsibility or the conflicted role of the 'compliance officer' inside corporations (Parker 2013). It is clear, however, that there is a core aspect of the compartmentalized self that 'does the business' (cf Hobbs 1988) which brackets ethical or socially responsible considerations while prioritizing the rational and satisficing (Simon 1982) decision-making that aims for profit. Professionals:

> often claim they act as representatives of an organisation rather than as individuals free to make their own decisions. Consequently, their moral responsibility appears heavily mitigated in so far as they do not create or define the roles they are requested to endorse. (Rozuel 2011: 687)

Rozuel agrees with Flores and Johnson (1983) that this does not of course stack up as a defensible argument against the taking of moral responsibility for consequences on the part of the professionals in question. Still, we might rejoinder that we are not concerned here with arguing about the actual moral responsibility of traffickers, only their impression of what it means to fulfil a business-like role in practice and the various rationalizations and neutralizations that come into play in forming that impression. It is well recognized that social structures, and the roles they create, can be destructive of individual morality (MacIntyre 1999), and it is more important for social scientists to trace how that occurs than to construct arguments for holding individuals in particular circumstances morally culpable. On both the former and the latter, MacIntyre has something to say though: his image is of 'the lacks or absences of the divided selves of a compartmentalized social order [as being] better described as active refusals and denials' (MacIntyre 1999: 327). In other words, in our context, traffickers thinking of trafficking as 'just business' is both a product of the cultures and social structures framing international illicit trade and, on at least some level, an active agency in respect of a self-serving compartmentalization. MacIntyre's argument relates to those social structures that allow people to 'lead blamelessly compliant lives, able to plausibly plead lack of knowledge as well as lack of control over outcomes', in which they 'inhabit a type of social and cultural order whose structures to some large degree inhibit the exercise of the powers of moral agency' and with which structures 'they share in responsibility for having made themselves into the kind of diminished agent that they are' (1999: 327). But the argument applies equally to traffickers, who may hardly argue that they lead 'blamelessly compliant' lives but who nonetheless construct and are structured into a fractured relationship between their acts of illegal enterprise and the harms they cause.

Compartmentalization goes along with the attribution of particular traits or dispositions in respect of the roles we play: 'e.g. as a parent, I am patient, kind, loving, energetic, confident, or as a manager, I am confident, trustworthy, efficient, ambitious' (Rozuel 2011: 690). Often these attributes of roles are aspirational: not so much perhaps how we actually see ourselves in these roles but what we aim for and how we would like to be seen. They are personal and usually socially validated impressions of indicators of what it would take to perform the role well (Gioia 1992). We can also quite easily come up with attributes of roles that would not allow them to be performed well. Business managers, if not entirely ruthless, cannot afford to be too empathetic as how then would aggressive competition in the marketplace be possible? Emotion management is a requirement of all business, training oneself to bracket out compassion insofar as it hampers performance (Gioia 1992; Lois 2003). Relatively few people want to be, or be perceived as, completely heartless though, whether in business or in trafficking, so compartmentalization of the less savoury aspects of personality is required, reserving them for display and implementation only in structural contexts where they are valued and perceived to be necessary. Roles are accompanied by scripts, or narratives, which describe and prescribe the story of the role, encapsulating in culture what the defining features of the role are and the ideal or essential attributes of those who would step into the role (Gioia 1992).

Compartmentalized knowledge is not suppressed, it is put aside. The harm of trafficking is not denied, although it may certainly be somewhat neutralized, that is, justified or excused (see Sykes and Matza 1957; Scott and Lyman 1968 and the discussion about neutralization to follow in various chapters here). The harm is known, and yet considered 'just business'. Compartmentalization in sociological criminology has strong foundations, although it has rarely if ever, as far as I am aware, been set out as an etiological factor in the sociology of crime (as opposed to psychological criminology where compartmentalization and cognate concepts are better recognized). Consider though, for one example, the institutional anomie theory of Messner and Rosenfeld (1994), which attributes the structural causes of crime in industrial and post-industrial society to the growing pre-eminence of the economy as the institution which governs social decision-making, to the increasing exclusion of other institutional structures that have historically provided conventional and pro-social bonds and norms, like the family and the church. Such an institutional anomie thesis can be seen to be very closely reflected in the philosophical definition MacIntyre constructs for the process of compartmentalization, as:

> the extent to which each distinct sphere of social activity comes to have its own role structure governed by its own specific norms in relative independence of other such spheres. Within each sphere those norms dictate which kinds of consideration are to be treated as relevant to decision-making and which are to be excluded. (MacIntyre 1999: 322)

Just as with Messner and Rosenfeld, then, MacIntyre is talking about a social-structural kind of compartmentalization, rather than the inside-your-head compartmentalizations of the self that the psychological field considers – but the two processes of structural differentiation and individual self-stratification are clearly engaged in a dialectical relationship in practice.

The banality of commercial evil

Compartmentalization of the self – the internal arrangement and rearrangement of items in our inventory of identity – is connected to the structural compartmentalization of tasks and roles in illegal enterprise. In order to fully grasp the nature of this relationship between compartmentalization, self-definition and the social structure of contemporary business enterprise, we can look to Hannah Arendt's writing on evil.

Arendt considered the banality of evil to be an effect of modern bureaucratic structure on the moral sense of responsibility of 'office criminals', who she described as committing 'administrative crime' (Arendt 1963). Given that her subject was the holocaust, one can see why a superficial (mis)interpretation of her propositions, of banality and administration, caused such outrage. The banality of the evil she detected in Eichmann did not, however, for her diminish his culpability; it merely explained how he had come to play a key role in orchestrating mass murder. The popular conception of Eichmann before Arendt's reports from the trial was that he could only surely be a monster, depraved in spirit and poisonous in the exercise of cruelty. She instead described a picture of an ordinary man excelling in the performance of his tasks within an administrative structure that rewarded those who expedited the will of the Führer, dehumanized victims, focusing instead on considerations of efficiency, and socially constructed the routines of mass killing as the design and carrying out of a logistical quasi-industrial process of technical accomplishment. So we see Eichmann on this view as co-ordinating a production line of death.

Bauman had a similar view of the relationship between modernity and the holocaust, using examples of individuals and groups beyond just Eichmann to expand on Arendt's portrait of the design and accomplishment of horror achieved by unthinking individuals choosing only to see the challenges of optimizing the technological aspects of an industrial task and not the effects of these processes (Bauman 1989). Such wilful blindness is the 'unthinking' that Arendt critiques – clearly the actors are thinking but they have switched off the moral compulsion to think about the harmful consequences of their action on others. Repetition breeds routine, which in turn leads to normalization, so the performance of the acts required to effect harm comes to be seen as unremarkable. The performance of the acts is also decoupled from the harmful effects, in this 'banality' of process. The banality of evil is therefore a depersonalizing performance of work evaluated not in human terms but in terms that consider the effective achievement of a series of tasks that in aggregate amount to the completion of an overall project.

The banality of evil is therefore a description of, among other things, a process of compartmentalization. Arendt does not use the term, but it is close to what she means when she calls Eichmann an 'unthinking entity'. He is not unthinking, he is just not thinking about the right things: his mind has not been the host to 'the silent dialogue between me and myself' (Arendt 1958) that is the foundation of moral or compassionate decision-making and action. In his study of the Rwandan genocide, Tanner finds a comparable frame of unthinking mind in the Hutus who killed their Tutsi neighbours (Tanner 2011). He illustrates with a quote from a Hutu man who spoke to French journalist Jean Hatzfeld for his book *Machete Season* (Tanner 2012):

> It was a madness that took on a life of its own. You got on board or got out of the way, but you followed the crowd. If you had a machete in your hand, you didn't listen to anything. You forgot everything, starting with your intellect. This repeated program freed us from thinking about what we were doing. We went out and came back, without a thought in our heads. We hunted because that was our daily routine until everything was over. Our arms drove our minds, or in any event our minds never spoke up. (Hatzfeld 2003: 60)

So the banality of evil 'implies a radical rupture between the daily technical and bureaucratic tasks, on the one hand, and the consequences, albeit extreme, at the end of the line, on the other' (Tanner 2012: 2). Tanner has developed the concept of the banality of evil to apply it beyond the crimes of the 'pen and administrative form' that are carried out by Arendt's 'office criminals', who are participants in a bureaucratic machinery. He has suggested thinking more expansively about its value as an explanation for how those who directly carry out acts of harm, as opposed to organizing them from a distance, may come to experience the '*absence of thought and moral judgement*' (2012: 3, his emphasis) which makes their crimes possible, and banal.

It seems to me that this extension and application of the banality thesis is helpful in throwing some etiological light on the activities of global traffickers. These actors are hardly Nazi war criminals or genocidal Hutus, but their activities bear the marks of both sides of Arendt's banality coin: on one side, organization, routine, project-based enterprise with goals that can be administratively cast and tasks which are structurally similar to those carried out in conventional business; and on the other, seriously harmful social effects from which offenders are emotionally disconnected. Many of the tasks undertaken as part of global illicit trading networks are similar, if not identical, to the routines of legitimate business, and for many of the actors involved in cross-border illegal trade, these legitimate and illegitimate actions interlace. Consider, for example, the conflict diamond fence who is a legal trader in the market but accepts and facilitates the insertion of stolen gems into the trading pipeline, or the antiquities dealer who sells both legal and looted artefacts, or the human trafficker who runs a travel agency, arranging the international movement of persons both legally and illegally. In these trading examples, the banality proposition may assist our understanding of how 'good people' do 'bad things'. The 'good people' here are not 'paragons' (Smith Jr 1980), nor in their bad deeds psychopaths, sociopaths or monsters, but merely ordinary – unremarkable – and therefore susceptible to the social forces which support doing dirty business as well as clean business in the world. Those social forces render, on one side, trade and, on the other, advertence to consequence, to be separated by a chasm that takes moral effort – Arendt's 'thinking' – to bridge, effort which many on the spectrum of enterprise decline to apply. With repetition, normalization and habituation develop – an observation made by Matza in relation to delinquency decades ago (Matza 1969) but one which seems particularly apt when thinking about the routine performance of illegal business transactions.

While the application of the constellation of indicators of banality may be more obviously applied to particular actors in global trade networks who mix illegal and legal pursuits, it can apply equally I think – but perhaps less obviously – to the 'darker' end of the spectrum of enterprise, where the less ambivalent purveyors of criminal enterprise rest. These actors are comparably 'unthinking' in the sense that they compartmentalize trafficking as a business enterprise rather than an indelible mark of identity, and seeing it as 'just business' they work on the technical aspects of achieving the tasks involved which as a banal preoccupation reduces feelings of responsibility for harmful consequences that might otherwise be experienced. In this way, traffickers are simply adopting the norms and values of globalized neoliberal capitalist markets: profit and power first, ask questions later.

The globalization of indifference

A well-known and controversial account of the North American workplace can be found in Howard Stein's book *Nothing Personal, Just Business* (Stein 2001). He portrays organizational business life as:

> a place of darkness, where emotional brutality is commonplace and different forms of psychological violence and dehumanisation – including degradation, humiliation and intimidation – have become the norm … the core, if unacknowledged, euphemism that inspires the title of Stein's book is that of 'collateral damage' – the view that no suffering, no lie, and no savagery is too great, as long as it is justified by the bottom line. People become dispensable pawns, resources to be used, exploited and discarded. (Gabriel 2003: 343)

Indifference to suffering is a useful concept because of the double meaning of indifference. Indifference can be first apathy, a lack of compassion or sympathy, as where we say 'he was indifferent to her distress'. Yet it can also be, second, an ordinary commonplace, unremarkable thing or occurrence, as in 'she made an indifferent effort to compete in the race'. That indifference to suffering might be a feature of economic globalization is deeply troubling. That it might become indifferent in the second sense – so common and routine as to seem unremarkable – ever more so. Yet the weight of evidence presented in this book suggests that we have witnessed a globalization of both kinds of indifference in the development of trafficking around the world concomitant upon the globalization of conventional trade.

The compartmentalization that the increasing dominance of economic ways of thinking represents is described by one of Rozuel's research participants, a marketing accountant, as an:

> overwhelming 'capitalist – you make your own money, you look out for yourself' persona. Consequently, her initial moral reluctance fades away which allows her to do her job efficiently. (Rozuel 2011: 694)

In revealing quotes like these we can perhaps see the coming together of all the concepts we have discussed in this chapter: the compartmentalization of harmful actions in business settings; the banality of the routine of such harmful actions; the differential association that characterizes business life and the associated ideas of obedience and role interpretation that dull the moral senses in this context; the spectrum of enterprise as drawing attention to the harms effected in business settings and through business mindsets whether through commerce that is ostensibly legal or illegal; and overall the structural parameters of what we might diagnose as the 'moral anaesthesia' of much contemporary commercial enterprise. In Candace Clark's work on the sociology of the emotions (Clark 1997), she considers sympathy to be a socially structured display – an emotional regime – with certain 'rules' that we come to intuit about who deserves sympathy, in what form and when. So what may feel like an emotion that comes from some wellspring inside us, manifesting as action in the outside world (let us say, inside-out), is actually more like outside-in when we consider that the social rules of sympathy routines are interpreted by individuals from social norms that they then internalize and subsequently act out. From such a structuralist perspective on emotions, it becomes easy to see areas of social life where an ethic of care is inscribed as normative (family life, for example) and other areas where it is not (business life, for example). The essence of the project this book sets out to accomplish is to follow that observation to some of its conclusions in respect of the criminology of trafficking seen as a form of transnational crime. Do traffickers think, in a compartmentalized way, of their illegal enterprise as a form of business, and if so, does this way of thinking bracket out the ethic of care that would provide some resistance to the performance of harmful criminal behaviour? In what follows, I suggest that the answer to both of these questions is yes, and I aim to show that we can find evidence for this argument in the literature on trafficking and in the accounts of traffickers themselves.

The book is not only an extended argument for the spectrum of enterprise approach to this type of transnational crime though, nor is it just an attempt to illustrate where the characterization of cross-border criminal markets as morally indifferent business takes us in terms of increasing our understanding of the causes of crime (although it is certainly all of these things). The book is also intended to be a summary and primer on the main features of each trafficking market covered, so that readers who may dispute, or be indifferent to, the overall argument can still use the text to improve their understanding of these contemporary transnational crime and security challenges in outline.

With reference to the effort to both provide coverage and develop theory, I should acknowledge the influence on my thinking of the many great works on transnational crime that have over the years helped me to build my own interpretation of the field. Many of those books are referenced throughout what follows so I will for the most part leave the text of this book to pay my academic respects to key inspirational works. But here I will just point out that in criminology and beyond, books collating evidence on criminal markets have tended to be either (a) monographs dealing with only one type of trafficking (see, for example, Green 2000; Mackenzie 2005b; Siegel 2009; Lee 2011; Levi 2015; van Uhm 2016) or perhaps several types but through one common theme (such as criminal finance, Naylor 2004), both of which approaches are a reflection of the particular specialism or interest of the author, or (b) edited collections where a contribution on each type of trafficking is made by an expert in that subject (see, for example, Beare 2003; Sheptycki and Wardak 2005; Passas 2013; Reichel and Albanese 2016; Beckert and Dewey 2017; Natarajan 2019b). In diverging from these approaches and writing about six global criminal markets in one book, the aim has been to build on what I have learned from these prior works and develop the kind of sustained theoretical analysis this single-author, multiple-case format allows.

The following chapters in the book will therefore address a number of different trafficking markets, tracing their structure and function while also pointing out links between them. Sometimes those links are best understood as part of the structural interplay of supply and demand in global illicit commerce. Shelley (2019), for example, gives a good precis of the period following the end of the Cold War, which ended one major conflict but ushered in myriad regional conflicts, for which guns have been in high demand. Financing the purchase of these guns was sometimes through trafficking deals in drugs and diamonds (Nordstrom 2007), and an effect of the conflicts has been the creation of refugees looking for safe haven abroad, economic migrants seeking escape from decimated local economies, and states unable to protect vulnerable women and children, all of which creates opportunity for human traffickers and smugglers. Sometimes though, and not incompatible with the 'structural causes' approach to comparison and synthesis, the links between the illegal markets will be seen to be conceptual, illustrating the themes of spectrum of enterprise, banality of evil and globalization of indifference that have been explained above.

I will consider each market through the same structure: the nature and extent of the harm; the structure of the transnational criminal market; issues of regulation and control and then a final section in each chapter which will contain evidence and discussion on the question (and implications) of taking a spectrum of enterprise approach to the interpretation of each form of trafficking – that is, thinking of it as 'just business'.

2

Drug Trafficking

The nature and extent of the harm

Drug trafficking is considered to be the largest revenue generator globally among the variety of transnational criminal markets (Reuter 2014), and despite the huge criminal justice infrastructure aimed at reducing drug trafficking, the problem is getting worse. The number of people using drugs worldwide was estimated by the World Drug Report to be 30 per cent higher in 2019 than it was 10 years earlier, in 2009 (UNODC 2019). Globally, 11 million people injected drugs in 2017, while 271 million people were estimated to have used illegal drugs in that year, which is 5.5 per cent of the global population aged between 15 and 64. The harm caused by drug misuse is a continuing global crisis. In the US alone, 47,000 opioid overdose deaths were recorded in 2017, up 13 per cent from 2016. More drugs are being illegally produced than ever before (for cocaine in 2017 a 25 per cent increase on 2016, at 1,976 tons), and more are being seized. Synthetic drugs are a growing part of the problem, with synthetic opioids such as fentanyl finding a market in North America and tramadol in West, Central and North Africa (UNODC 2019).

The picture, as we shall see, is one of a catastrophic failure of law and policy to control this global criminal market. The criminal justice supply-chain intervention approach has not reduced illicit drug consumption despite sometimes very large seizures. At the demand end, government initiatives targeted at treatment and prevention are not reaching enough users, with the 2019 World Drug Report finding that globally only around one in seven people with drug disorders received treatment. The figure is considerably less than this in prisons where clandestine but widespread illicit drug use takes place, usually without access to standard harm-reduction measures such as needle exchange programmes or substitution therapy, giving prisoners an elevated risk of contracting serious diseases like HIV and Hepatitis C (UNODC 2019). Drug policies are a source of racial injustice, such as the much-debated difference in sentencing dispositions for crack versus powder cocaine, the first more likely to be found in the possession of black offenders, the second in the hands of whites.

Crack attracts significantly higher penalties purportedly because of the nature of the drug, but the effect is indirect racial discrimination. Racial discrimination is in fact evident throughout the criminal justice response to drug offences, such as in stop and search, arrest decisions, prosecution decisions and sentencing (Glasser 2000; Eastwood et al 2013; Shiner et al 2018). These, to be clear, are harmful effects caused or exacerbated by the legal response to drug trafficking and use.

In 2012, UNODC reported that one in every one hundred adult deaths in the 15–64 age group was due to drug use (UNODC 2012), and in 2017 they identified that globally, but excluding sub-Saharan Africa, injecting drug users accounted for nearly one-third of new HIV infections (UNODC 2017b). Drug production and trafficking in producer and transit countries are security and development issues, adversely affecting millions with violence and disrupting state capacity to function effectively. In the richer, consumer, countries the end points of the drug trafficking chain of supply create serious public health issues (Middleton et al 2016; Christie 2019; Hurley 2019; Csete et al 2016) as well as harms associated with the functioning of the trade such as violence and knock-on crime events where users turn to robbery or burglary to fund addiction (Bennett et al 2008; Jacques et al 2016; Werb et al 2011).

The structure of drug trafficking: source, transit, market

Analysts tend to split drug trafficking into layers. The 'high' or 'upper level' of drug trafficking includes organizing production, refining and exporting in producer countries and arranging their transport to and import into consumer destinations. In those consumer countries, the regional wholesale distribution of drugs is the activity of the middle-market or mid-level trade, and at the bottom of the chain of supply is the retail trade, so-called lower level distribution (Natarajan 2011). Just as in legitimate trade circles, wholesalers sell to other members of the trade, while retailers sell to consumers, usually in smaller amounts than the larger sales made by wholesalers.

The literature on drug trafficking is huge, and spans disciplines. Perspectives on this trade can be found in politics, international relations, economics and anthropology, as well as in sociology and criminology. Much of the criminological research has been focused on the lower levels of the global trade, for various reasons. The street-level retail markets have been more visible to researchers, the public and politicians in consumer nations than are the more distant upper echelons of the trade, appearing as day-to-day problems in their neighbourhoods. Criminology in the US has grown up to meet the challenges of such neighbourhood crime problems, especially from the 1960s Chicago School era onwards with its emphasis on understanding the causes of delinquency. So we have less research in criminology about the upper levels of the international drug trade (Desroches 2007) and here we need to draw more on the research in some of the other disciplines mentioned.

The mechanics of drug trafficking vary depending on the type of drug in question. The production locations for both heroin and cocaine are few: six countries account for 98 per cent of the world heroin production, with Myanmar and Afghanistan leading the way, having produced more than 80 per cent of the world's opium since the mid-1980s, while the world's coca production is based in Bolivia, Colombia and Peru (Reuter 2014). The long trafficking chains these drugs move through as they transit from producer to consumer countries may look like an unduly cumbersome way to do business, but moving production closer to consumption brings a considerable escalation in the law enforcement risk, whereas the situation in producer countries is far more conducive to uninterrupted production with minimal risk. This may involve state and police negligence, corruption or collusion, or in some regions the effective capture and replacement of the local governance infrastructure with drug business interests: so-called 'narco-states' (Paoli et al 2009). Participation in the markets for heroin and cocaine takes an hourglass shape overall (Reuter 2014), with large numbers of farmers growing the crops, large numbers of street-level retailers in consumer countries and relatively fewer traffickers connecting these two ends of the market. For cocaine and heroin, Reuter estimates that the producers (that is, the growers) get around 1 per cent of the revenues, while 70 to 80 per cent of the revenues are 'generated by the last two or three transactions, as the drug goes from ounce purchases by low-level wholesalers to a fraction of a gram at the retail level' (Reuter 2014: 364). Although the bulk of the revenues goes to these low-level dealers, the large number of these retail deals and dealers means that 'the fortunes are made by those at the top of the trade' (Reuter 2014: 365).

While cannabis is mostly produced within the consumer nations, there is a cross-border trade in it, exported mainly from Jamaica, Colombia and Mexico, and in Europe from Morocco and Albania (Reuter 2014; Natarajan 2019a). Likewise, synthetic drugs are produced both in consumer countries and abroad, with various producer locations depending on which consumer country is at issue: for example, in the case of methamphetamine Mexico produces some of the US's supply, although domestic production in the US is on the rise, and other production and consumption locations span the world from Western and Central Europe to recent manufacturing increases in North Africa (Natarajan 2019a). The East and Southeast Asia and Oceania region is currently grappling with significant flows of methamphetamine being produced in Myanmar and the surrounding Greater Mekong region, especially the so-called 'golden triangle' of Thailand, Laos and Myanmar. Ecstasy is produced in many European countries, particularly Belgium and the Netherlands, as well as 'Australia, North America, South Africa, China, and Southeast Asian countries (where they are much cheaper to produce than in Europe), and more recently in South and Central America' (Natarajan 2019a: 7).

Several of the producer countries are characterized by a drug trafficking culture that is violent and cartelized. Colombian drug production was dominated through the 1980s by the Cali and Medellín cartels, which were ultimately diminished in their powerful grip on the trade in the early 1990s after pressing their political ambitions too far when the Medellín assassination of a presidential candidate led the state to initiate a military crackdown. Since then, smaller and more numerous 'cartelitos' have developed, although less stable, less political and part of a generally more fragmented scene. In Mexico, for decades a small number of large cartels have fought for a share in controlling the drug trade, with seven identified in 2010 (Astorga and Shirk 2010), and the result has been such an extraordinary level of violence that Ciudad Juárez, across the border from El Paso in Texas, is now the world's most dangerous city.

Drug traffickers are either organizers – so-called 'king pins' and their middle managers who control the business – or mules/couriers (Dorn et al 2005). Mules run the greater risk: border seizures of illicit drugs are common. Street dealers run considerable risk too, being visible and engaged with end consumers who may not have much incentive to maintain the secrecy of the supply chain. Notwithstanding the fairly well-known large cartel structures, particularly in Colombia and Mexico, and the documented participation of mafias and other organized crime groups in such a lucrative market (Natarajan et al 2015), most research studies have generated a picture of the upper level of the international drugs trade as represented by:

> informal and loosely organised associations of relatively small syndicates or crews of independent drug entrepreneurs. They compete for market share and deal primarily or exclusively with trusted associates chosen from ethnic,

> kinship, and friendship networks. Most dealers are highly cautious, eschew the use of violence, typically make huge profits, attempt to maintain a low profile, rationalise their conduct as business activity, and operate within geographically niche markets. (Desroches 2007)

Drug trafficking is necessarily clandestine, unlike some of the other markets discussed in this book such as antiquities, wildlife or human trafficking. In those markets the objects of trafficking themselves may not need to be disguised or hidden in transit, one smuggling strategy being simply to present the objects in transit as part of the legitimate trade, using false documents or other misrepresentations. This approach is not available to drug smugglers, and as such the structure of the international traffic in drugs is shaped by the requirement to avoid detection, with network security and minimizing risk being found to be 'key organising principles of drug trading organisations' that need to be considered as mitigating the view that drug trafficking is an enterprise purely structured by rational efficiency considerations (Benson and Decker 2010: 130). This has been put forward as one of the main reasons for findings of drug trafficking networks being constituted by smaller groups, not formally connected to each other but more like a network of connected nodes without a vertical or horizontal command structure. This arrangement, or more accurately lack of arrangement, serves to protect each participant node in the network from the law enforcement risk that would attach were the structure more monolithic (Williams 1998a; Morselli et al 2007). In such decentralized networks, power and status can be linked to function, so particularly effective brokers who are able to serve as 'network vectors', linking separate parts of the trafficking chain, may find themselves highly prized (Morselli 2001).

Methods of movement cover land, sea and air, including everything from using the postal service to concealed compartments in vehicles, bodily insertion, private jets, speedboats and submarines, fishing boats and, most often, large commercial freight trucks and container ships. Despite the significant attention to drug smuggling at the border in consumer countries including the US and European countries, the massive daily global movement of commercial shipments means that without insider intelligence, container deliveries can still make it through the security barrier in large numbers. Not only, then, do the main drug trafficking methods follow the routines of transit in legitimate global business, they are disguised by the volume of that legal trade.

In addition to conventional business trade routes, another observable trend over recent decades has been an increase in leisure travel due to the fall in price of aeroplane seats and other forms of transit. Several studies of drug traffickers have picked up on the exploitation of this trend in illicit trade. Holiday travellers are exploited to traffic illicit drugs (Marsh et al 2012: 171–2), sometimes persuaded to do so with the treat of a free holiday. Speed and regularity of transit connections is a factor in this tactic. For example, as it has become common for people to take day trips on the cross-channel ferry from the UK to France, sometimes in a van to take advantage of duty-free prices in Calais on wine and food, trafficking illicit goods alongside this movement of people and legal goods has become easier to disguise (Hornsby and Hobbs 2007).

As the global supply routes for illegal drugs develop in response to regulatory pressures, traffickers take the opportunity to develop local markets for their commodity along the way. So transit countries, which neither produce nor, initially at least, consume the drugs, become affected by the trade over time and develop as consumer markets in their own right: this is why there has been 'a surge in drug use among the general population in Nigeria and other African countries as well as in the Indian subcontinent' (Natarajan 2019a: 8).

In the consumer countries, official agency reports have tended to create the impression of a marketplace controlled by criminal syndicates. To the contrary, ethnographic, interview and other sociological studies have often struggled to find evidence of such syndicates, coming instead to an impression of drug dealing markets as comprised of 'small groups of wheeler-dealers who operate competitively and entrepreneurially' (Adler 1993: 2). The several findings of such an opportunistic entrepreneurial marketplace do not rule out the presence of larger criminal organizations, and there is clearly evidence that in certain times and places these do indeed enter the trade (Fuentes 1998), but it is a general theme in the organized crime research literature that smaller, fragmented entrepreneurial groups and partnerships are more usual while the presence of mafia is often wrongfully imputed (Reuter and Haaga 1989). Two studies of the UK market for imported drugs involving Dick Hobbs, several years apart, found a situation similar to the earlier studies of Adler and Reuter in the US: networks of dealers working as sole traders or in small groups (Pearson and Hobbs 2001, 2003; Matrix Knowledge Group 2007). The impression we have from Hobbs is of the importing end of drug trafficking, as well as other branches of organized crime, as a market where flexible systems of enterprise flourish, while the larger centres of gravity of bigger and more stable organizations cannot adapt to avoid law enforcement intervention or the changing social and economic contexts of late modern capitalism (Hobbs 2001, 2013). Similar findings can be found in other studies, confirming the picture of drug trafficking as generally more like a 'cottage industry' than a 'concentrated industry' (Eck and Gersh 2000): populated, that is, not by a few highly organized groups that control supply but by a large number of smaller groups and individuals where the groups may have fluid membership, no long-term established leaders and no access to sophisticated technology beyond common items such as cell phones.

Many commentators have noted the parallels between the organization of illegal drug trafficking and how successful contemporary legal business structures itself to take maximum advantage of globalization opportunities. For example, Shelley, summarizing Thoumi's 2003 study of the Andes region (Peru, Colombia and Bolivia), suggests that Colombian groups have based their success:

> on many of the same principles found in the globalization of large legitimate corporations. They run network-based business, not top-down hierarchical structures. They integrate their business across continents. Drug cultivation and processing are done at low-cost production sites in Latin America, their products are marketed to the lucrative Western European and American markets, and the profits are laundered at home, in offshore locales such as Panama, and in international financial centres. (Shelley 2019: 226)

Aside from the publicity surrounding the South American cartels, one of the contributing reasons to the general impression that drug trafficking is the remit of large criminal organizations is the over-representation of ethnic minorities in drug trafficking in the US and the UK and the unreflective assumption that goes along with this observation that these are surely part of larger, ethnically based mafias. Yet there are good reasons for this over-representation, and we do not need to reach into underground alien conspiracy theories to find them (Woodiwiss and Hobbs 2009; Hobbs and Antonopoulos 2013). As ever, we need only to look to the evidence provided by social structure and the normal routines of market forces. Ethnic minorities are restricted in opportunities to enter the legitimate labour market, discriminated against and therefore more likely to suffer economic strain (Merton 1968) and look for alternative ways to make money (Decker and Townsend Chapman 2008:

97–8). They may be part of a diaspora and have links to source countries, which makes participation in transnational networks of illegal trade easier and more resistant to law enforcement attention, disguising communications about crime among more routine global conversations among families and friends. Such family and friendship bonds may be stronger than the ties between unrelated professional criminals and therefore more likely to provide the basis of a resilient structure of criminal enterprise (Paoli and Reuter 2008). One can see how some of these arguments could be pulled into the orbit of an alien conspiracy version of transnational organized crime, but equally from the perspective of how to think about the costs, risks and benefits of setting up a transnational business that trades commodities, these considerations seem fairly mundane as producers of certain overall demographic patterns in those markets. That is to say, of course certain people are more willing, or better socially equipped, to become participants in drug trafficking networks than others, but these aggregate ethic differences are the result of the opportunity structure the particular forms of enterprise present.

Regulation and control of drug trafficking

Social scientists have come to see enforcement and control as more instrumental in positively shaping the markets they apply to than might at first seem to be the case if we think of criminal justice as simply a series of prohibitions. The usual starting assumption would be that regulation is a response to criminal behaviour and simply seeks to eliminate it. Yet a pattern emerges where criminal behaviour, not amenable to being entirely suppressed, adapts to regulatory interventions, interfaces with them, and the outcome is an amalgam of the original phenomenon and the official response. Reuter explains how this can look, in describing the dominance of large criminal drug trafficking groups in Tajikistan:

> The progress in border control and law enforcement that Tajikistan has achieved since the late 1990s – thanks to the support of international agencies and foreign donors – has facilitated the large groups' domination. By 2001, for example, a total of 12 to 13 police and customs posts could be found on the route from Khorog to Osh, a distance of only 700 to 800 kilometers. The roads from the Afghanistan border to Dushanbe are checked even more strictly. Rather than create insuperable barriers to drug transportation, this

> has generated large payments to border and police officials. (Reuter 2014: 367)

In such examples, large criminal operations can minimize law enforcement risk by buying it out, so the law enforcement structure can serve to embed the power of mafias and cartels rather than disrupt them. In other cases, however, the threat of serious law enforcement intervention which cannot be fully neutralized through corruption exerts a pressure on high-level traffickers to insulate themselves from investigation. This is accomplished by minimizing the number of people they deal with in the supply chain and layering the overall operation into severable parts to make such insulation possible through delegating colleagues lower down the chain to have more exposure to risk. Drug mules will have little knowledge of the overall drug trafficking network, a sensible precaution by the organizers in case the carrier is intercepted.

Law enforcement affects the geographical routes of drug trafficking too, seemingly pushing routes around the globe depending on where the policing resource is allocated from time to time (Andreas 2000). The usual metaphor is pushing a balloon: one side is pushed in, the other pops out in equal measure. Perhaps a better metaphor for transnational criminal markets is an electric current, seeking out the path of least resistance, always ready to divert in response to increasing friction in any particular route.

In all of these various ways, 'criminalisation steers the flow of events within the market in distinctive ways' (Seddon 2019: 10), and the relationship between illegal drug markets and regulation has been argued to be constitutive, in the sense that Shearing has identified (Shearing 1993). He sees markets, legal and illegal, as a 'regulatory accomplishment' (1993: 72): regulation shapes the opportunity structure of markets *ex ante* and then the market and the regulation evolve in a process of mutual observation and co-production (Seddon 2019). From this perspective, the war on drugs should be seen as a slow waltz of market and regulation, where sometimes one partner leads, sometimes the other.

The global policy and law enforcement attention to drug trafficking internationally is massive. The United Nations Office on Drugs and Crime (UNODC) spearheads a large group of intergovernmental organizations which address the issue, alongside others: Interpol, Europol, the World Customs Organization (WCO), the UN International Drug Control Programme and more. Most consumer nations have dedicated police drug enforcement squads and dedicated legislation prohibiting use, possession and supply. There is no shortage of legal prohibition and the supporting enforcement apparatus in consumer countries, but the situation in producer and transit countries is much less conducive to energetic control and that is a context which will surely not change soon. Drug trafficking is often held up as an example of the failure of prohibition strategies which, as was the case with alcohol in the US in the 1920s and '30s, target the supply of an illicit commodity without doing enough to decrease the demand for it. This is slightly misleading though because while the predominant international supply-intervention strategy has certainly not stemmed the flow of illegal drugs, there is a considerable demand-end response too organized internally by national governments, including a mix of policing, education and awareness raising, and drug rehabilitation for users. All of these interventions can be criticized, but rather than labelling the war on drugs only a failure of supply-side prohibition, it would be more accurate to say that there are many features of global criminal markets that make these hugely profitable enterprises hard to control.

The decades since 1950 have seen two trends in particular in relation to drug trafficking (Seddon 2019: 4, his emphasis):

> First, a *trend of rising drug consumption and the geographical spread of the drug trade into parts of the world that had previously avoided it*, starting with Eastern Europe (Csémy et al 2002), moving across parts of Asia and, most recently, into Africa (Carrier and Klantschnig 2012; Dewing et al 2006), leading to today's globalized drug market (UNODC 2012: 69). Second, at the same time, a *hardening of the international prohibition regime* (Bayer and Ghodse 1999) ... The fact that these have been parallel developments – the tighter the screw is turned, the worse the problem gets [is the] 'paradox of prohibition'. (Marks 1990)

The trends in illegal drug use globally of increasing production, increasing numbers of users, and decreasing prices, during the decades when the war on drugs has been ostensibly aiming for complete prohibition, show that law enforcement does not have the capacity to reduce, let alone eliminate the market – although it may have reduced the velocity and extent of these trends compared to the alternative of having no enforcement (MacCoun and Reuter 2011; Pollack and Reuter 2014). There is almost universal agreement in the literature that supply-focused intervention strategies have failed, and many analysts have seen this failure as placed within a context of globalization of communication, transport and trade that has for some time been supplying an opportunity context in which illicit global trade can grow. Where these globalizing trends have far outpaced the capacities of nation states to exert control over the innovations of free market entrepreneurs, legal and illegal, contraband goods will cross state borders as sand runs through fingers.

When sand runs through your fingers, though, the instinctual reflex is to tighten your grip. This has been the bind that the war on drugs has created: a public which accepts that the war is not working but is reluctant to give up on it despite regular interventions from experts pleading with governments to look for 'options beyond eradication, interdiction, criminalization, and incarceration to limit the social consequences of drugs' (Naim 2009: 168). One result of this constant pressure to reform is that, looking around the world, we can see that there is an increasing move towards decriminalization (that is, not applying criminal penalties) and legalization (that is, doing away with criminal drug laws altogether) for some drugs (Eastwood et al 2016). These moves are often presented initially as social policy experiments, with the implication that things can go back to the way they were if the new deregulatory ethos does not work out. The dilution of drug law prohibitions has been most notable in relation to 'softer' recreational drugs like cannabis and is justified on a variety of inter-related grounds, including that the harm caused by recreational use is not significant or at least is contested, criminal justice intervention is harmful and inequitable, and illegal use has been so widespread for so long, and for some drugs in some social groups and contexts has for a long time been quite normalized, that it is clear the old approach to attempted control has failed. The movement from illegal to legal cannabis production, dealing and use in some jurisdictions surely shows the value of the spectrum of enterprise analytical approach. The somewhat arbitrary, or at least contingent, application of the criminal law to some drugs, like cannabis, but not others, like alcohol or tobacco, is the main operative distinction between conventional and criminal enterprise here. Moving that line of il/legality on the spectrum of enterprise changes the opportunity structure for the market, but the underlying dynamics of supply and demand remain similar. Cannabis is now becoming 'big business' in some of the legalized jurisdictions (Richter and Levy 2014): big *legitimate* business.

Drug trafficking as illicit business

As we have seen, Desroches in his literature review on upper-level drug dealers (2007) finds that they 'rationalize' their conduct as business activity. Rationalize here is his word: I would go further and say that to most intents and purposes it *is* business activity. Desroches notes (2007: 830):

> A number of studies of higher level smugglers and wholesalers note that the language used by traffickers is the language of business, dealers view themselves as entrepreneurs, and that being a good 'businessman' is the ultimate compliment in the drug trade. (Adler 1985; Adler and Adler 1992; Desroches 2005; Hagan and McCarthy 1998; Reuter and Haaga 1989; Zaitch 2002)

Certainly there are constraints on the way the business can be carried out, imposed by the illegality of the market. However, some of these constraints do not distinguish these markets from some legal trades. For example, illegal businesses cannot publicly advertise, while also remaining hidden from law enforcement. But the legal cigarette trade cannot publicly advertise in some countries either. Illegal businesses cannot borrow money from banks unless under false pretences, through intermediaries like front companies, or else they have to seek finance from an alternative, underground, finance system. Yet in reality they do both: the recent growth of money laundering laws globally has developed precisely to try to identify the criminal money that washes through conventional financial systems. Even the impossibility of recourse to law which is much remarked upon in the literature is overblown. Organized crime has to settle its own contractual disputes, it is said, as it can hardly turn up in court to ask for an official determination. To a significant extent this is of course true but sophisticated operators in many of the trafficking markets we study in this book do use the law to protect their enterprises, purporting to be legal traders when in fact they are not. So without denying the well-founded observation that illegal business is in some respects different from legal business, the difference seems almost entirely to be in the social and political response to the trade, in other words in the simple fact of its being labelled as illegal, and the economic prerogatives for the business that follow on from that. And even these economic prerogatives are not so clear-cut in practice as they are sometimes imagined to be.

As such, in a world context in which 'globalization has greatly increased the volume of containerized trade, the frequency of international flights, the availability of international delivery services, and global access to the internet' (Natarajan 2019a: 7), it is hardly surprising to find these methods exploited by illegal entrepreneurs for the acceleration of the transnational illicit trade in drugs. Researchers in recent years have noted the illegal drug trade making use of the 'darknet' to organize sales, with Silk Road having been a notorious example (Bilton 2017). The darknet is probably quite obscure as a concept to many non-users but the drug trade has also benefitted from the development and growth in general use of many less arcane or sinister technologies (Marsh et al 2012). Drug deals are done in internet chat rooms and closed Facebook groups. Cell phones are used to make arrangements: either 'burners' where pay-as-you-go SIM cards are purchased for single use then destroyed or 'cloned' phones which ape the identities of legitimate customers. Money laundering is facilitated by the normalization of electronic transfers, in which the task for the specialist forensic accountant policing staff becomes identifying patterns of suspicious behaviour among the millions of financial transfers occurring daily. File encryption allows illegal entrepreneurs to hide evidence of their trade just as it protects the data of legitimate actors.

The structure of drug trafficking overall represents a series of responses to business decisions that affect all traders – for example availability of product, conducive political context for doing business, access to a suitable workforce – combined with a series of responses to the need to minimize the risk of detection by law enforcement or threats from rivals, like dealing with trusted collaborators (Decker and Townsend Chapman 2008), and projecting an impression of violent resolve while minimizing the use of actual violence which would be detrimental to business (Reuter 2009). Just like conventional business, the drug market has successfully developed new products and diversified its supply chains through moving into new regions and using new technologies, all of which has increased its customer base globally. Just as with the globalization of legal business, this has been achieved in aggregate through the enterprising profit-focused decisions of individual entrepreneurs and their networks, groups and firms. In this way the micro-sociological relationship between individual choice and opportunity produces a global structure of illicit economy.

It is axiomatic that drug trafficking is driven by demand, and this is often put forward as a reason supply-focused intervention strategies fail. Illegal entrepreneurs will always work to find a way to meet consumer demand where that exists. However, this is a rather simplistic view of the relationship between supply and demand and on closer inspection it seems that relationship is more dynamic than might usually be thought: it is not just one-way. The development of new synthetic drugs, for example, may be considered an ongoing attempt by drug traffickers to test the waters of demand, and sometimes the new product may not fulfil expectations. We can perhaps see this in the New Psychoactive Substances (NPS) part of the UN's tracking of world drug trafficking, where the 2019 report did not find these to have been taken up in the market as much as had been previously feared and forecasted (UNODC 2019). Supply can therefore create demand, as well as fail to do so, and again the sociology of consumption that addresses legal trade is well aware of this fact. Legitimate businesses often aim to create new markets in products that consumers were hitherto unaware that they needed or wanted. Free trials, or the 'slippery slope' offers of different, 'harder', drugs for purchasers of 'soft' or 'recreational' drugs in illicit drug markets, would be an example of the lower end of that supply-creates-demand dynamic. The development of a new international trade in NPS would be at the higher end of that scale, as would the growth of consumer markets for illegal drugs in transit regions.

Decker and Townsend Chapman's interview study of drug smugglers clarifies the business nature of the enterprise. Among their respondents, roles taken in trafficking are determined by the usual needs of a transnational commercial supply operation: organizers, brokers, those in charge of freight, providers of warehouse space or personnel and those who deal with the finance and money laundering. Like all business enterprises, participants in drug trafficking operations understand the business as comprising roles and duties and talk about trafficking in these terms. In larger organizations, these roles and duties may be well defined, but in smaller projects the participants may be required to multi-task:

> You see, it's like any small business. Sometimes you are the only person there. Your duties won't be completely limited to accounting. You may have to do some driving or something like that, which I would do. Usually, a lot of times I'd get stuck in the so-called safe house or the warehouse. Someone has got to control the inventory, keep track of what goes out and what comes in. That would be my job. (Decker and Townsend Chapman 2008: 95)

Trafficking as business is more nepotistic than conventional business, suffering none of the legal or conventional restrictions on favouring giving jobs to friends, family and recommended acquaintances. Potential participants who are vouched for are more likely to be recruited, where trafficking careers are based on contacts and reputation:

> If you are in the business, you can trust that you are working with serious people. It is easy to get involved because you know people … (Decker and Townsend Chapman 2008: 106)

At the root of all of these references to 'the business' by drug traffickers is a declared self-image as a business person. In *Drug Smugglers on Drug Smuggling*, the authors relay the words of five different drug traffickers, who all consider their crimes to be simply business and through that construction of the activity separate themselves from the harmful consequences of the trade. Some of these quotes are worth reproducing here in full, as they reveal precisely the identity as part of the world of business dealings that I am suggesting throughout this book is the framework that serves to obscure the individual's perceptions of the harm they are doing. The numbers refer to the identification codes used in the study from which these quotes are drawn, used here only to show these are five different respondents speaking (Decker and Townsend Chapman 2008: 108):

> You don't see the damage that drugs do to people because you only deal with classy people, you know? … You never see nobody smoking crack … You don't see yourself like a drug dealer. You see yourself like a businessman. (32)

> I never sold on the streets, never … I am a businessman. (29)

> Organizing and touching drugs is lower-class work, I am a businessman. (15)

> No, it's business. The guy is doing it, and I'm doing this for this amount of money, and that's all. He's not thinking about who's going to smoke that or who's going to die or who's going to do that. I mean, it doesn't even cross his mind. (13)

> A person is only thinking of the money without thinking of the consequences and tragedies it brings along. (720)

Seeing yourself as a businessman taking part in profitable illicit enterprise rather than a criminal causing widespread social harm is a frame of mind that sustains the successful drug trafficker. It allows traffickers to compartmentalize their illicit business activities in two ways: firstly so that the business of drug trafficking is held separate in their minds from other aspects of their personality outside this sphere they perceive to be business enterprise; and secondly so that within that sphere of illicit business there is a stratification between what they are doing (just business) and what other less auspicious participants in the drug trade may be doing (lower level dealing, causing harm). These approaches to compartmentalization achieve a double-layered insulation of the self from the implications of participation in harmful illegal enterprise: in the first place, separating the private person from the business person, and in the second place, relieving that business person of the responsibility for the harmful effects of the trade by placing that responsibility with other less professional criminals in the global system of drug supply.

3

Human Trafficking

The nature and extent of the harm

Human trafficking is an industry. It supplies cheap labour to markets where this can be exploited, and sex workers to sources of demand for prostitution. To call it an industry does not imply corporate levels of organization; the term simply reinforces the widely accepted point that, like other resource-extractive industries, the aim is the sourcing of suitable 'raw materials', the transformation of those raw materials into a product, the movement of the product to a receptive marketplace, and then the final step, turning the product into money in the market.

Much of the discussion about human trafficking to date has focused on sex trafficking, but labour trafficking for business sectors other than the sex industry is also a significant part of the problem. In 2016, an estimated 25 million people worldwide were exploited in forced labour including the sex industry but also working under threat or coercion as domestic workers, on construction sites, in clandestine factories, on farms and fishing boats, and in other sectors (ILO 2017). Women and girls were found to be 99 per cent of those victimized by sex trafficking and 58 per cent of those trafficked into other forced labour sectors. Around one-fifth of the victims of sex trafficking in 2016 were children (ILO 2017). As well as trafficking victims into the sex industry and other legitimate industries, human trafficking also feeds war and crime, as where trafficking 'occurs for the purpose of child soldiering, forced begging, and other criminal activities, and organ harvesting' (Aronowitz 2019: 12).

Human trafficking victims are subjected to serious physical, emotional and sexual abuse (Bales 1999). They have their liberty curtailed, often being held captive in part physically (such as with the removal of passports or being locked into rooms) and in part psychologically (such as where escape is disincentivized with threats of violent repercussions). Their living circumstances are often abject, and in addition to being forced into sex they may also be forced into drug and alcohol abuse, all of which risk serious disease. Health researchers have performed two systematic reviews of the research literature on the physical, mental and sexual health problems associated with human trafficking (Oram et al 2012; Ottisova et al 2016). These have found that trafficked men, women and children report high levels of violence and that in mental terms, unsurprisingly, trafficking victimization induces anxiety, depression and post-traumatic stress disorder. Women and girls self-report 'symptoms suggestive of a high prevalence of infections' (Ottisova et al 2016). In labour trafficking, human trafficking victims may suffer dangerous working conditions in jobs that are typically for low-paid, seasonal workforces.

Human trafficking victims are often said to be vulnerable, and indeed vulnerability is generally considered one of the main factors that puts people at risk of being trafficked (Wilson and O'Brien 2016; Bales 2007). The vulnerability conceptualized here is a combination of socio-economic precarity and psychological impressionability. This vulnerability is, in essence, an ongoing harm in itself, rendering human trafficking often something like getting out of the frying pan into the fire – seeking to escape one set of strained circumstances only to find another, considerably worse, situation. Key to the harm caused by human traffickers to their victims is commodification. The human rights of individuals to be treated as such are denied and they are used by traffickers as 'things', to be moved around the world to feed receptive commercial systems just as goods are transported to market. The process and mindset of commodification is a key part of the exploitation that occurs in human traffic.

The true extent of the harm caused by human trafficking is difficult to estimate. So much of the phenomenon happens in informal economic sectors, among a workforce that is largely hidden from official statistics: undocumented workers in the fields, sex workers on the street and domestic labourers in the home, for example. Most of these instances of victimization will not be reported, and therefore will remain unknown to authorities. Some victims 'may not consider themselves to be victims, instead viewing themselves as migrants whose journeys went wrong, and they prefer the current exploitative situation to their original situation' (Kleemans and Smit 2014: 393), others fall into a depressive fatalistic mindset, coming to think that they are deserving of their fate, others still may not report for the same reasons that victims of other types of fraud are similarly reluctant – shame and embarrassment at having been deceived (Mackenzie 2010b).

The structure of human trafficking: source, transit, market

Unlike some other forms of global trafficking where 'trafficking' is a rather loose catch-all term applied to certain patterns of illegal global trade, human trafficking is a tightly defined concept. The *United Nations Convention against Transnational Organised Crime*, usually referred to as UNTOC, contains several protocols, one of which addresses the particular issue of trafficking under the title *The Protocol to Prevent, Suppress and Punish Trafficking in Persons, Especially Women and Children*. It offers the now generally accepted definition of trafficking as involving acts, means and goals: acts being the types of movement of people that are prohibited, means being the ways in which people are forced or enticed into being trafficked and goals being the ultimate aims of the enterprise. At least one element from each of the acts, means and goals must be present for the activity to constitute human trafficking. The particular acts identified are 'the recruitment, transportation, transfer, harbouring or receipt of persons'. The means are 'the threat or use of force or other forms of coercion, of abduction, of fraud, of deception, of the abuse of power or of a position of vulnerability or of the giving or receiving of payments or benefits to achieve the consent of a person having control over another person, for the purposes of exploitation'. The goals are the ends of that exploitation: 'at a minimum, the exploitation of the prostitution of others or other forms of sexual exploitation, forced labour or services, slavery or practices similar to slavery, servitude or the removal of organs' (United Nations 2000). We will not specifically cover organ trafficking in this book due to space constraints but there are very good sources available that provide revealing investigative detail and critical analysis of the trade in body parts (see, for example, Scheper-Hughes 2001; Lundin 2015; Columb 2020).

The key to the definition of human trafficking is exploitation, and the question of whether there has been exploitation is really one of consent, with strong presumptions against the inference of consent where the circumstances suggest that it may not have been freely given. Genuine consent to movement would render the act one of human smuggling rather than trafficking, and smuggling is governed by its own protocol to the UNTOC convention. Human smuggling may turn into trafficking if exploitation follows, so to that extent the issue of consent is confused since human trafficking also usually begins with consent to travel (Andrees 2008). A key difference between human trafficking and human smuggling is that the relationship in smuggling will end when transport is completed, whereas for trafficking the end of the transport phase may be simply a gateway to the next phase of the exploitative relationship. The trafficking protocol is quite clear that consent to trafficking can never be given by children (defined as under the age of 18) and neither can it be considered as having been given by an adult if it were obtained through 'the threat or use of force, coercion, abduction, fraud or deception' (United Nations 2000).

Debt bondage plays a significant role in human trafficking. In the year that the International Labour Organization studied, 2016, over 70 per cent of adults who were trafficked into forced labour in the agriculture, domestic work or manufacturing sectors were being pressured to do so because of a personal debt they owed (ILO 2017). In many instances these debts are created by the traffickers themselves, who tell the victims they must work to pay off the cost of the transit from their home countries. In one common version of this routine, victims are housed in poor quality, overcrowded lodgings for which they are charged an absurd rent, adding to their debt at the same time as they work to try to reduce it. The threat, and sometimes the reality, of non-payment of wages also exerts undue pressure on labour trafficking victims to submit to their exploited situation, as do threats and acts of physical and sexual violence and threats against family members. Their passports having been confiscated and with no right to work in the country as irregular migrants, recourse to the police seems unlikely and unattractive and victims have little choice but to comply with the circumstances they are presented with. Sometimes the traffickers are more subtle in their methods of control, sharing a small amount of the proceeds of the work with the exploited victims to make them feel complicit and thus discourage them from seeking help from the authorities (Kleemans and Smit 2014).

The usual global trafficking analytical framework of supply–transit–demand applies equally well to human trafficking as it does to other forms of cross-border illegal global commodity trade. Many authors use slight variations on the overall schema – for one illustrative example, 'recruitment, transportation (movement within or into a country), exploitation, and victim disposal' (Aronowitz 2019: 13; 2009) – but these are really just ways of specifying more particular elements involved in the crime rather than any serious departure from the overall economic supply–demand pathway. Like drug trafficking, there is a wide variety to the structure of human trafficking networks. As with drugs, most usual are individuals and small groups linked together as a network into a group of nodes which taken together form the human trafficking chain. Larger organized groups do exist, and so do solo traffickers, who are individual entrepreneurs moving only a few people at a time. The usual practical necessities of trafficking present themselves in human trafficking as elsewhere, in particular corrupting police and border agents and arranging false documentation. Human trafficking is modern day slavery, but Shelley points out that historically not all slavery was the same (Shelley 2010). Patterns of the slave trade varied according to region, and some of those same patterns have cultural and historical resonance in the human trafficking networks operating now.

In the chapter on drug trafficking, we noted that researchers had suggested one of the constraints on that criminal trade, which differentiated it from legal trades, was that drug traffickers cannot advertise. That is one of the constraints of a transnational crime that is prohibited at all stages, and does not become confused at any point with a commercial enterprise that is legal or that is a grey area in terms of il/legality. Human trafficking is not like that – or at least it would be more accurate to say that not all kinds of human trafficking are like that. Sexual services, for example, can be advertised freely in countries where this is legal, and even in countries where aspects of selling or buying sex are illegal, adverts are often widely condoned. Where once it was cards in public telephone boxes, this has now been made redundant as cell phones have killed off public phones and the internet has superseded telephone calls as a means of communication anyway. Human traffickers use advertising for sex to reach large numbers of people, most often via the internet.

The map of human trafficking around the world is closely tied to issues like regional conflict, economic imbalance, unprotected borders and other 'global asymmetries' (Passas 1999) that generate push and pull factors from one country to another, with un- or under-regulated passage in between. Regional human trafficking flows run from surrounding countries into Europe, where entry by the weakest link in the border allows subsequent unrestricted passage throughout the EU, so we see migrant flows from Africa into the EU via Italy's Mediterranean coastal border and other flows from Russia and the Balkans into Eastern Europe. The Golden Triangle zone in Asia has borders across which human trafficking joins other traffic such as, most famously, drugs but also other illicit commodities such as timber and wildlife. Many of the border zones in South America are similarly hot zones of cross-border trade – the illegal and the merely informal – including human trafficking, and the border between Mexico and the US is permeated by human trafficking and smuggling as well as drugs (Andreas 2000).

Human trafficking is a diverse business with different patterns developing from the culture and history of various regions of the world. It has become integrated into the routines of the host societies to the extent that many of the legal and illegal business sectors in these destination countries now depend to some degree on trafficked migrants to fill jobs. Apart from the most discussed realm of sex work, enterprises which use illegal migrant labour include the service industries, like office cleaning firms and domestic labourers, and the night-time economies of many cities, like nightclubs and bars. They also include transport companies, and farming, where salaries for menial labour in fields and factories are so low as to be viewed with derision by local workers, becoming instead the realm of the untaxed, underpaid and possibly indentured victims of international labour trafficking. Some businesses are prepared to turn a blind eye to the use of illegal trafficked migrant labour given the benefits it has for their bottom line.

So human trafficking does not just 'inject' illegal workers into a clean economic system, 'infecting' the labour force and practices of the 'host' country, to apply the epidemiological metaphor, but rather the host is in many ways a willing participant. A better metaphor might be the iron filings drawn to a powerful magnet, as the dominant world economies are built on dubious labour practices, exploitation of the poor and desperate, and willing accomplices in and facilitators of the use of undocumented labour. These powerful economic forces create a demand for cheap labour and other kinds of bodies to be exploited, which makes for a context in which human trafficking is a rational response. Some of the profits of human trafficking are reinvested in the tourism sector as, for example, where Asian trafficking groups buy 'hotels, golf courses, and restaurants' and 'profits from Chinese labour help buy restaurants' (Shelley 2010: 137). This kind of money laundering further integrates the legal economy with the illegal, tying one end of the spectrum of enterprise in with another and further complicating the divide between business that is above board and that which is not.

Methods of recruiting victims into trafficking are varied but most involve some kind of misrepresentation about what is really going on, often tied to the alleviation of deprivation and desperation. Young girls are promised marriage to attractive 'loverboys'; young adults are promised work and the ability to send payments back home to support parents; children are promised toys or educational opportunities; jobseekers are promised arranged employment via agencies that claim to have contacts abroad; some trafficking victims become complicit with their captors and recruit new victims with false accounts of a better life. Promises broken, so do the victims become broken, as they find they have been exploited, lured into forced participation in prostitution or slave labour. For these reasons coercion in the transit phase is the exception rather than the rule, as having been the subject of a misrepresentation during the recruitment phase, the trafficking victim tends to believe the story and travel willingly, only to find out the reality later. Many victims are genuinely deceived but as with all knowledge in society there are shades of understanding, woven with unrealistic hopes and dreams. In his study of sex trafficking, Kara says that 'people know that many such job offers are false, but as many interviewees told me, they are so desperate that they accept them hoping that "nothing bad will happen to me"' (Kara 2017: 7).

While deceit is the most common recruitment method, human trafficking can also occur consequent upon sale of the person by family members, usually 'heartbreaking decisions that parents are forced to make due to extremes of destitution few Westerners can imagine' (Kara 2017: 8), or other forms of abduction against the will of the trafficking victim. Given that most human trafficking is based in deceit, the victim usually moves willingly, and the increasing volume of both commercial and leisure travel that globalization has brought, together with its lower cost, both facilitates human trafficking and makes it easier to hide among the hundreds of thousands of daily journeys that take place worldwide. Added to this high volume of movement, the fact that many human trafficking victims have the correct documents to travel, including the use of tourist or student visas, makes trafficking very hard to detect (Viuhko and Jokinen 2009).

At the demand end of the chain of global supply in trafficking markets we can see so-called 'pull' factors and these are present in the markets for trafficked people just as they are in other illegal cross-border trade. They include the receptive industries mentioned above – construction, farming, sex and more – and their capacity to integrate low paid illegal migrants into their work. Unlike other trafficking markets though, human traffic has been identified as having 'push' factors too. These include the precarious economic circumstances back home, which may offer few opportunities for stable employment, combined with and in some cases a result of high population growth, civil conflict or political instability, oppression and human rights violations based on race or gender, and other local or national instabilities such as corruption and persecution by political violence or the collateral damage effects of unchecked organized crime (Bales 2007). Whereas humans can be 'pushed' in such ways, unconscious chattels hardly can, so there is not a developed discourse of push factors for global markets in illicit commodities, where the main analytical tool is the pull of the market. Certainly many of these social contexts of conflict, unemployment and instability are implicated in the outflow of trafficked goods from source countries, but the language of the 'push' applies more readily to humans than to inanimate objects.

Regulation and control of human trafficking

The major ongoing debate in relation to human trafficking policy is whether it is more appropriate, or more productive, to take a criminal justice approach or a human rights approach to the problem. Observers of the discourse of human trafficking at the UN level see an amalgam of these perspectives in the current approach, which has moved from primarily human rights oriented to incorporating ever greater reference to and framing of the problem as transnational crime (Lloyd and Simmons 2015).

Proponents of the human rights approach point out that the victims of human trafficking have usually been seen in destination countries not as victims but as perpetrators of crime (Lee 2011). Their exploitation unrecognized, they are too often considered illegal migrants and/or sex workers in destination countries, to be deported and therefore re-inserted into the same social and economic context that generated their trafficking victimization in the first place. This sense that trafficking victims are complicit in the criminal situation they have been forced into is compounded by several features of the usual victim response to their exploitation: a reluctance to inform the police; shades of denial that render them incapable or unwilling to come to terms with their victimization; a sense of shame and the consequent desire to keep their exploitation a secret; and the fact that their exploitation by the traffickers is constructed as a dependent relationship, so breaking out of that dependence would bring circumstances unknown, and therefore feared.

Awareness raising is thought to be important in combatting recruitment, given that the problem has been characterized as vulnerable individuals being sucked in by misrepresentations made by traffickers. In that context, it makes sense to try to sensitize people to the risk involved, aiming to make vulnerable populations more resilient overall to these predatory approaches. Awareness raising can occur through adverts in the print, online and TV media and advice hotlines. These may be useful in their own right, but in the case of the internet particularly, they may counteract the use of social media platforms to recruit victims through these channels. The internet has made it easy for traffickers to strike up online conversations with prospective victims, including young people, and to hide behind false identities, as in the case of fictitious labour employment agencies.

Awareness raising is not only targeted at potential victims but has also been thought important for officials who may come into contact with human trafficking, such as police, border control authorities, embassy staff, labour inspection agencies that monitor and enforce labour laws, and employers in the private sector.

Technological developments of course play a role in human trafficking, as suggested above in relation to the use of social media. Like drug traffickers, human traffickers use cheap, readily available technology to aid communication and avoid detection. Burner phones and disposable SIM cards are common in human trafficking (TRACE 2016), just as in drug trafficking. Business enterprises, legal and illegal, use infrastructure to facilitate trade, and communications technology is simply one – constantly advancing – aspect of the infrastructure that forms the context in which trade can happen.

The ongoing confusion created by a problem of extreme human rights infringement that is policed by a criminal justice system based on a flawed understanding of, and quite possibly a structural inability to ever clearly see, the real nature of the problem has led to a global trafficking problem that remains ineffectively controlled. Police organizations and their policy counterparts worldwide have traditionally focused unduly on the movement, or transit, phase seeking to interdict traffickers on the move, especially at the border. International movement is only one aspect of the problem, however. There is a disjuncture between, on one hand, the nomenclature used to label the problem – human trafficking – and, on the other, the fact that the core definition of the problem in the UNTOC protocol focuses on exploitation rather than movement. Movement is part of the problem, to be sure, but it has been watered down to the extent that it includes internal trafficking – that is, movement within a country, not crossing an international border – rendering various kinds of within-country exploitation 'trafficking' and confusing the issue for law enforcement as well as for students of the phenomenon. While national police forces attempt to intercept human trafficking in transit, therefore, much local exploitation in both source and market countries continues unchecked.

The historical failure of law enforcement agencies in destination countries for human trafficking to treat victims as such, casting them instead as part of a network of illegal migration, undocumented labour or unlawful sex work, has significantly hampered the ability of the police and prosecutors to collect actionable testimony from victims. Suspecting they are likely to be criminally charged and/or deported, many human trafficking victims prefer not to engage with police interrogators at all. It has now been acknowledged that this is a significant and unnecessary intelligence gap for the police, and the use of translators and a generally more willing approach to acknowledging victimization is becoming more common.

As with drug trafficking, and as we shall see the same is true of all of the other trafficking markets examined in this book, corruption in the agencies of control is a significant facilitator of human trafficking and a key sticking point in attempts by national law enforcement agencies to exercise greater control. At all points – police, border agents, prosecutors, judiciary – the proper enforcement of the law is compromised by actors who take bribes in order to overlook their official duties. For the case of sex trafficking, Kara summarizes the problem:

> Police take bribes in every country I visited to allow sex-slave establishments to operate, warn brothel owners when investigations are imminent, and permit the exploitation of minors with impunity. Border guards do the same to allow traffickers to pass from one country to the next. Judges take bribes to lessen trafficking charges to minor infractions, such as pimping. In all cases, paltry civil wages allow traffickers to offer bribes that represent a rounding error in operational profits to them but a large increase in a civil servant's income. (Kara 2017: 39)

In both source and destination countries, specialist police units dedicated to human trafficking where they exist are small and often substantially under-funded. But perhaps the most obvious failure of the criminal justice/border control approach is that it does not take account of the fact, already noted above, that very many human trafficking victims travel willingly and with papers in good order, only to discover the nature of their exploitation on arrival at the destination. Border securitization has its challenges as an approach to a problem that is hard to see in those terms. Where, in extreme cases, border lockdown approaches do influence traffickers to try to circumvent rather than dupe control points, it can be counter-productive 'in terms of human lives, injuries, and perilous travel conditions, as is demonstrated by research on securing the US-Mexican border' (Kleemans and Smit 2014: 389; Frost 2007; Guerette 2007), and also, we might add, the many other cases of deaths and injuries in transit around the world in both human smuggling and trafficking, such as the 58 smuggled Chinese immigrants who were discovered suffocated in a lorry at the port of Dover in the UK in 2000 (Kleemans and Smit 2014).

Compartmentalization of human trafficking as just business

Reports of the abuses perpetrated by human traffickers sometimes suggest a mindset that would be hard to class as much other than pure evil. Consider this report by Kara of the typical experiences of sex trafficking victims in his study:

> A young woman named Tatyana, who accepted a job offer through *Makler*, told me, 'When I left home with the agents, they raped me and they did not feed me for days. They forced me to urinate in my clothes'. Another sex trafficking victim was taken to a hotel by her alleged job agent and raped by six German men for several days in a row. Another was dumped in the trunk of a car for a four-day journey from Poland to Italy, beaten daily, and given nothing to eat. (Kara 2017: 12)

Surely these quotes reveal a level of depravity on the part of the traffickers that would make an attempt to talk about compartmentalization redundant? Can such abusers really be thought of as possibly considering themselves generally 'good people' and as inflicting harm only in a way that makes it all 'just business'? To answer these questions we should remember that the issue of compartmentalization and a 'just business' approach sits within the theoretical framework of the banality of evil and the dehumanization and indifference to suffering that this involves. We should also remember that the original banal evils that spurred Arendt to her critique were the abuses of the holocaust, which are surely just as hard to witness and to try to understand. So let us begin this section by acknowledging that on the face of it, the compartmentalization and business approach we identified in relation to drug dealing seems more plausible as a meta-analytical framework for that kind of trafficking than it does for human trafficking. Yet despite this apparent diagnosis of human trafficking as the large-scale perpetration of outrageous personal violations, I will suggest that torture, rape, humiliation and merciless abuse are indeed amenable to being best explained as 'just business'.

There is some evidence that human traffickers compartmentalize. Following the classic and well-known work of Sykes and Matza (1957) on techniques of neutralization, some studies of human traffickers have sought to frame the discourse of traffickers as a neutralizing practice (Antonopoulos and Winterdyk 2005; Copley 2013). These papers use interviews recorded with traffickers and analysed by the researchers, and although that analysis is framed in terms of techniques of neutralization, the discourse as reported in these papers is notable for being entirely transactional. A trafficker of women and girls for sex considers that for some victims – those who initially consent, not knowing the reality of what they are getting into – the trafficking is effectively contractual: 'I offer, you accept, and the job is done' (Antonopoulos and Winterdyk 2005: 142). He rationalizes his role in organizing the exploitation of others in the same way a capitalist employer would focus on the ideology of the benefits of employment to their workforce, rather than the pains of indentured labour: 'when they were in their countries they did not have anything to eat … now, they have money, they live in good houses, they have clothes …' (Antonopoulos and Winterdyk 2005: 143).

As with white-collar crimes and other crimes of the powerful such as state crimes, the fragmented nature of human trafficking chains allows actors to use 'cog in the machine' arguments to distance themselves from a sense of personal responsibility for wrongdoing. In the business of human trafficking, as in legitimate business, you take care of the duties and responsibilities of your role while the ultimate effects of the industry are not your fault:

'I have no responsibility if anything bad happens to the girls. I do not do anything … I just get the papers …' (Antonopoulos and Winterdyk 2005: 143). We can hear echoes here of the 'I'm just a businessman' narrative that in the preceding chapter we found drug traffickers used when talking about their involvement in that crime (Decker and Townsend Chapman 2008).

Earning a living is the priority, a motivation created by the structure of economic life and its demands: 'if you have … children, and they go to school … and they want clothes, shoes, holidays, what can you do? Do you think it is enough money if you go legit?' (Antonopoulos and Winterdyk 2005: 143). Here we can clearly see the Mertonian strain of contemporary economic life (Merton 1968) pushing decision-making into the 'just business' compartment; it's just what you have to do to get by.

The human trafficker interviewed by Antonopoulos:

> placed the trafficking of women in a context that fits the legal business context of the night-time economy. In

> particular he perceived the trafficking of women in Greece as just another integral element of the night-time economy, a commodity, just as the alcoholic drinks, non-forced prostitution, or even bouncing … Framing, to use a term by Erving Goffman (Goffman 1974), the trafficking of women as 'simply business', by detaching the whole activity of trafficking from the women who are trafficked, and by ascribing trafficking a functional entrepreneurial nature … (Antonopoulos and Winterdyk 2005: 144)

The authors in that revealing study consider that the only technique of neutralization that is absent in the trafficker's discourse is the appeal to higher loyalties – for what loyalty higher than the law might such an enterprise criminal appeal to? However, it is clear on reading their report that they have overlooked the financially lucrative nature of the illegal business enterprise as providing the higher loyalty: a commitment, that is, to what is perceived to be the necessity of financial gain in a social, economic and political context where that is set up as paramount.

The defence of necessity is one of the additional neutralizations authors have suggested as expansions to the original five techniques set out by Sykes and Matza (Minor 1981; Maruna and Copes 2005). There can, of course, be all sorts of perceived necessities that help offenders to neutralize feelings of guilt and shame, and not all of the necessities in life are financial or business-like. Yet where that perceived necessity is for money, and the perceived best mechanism to get that money is illegal trade, we seem to have stepped beyond the realm of techniques of neutralization as guilt reduction and into the realm of a more whole-hearted adoption of a business mindset.

We could make a similar argument for others among the extended repertoire of techniques of neutralization. For example, the metaphor of the ledger, developed by Carl Klockars in his study of a professional fence (Klockars 1974), can be interpreted as a rapprochement between the compartmentalized business life and the personal, social life that is lived alongside it. The ledger metaphor has the offender saying 'yes I know this act is bad, but look at all the good I have done', thus considering the individual's ethics to be accounted for by way of a moral balance sheet, in which individual entries are less important than the overall positive or negative balance. There is strong evidence that many people do indeed implement practical day-to-day morality in this way, if not wholly endorse it as a justifiable abstract mechanism for judging good from bad. This is a metaphor that draws on business imagery, the accounting ledger, but its import in criminology has only been taken on as a relatively weak version of the impact of business on practical ethics. In this diluted business metaphor, people think about morality as if the right/wrong quality of acts were a series of entries in the credit and debit columns of an accounting ledger. However, the theory does not go so far as to suggest that this type of transactional ethical accounting may be part of a compartmentalized approach that takes moral turpitude in the course of a business enterprise, whether that be licit or illicit, as 'off the books' altogether as far as one's ethical accounting in personal life goes. If that latter version is true, it may be that what goes on in business stays in business, if the compartments of the soul are adequately constructed.

In addition to the papers that have engaged with human traffickers as users of techniques of neutralization, other studies contain interview data sourced from human traffickers that can be revealing in terms of the business orientation of human traffickers (Kara 2017; Molland 2010). Some of these show the limits to the 'just business' frame of analysis. Human trafficking is a complex area including not just enterprise criminals trafficking for profit but also cognate activities like soldiers, sometimes senior officers, trafficking women to serve the sexual predation of military troops (Allen 1996; Tanaka 2003), in some cases for political and symbolic ends (Salzman 1998).

Molland's study of sex trafficking along the Thai-Lao border engages with what he perceives to be the over-cooked impression among international agencies and other commentators that human trafficking is 'immensely profitable' (Molland 2010). An anthropologist, he introduces other cultural and social considerations in a finer-grained analysis than most high-level observers would undertake. He finds that traffickers act in a mindset of Sartrean 'bad faith', rationalizing to themselves and others that they are helping those they recruit into the sex trade, by giving them a way to improve on their socio-economic position. For Molland, this is bad faith because underneath these productive lies is the fact that the recruiter is clearly motivated by money. As such it seems to me that it would be useful to think of such lies, if not as transparent, then perhaps as translucent. The *translucent lie* is only half believable, and only half believed, both by those who hear it and those who utter it. The translucent lie of Molland's sex trafficker is that 'recruitment takes on a connotation of *helping*' (Molland 2010: 223, emphasis in original). In this way, exploitation is dressed up as altruism, considered to be playing a part in increasing the capacity of trafficked sex workers to acquire the trappings of cultural and economic capital (Bourdieu 1984, 1986). The fact that the trappings that can be acquired in the brothels in Molland's study amount only to trendy clothes and make-up does not seem to disturb the translucent lie of altruism being peddled by those involved in the trafficking.

Bad faith, as Sartre conceived it, amounts to the denial of one's own nature as a subject (Sartre 1956 [1943]). It involves the weaving of new webs of meaning that overlay the essence of the situation as it is understood, deep down, by participants, over-writing that with a new interpretation that participants and observers are invited to believe. Thus, 'social actors … deny to themselves alternative courses of action as well as alternative interpretations of them' (Molland 2010: 224). If trafficking is an act of helping, why would one stop? We can easily think of many examples of bad faith in the social construction of reality, and business enterprise is a good example among the many social contexts in which bad faith as a process of normative cultural narrative is rife. The discourse of helping is one of the major ways in which the harmful effects of profit-oriented business activity are recalibrated as externalities, considered peripheral to the main aim of the enterprise. Where the indicators of social status and success are themselves economic, giving people the opportunity to earn money, licitly or illicitly, can be portrayed as improving their situation. Minor economic rewards that can be transformed into the barest indicators of cultural and economic capital allow exploitation to be recast as helping.

Of course much human trafficking is not amenable to being characterized by the traffickers as helping victims; the serial rapes and other physical and mental abuses which are common currency in human trafficking are obviously outside an explanatory framework of a bad faith sense of helping. Ingrained and normalized gender bias can contribute in some regions to our understanding of the dehumanization and commodification of female bodies as saleable objects of use and abuse. These acculturated denigrating attitudes towards women in source regions for human trafficking like South and East Asia, and Central and Eastern Europe, combine with a ready market for sex among men in the destination countries for human trafficking to create an illicit economy which rewards recruitment, transport and exploitation (Kara 2017).

Vetlesen says that 'what makes us suffer evil is also what makes us want to cause it' (Vetlesen 2005: 289). The large-scale vulnerability caused by economic globalization with its reinforcement and acceleration of structural global inequality is at the root of the globalization of indifference to suffering identified in this book. The vulnerable and exploited, trapped by an economic system that excludes them, react to this marginalization by seeking their own victims, undertaking an existential project which seeks through exploiting the vulnerability of others to expunge that which they despise in themselves:

> In this perspective, evildoing is an existential project in which the individual, finding his non-chosen vulnerability intolerable, seeks ways to get rid of it, hoping to do so by transporting the vulnerability to others so as to feel some control over it. (Vetlesen 2005: 289)

And:

> In keeping with Alford's Kleinian insight into how psychic pain not only stifles vitality and self-worth but tends to be transported from one individual (the one originally affected) onto others, the suffering caused by economic-system injustices is today subject to various attempts among the victims to reclaim their threatened agency by turning it – be it by subtle psychological assaults, be it by violent physical ones – against selected others perceived as even weaker and more marginalised than themselves. (Vetlesen 2005: 291)

As with many other writers, including as he points out, Bourdieu (1998), Vetlesen sees economic globalization as 'a systemic evil, a systematically produced social injustice, that humiliates its victims, stripping them not only of material security but of positive sources of social respect and ultimately of self-worth' (Vetlesen 2005: 291). In the neoliberal globalization of marketization, where seemingly any sector of society is a ready candidate for reworking in line with the ideology of a competitive market, 'of making a profit of every single human activity and need, of seeing profitability as the sole source of justification for just about everything … evil breeds evil, since all non-episodic and enduring violence is eventually paid for in the utterly concrete form of human misery and suffering' (Vetlesen 2005: 291).

Here then we can conclude our analysis of human trafficking with the outline of an analytical framework that seems to provide some links between: first, the macro-level processes of global economic markets that have produced success and, disproportionately, failure and exclusion; second, meso-level narratives around business and enterprise that justify and excuse the externalizing of harmful effects from that enterprise, and push consideration of those effects aside; and third, micro-level adaptations by individuals to the strains and illicit opportunities that global markets present, including paying out the dividends of the symbolic violence they have suffered at the hands of the neoliberal global market by way of turning those market forces to their own illicit benefit and shifting the focus of the ills of economic exclusion and the commodification of the human body and soul onto the victims they traffic. This is the model by which human trafficking is cast for participants as a form of illicit business in which doing that business is considered simply a way of getting on economically in a hostile and uncompassionate world.

4

Wildlife Trafficking

The nature and extent of the harm

Wildlife trafficking as a topic of study in criminology sits in something of a position of tension. On the one hand, it is considered a 'green crime' and as such it is discussed as an integral part of the topic area of green criminology, which is concerned with harm to the ecosystems of the planet (for example, Ngoc and Wyatt 2013; Nurse and Wyatt 2020). On the other hand, as a form of trafficking alongside drugs, arms and so on, it is taken to be a type of organized crime, and so scholars working in that field concentrate on the ways in which it fits with that literature (for example, Lavorgna 2014). Wildlife trafficking is not alone in being treated as a topic of core interest to green criminology while also having been analysed from the perspective of another branch of criminology. For example, many green crimes are also white-collar crimes – think of corporate pollution, carbon trading scheme scams and so on – and green criminologists are generally quite explicit in their acknowledgement that their area is a hybrid meeting point of many different streams of thought, coalescing around a concern with environmental destruction. There are many effects of these 'multiple perspectives' issues in criminology, and for wildlife trafficking one of these is the different frameworks of harm assessment that green criminology and the criminology of organized crime bring.

From the perspective of green criminology, the harm wildlife trafficking causes should be assessed in terms of harm to animals, the environment and ecosystems. The harm to the environment and ecosystems is where the overlap with human harm is seen from the green criminological perspective. Flora and fauna are important resources for local communities around the world, and this is especially so in developing countries where they may provide a source of food, fuel (for example, in the case of timber), medicine and tourism. The removal of these community resources to feed an international trafficking trade can have considerable adverse effect on the locals who usually benefit from and co-exist with them. The longer term economic and cultural effects on local populations when the biodiversity that enriches their landscape is depleted can diminish the prospects of sustainable income through tourism, as well as the many other damaging effects that local ecosystem collapse may bring about. So the taking of species of animals and plants from their natural habitat is one damaging ecosystem effect of this form of trafficking but so too may be their unregulated insertion into other regions as a result of trafficking, where they might 'compete with local species for resources, alter ecosystems, damage infrastructure, and destroy crops' as well as introducing 'pathogens that threaten public health, agricultural production, and biodiversity' (Smith et al 2009: 594).

There is also another human cost to wildlife trafficking in that both poaching and anti-poaching can be a dangerous practice. Van Uhm talks of 'poor fishermen in the Caspian basin [who] poach sturgeon and risk their lives to feed their families' (van Uhm 2016: 258), and there are many accounts of rangers being killed and injured by the more violent among the poaching gangs (for example, Belecky et al 2019).

Focusing on the human costs of wildlife trafficking has been pointed out by green criminologists to be a typically anthropocentric view, and these writers also therefore draw attention to the great suffering of the animals involved (Nurse and Wyatt 2020). Animals are drugged, concealed in small smuggling spaces (Wyatt 2013), killed for their horns or tusks, boiled alive (Pantel and Anak 2010), caught in illegal traps, caged and so on. The regulatory conceptualization of the issue of wildlife trafficking as a problem of trade versus extinction, combined with the conceptual policy language of fighting crime, tends to gloss over the issue of animal abuse and non-human harm (Wyatt 2014a).

In figures, trafficking wildlife can be seen to be a seriously destructive crime. In 2019, despite an increase in numbers over the last decade due to conservation efforts, rhino populations have reached a tipping point with births no longer keeping up with poaching, so that 'two of the world's five rhino species could be lost in our lifetime' according to researchers (International Rhino Foundation 2019a, 2019b). The World Wildlife Fund estimates there are only around 3,890 tigers left in the wild due to killing for skins and traditional medicines (WWF 2016).

From the perspective of the criminology of organized crime, the harm of wildlife trafficking is often considered in monetary terms or number of seizures (the size of the illicit trade), in terms of its human costs (especially violence associated with the trade) and its destabilizing effects on states and governance (corruption of officials and drawing local populations into the source end of global crime networks). On the first of these, the size of the trade, the UN has estimated that wildlife trafficking 'ranks among the five most lucrative illegal trades in the world – costing approximately US$23 billion annually' (Kurland 2019: 55). These estimates and rankings of the hit parade of illicit trades are notoriously unreliable though and have been quite widely and consistently critiqued by scholars working in each of the ranked fields. It is also worth pointing out that although headline catching, the financial size of a given trafficking market is hardly a measure of its harmful impact, merely an indicator of the amount of money changing hands. Seizure statistics are available through the first UNODC Wildlife Crime Report, which used WorldWISE, the World Wildlife Seizure database, to paint a picture of current trends (UNODC 2016). The database included some 164,000 seizures from 120 countries and a follow-up report in 2017 tracked the trends from there (UNODC 2017a). Other seizure reports are available that track trends focusing on specific types of animals (see, for example, Wong and Krishnasamy 2019). These tend to acknowledge that seizures alone are not enough to prevent or reduce wildlife trafficking.

The structure of wildlife trafficking: source, transit, market

Wildlife trafficking, as it is usually conceived by criminologists, involves the trafficking of protected species of animals and plants, and parts of them (such as ivory or pangolin scales). Timber is usually treated as a separate category of trafficking, so not normally included in discussions of wildlife trafficking, and neither is illegal, unreported and unregulated fishing, which again has its own literature. Whether these distinctions and exclusions are justifiable is open to question (Kurland 2019).

In general, and in common with the other transnational criminal markets referred to in this book, illegal wildlife flows originate in developing countries and connect to the sources of demand in consumer markets which exist particularly in Europe, the US, the richer states of the Middle East, and Asia (Duffy 2010). Each of these flows has a different dynamic, with the demand being based in some cases more for traditional medicines, in some for high-end status symbols and in others for the more routine wildlife trade of pet stores and specialist private collectors. Like some other trafficking markets, for example antiquities, although the overall picture is of resource drain from developing to developed nations, some developed countries which are the source of particular types of sought-after wildlife suffer from trafficking that extracts flora and fauna. For some examples: New Zealand has rare reptiles such as gecko and tuatara, and unusual wild birds and insects found only there; Australia similarly has a number of idiosyncratic species; and the UK and Russia are home to a variety of wild birds of prey such as falcons and osprey that are prized in the falconry markets of the Middle East (Elliott 2009; Wyatt 2009).

The picture of trafficking networks for wildlife is in some ways similar to the cases of drugs and human trafficking already covered. That is, if the initial impression from media and policy output is of global organized crime syndicates running the trade, the reality is usually considerably smaller scale and more mundane, and substantially more so than drugs and human trafficking. Wildlife trafficking, like other forms of transnational crime, is better thought of as a 'crime that is organized' rather than as organized crime (Pires et al 2016), and indeed while some of the policy literature suggests wildlife trafficking to be huge business, reliable evidence of this purported large-scale global threat is hard to find in the literature. Trafficking wildlife seems to be the remit of solo freelance operators or small networks with links to the legitimate trade (Reuter and O'Regan 2017). The literature review conducted by those authors found minimal links between wildlife trafficking and other types of trafficking such as drugs, humans and arms. Although there are reports of some such links available, Reuter and O'Regan consider these to be the exception, where the rule is fairly rudimentary trafficking methods employed by actors with ties to the industry, which the authors consider to be 'relatively small scale across the Western Hemisphere' (Reuter and O'Regan 2017: 90). Kurland characterizes this as '"crimes that are organized" by largely legitimate businesses that take advantage of opportunities arising in day-to-day operations to make some additional money' (Kurland 2019: 58). It is hard to reconcile assessments of the modest size and structure of wildlife trafficking with the ubiquitous statements of apparently reliable expert sources along the lines that 'the illegal wildlife trade is one of the most profitable illegal industries in the world, only behind the trafficking of drugs, guns and humans' (Pires et al 2016: 4). Can 'crimes that are organized' by largely legitimate businesses and small-scale actors with ties to them really amount to a massively profitable illicit global industry?

The answer is perhaps found in the need to differentiate between regional types of poaching and the dynamics of the particular markets they feed. Pires et al suggest this may be the right approach:

> Claims that organized crime groups are involved in the poaching and trafficking of elephant tusks and rhino horn may be accurate, but it does not necessarily insinuate

> their involvement with hundreds of other species that are commonly poached and trafficked around the globe. The illegal trade in endangered flora and fauna can (and does) differ vastly from species to species. (Pires et al 2016: 8)

Certainly, poaching rhino horn in South Africa seems to have a level of organization above many more opportunistic wildlife trafficking crimes. Rhino poachers have high-calibre weapons and other sophisticated hunting equipment and vehicles, are prepared to use threats, bribery and violence in pursuit of their enterprise and are connected to the international operations of organized trafficking networks (Hübschle 2016). Likewise the trafficking of illegally sourced caviar is a business where 'networks regularly maintain their position by the use of excessive violence illustrated by military attacks, bombings and kidnappings' (van Uhm 2016: 263). Other activities at the source end of wildlife trafficking markets are less dramatic, however, such as where hunting is regulated through permit systems that can be abused:

> A Russian professional trapper told one source how he uses the same permits multiple times to take more than his licensed amount of furbearers ... For instance, he will trap 20 squirrels, or whichever amount is shown on his licence. If the inspector does not stop to check his documents, then he will go every day to take as many squirrels up to the limit of 20 as he can, until the inspector stops him and stamps the date and fills in the rest of the permit ... Trapping occurs during the peak of winter when the pelts are at their fullest, so this trapper also hides pelts in the snow, showing the inspector only the number of pelts that corresponds to his permit. (South and Wyatt 2011: 548)

This kind of routine abuse of licencing systems finds a close parallel at the source end of some other trafficking markets. Notably, using one permit or licence document to launder multiples of the apparently authorized item has been found to be a method used by local antiquities dealers in Israel (Kersel 2006). Another version of this type of permit laundering has been observed in the Southern African trade in exotic birds:

> A bird dealer or pet shop owner may legally have a pair of exotic birds with the legitimate CITES permits required for ownership. This dealer or owner may continually buy

> poached birds of the same species at regular intervals for resale, claiming that these are the offspring of the original pair. (Warchol et al 2003: 23)

Comparable with antiquities trafficking, where cultural artefacts are often looted in secluded locations, much wildlife in source countries is found away from the large centres of human habitation, in forests, savannahs and game reserves. The risk of detection that poachers run is therefore, as with antiquities looters, relatively low. Another clear parallel with grey markets such as those serviced by antiquities trafficking and diamond trafficking, as we will come to see, is in the interface between trafficking and legitimate businesses. As intimated above, flows of illegal wildlife regularly enter the legal trade through people and businesses that essentially 'launder' the illegal things so that, when sold, they have taken on the appearance of legal sales (Lyons and Natusch 2011; Wyatt 2009). These legitimate enterprises that mix legal with illegal trade, covering up wildlife crime by wrapping it up in the presentation of legal business, include pet shops, restaurants and dealers (Wyatt 2013). Following the remarks made above about the different perspectives one could use to think about wildlife trafficking, these above-board business entities that launder illegal wildlife into the legal trade could be viewed through the lens of organized crime, as facilitators to organized criminal network activity, or alternatively through the lens of white-collar crime, as legal businesses doing some underhand trade 'on the side'. Green criminology has even invented its own terminology for the illegal environmentally destructive business activities of legal enterprises: dirty collar crimes (Ruggiero and South 2010) or green collar crimes (O'Hear 2004). Both of those terms could be usefully applied to white-collar criminals in the wildlife trafficking area, suggesting an emerging frame of reference which is moving towards a synthesis of relevant theoretical considerations from white-collar crime, organized crime and green criminology. Sometimes these upperworld organizations are essentially fronts for underworld (that is, organized crime) enterprises – van Uhm refers to the example of 'a syndicate [that] was active for over four years keeping rhinos for conservation purposes, while the rhinos were actually dehorned and killed to make profits of their illegal sale' (van Uhm 2016: 266; Rademeyer 2012; Ayling 2013) – but more often they are genuine legal businesses running a mixed economy of licit and illicit trade.

Poachers connect with the market in various ways. In their study of the parrot trade in Peru and Bolivia, Pires et al found poachers gathering birds in a fairly uncoordinated way using basic methods like nets. They then either sold the goods to middlemen or to marketplace sellers, who would sell to consumers, or in some cases they simply sold direct to consumers themselves. In the last two cases, the poachers were also therefore, technically, the traffickers (Pires et al 2016: 14). This kind of loosely organized and opportunistic structure may work in this region because the demand for parrots is local rather than international. Therefore the challenge of international transit and penetrating the customs barriers of distant countries does not present itself. Other studies of local markets, for example unregulated markets for elephant ivory in adjacent countries to the source, reveal similar trafficking patterns that take advantage of these nearby opportunities (Lemieux and Clarke 2009).

Family and friendship networks regularly form the basis of wildlife trafficking connections. Van Uhm (2016) notes such family and friendship ties in his studies of the Russian caviar trade, the Barbary macaque traders in Morocco and the Chinese cultural practice of *guanxi*. *Guanxi* supports illicit wildlife trade by way of a deeply ingrained and widely understood system of social relations encapsulating loyalty, reciprocity and trust, therefore providing some social and cultural 'glue' to illicit exchange relationships (Zhang et al 2009).

Like drug trafficking, the methods of transporting wildlife illegally across borders include concealment in legitimate shipments, in luggage and on the person and/or corruption of officials. Unlike drug trafficking but like other trafficking markets where the product is hard to distinguish on inspection as either licit or illicit, for example antiquities, guns or diamonds, import/export document fraud can be enough to allow uninterrupted transit. Facilitation is sometimes provided by transport haulage firms, airline, railway and shipping personnel, baggage handlers and tour firm employees (South and Wyatt 2011), among others.

Consumer markets in wildlife are varied in their orientation and purpose, including markets for status pets, local cultures of consumption (for example, of bush meat in Africa) and traditional medicines which comprise protected flora and fauna (Warchol et al 2003). In many of these markets, the symbolic value of particular kinds of wildlife mixes with the functional value of the thing, so that the motivation to purchase or consume is a mix of cultural tradition and impression of the importance of the consumptive practice to personal or communal health and wellbeing. In the case of traditional Chinese medicine (TCM), form and impressions of function are clearly fused in this way (Coggins 2003). In other markets for trafficked wildlife products, questions of function seem almost entirely over-written by symbolism, for example the reality of fish eggs versus the high-rolling imagery of caviar (Saffron 2002).

Poverty, unemployment and social exclusion are often the context for wildlife poaching. As with many other transnational criminal markets, the first steps at the source stage of the raw materials for illegal cross-border trade take place in a context of local and regional economic strain, relative inequality and deprivation. The source end of wildlife trafficking chains of supply is also notable for being relatively violent compared to some other resource extraction-based trades such as antiquities. The presence of weapons used as instruments of poaching plays some part in this, as carrying firearms, which are sometimes high-powered and semi-automatic, makes a deadly gunfight more likely to ensue if park rangers or other law enforcement agents attempt to intervene.

Regulation and control of wildlife trafficking

The Convention on International Trade of Endangered Species of Wild Flora and Fauna (CITES) is an international agreement to regulate trade in protected wildlife. It sets up a series of categories into which animals and plants are placed depending on the gravity of their threatened status. Appendix I flora and fauna are considered threatened with extinction, and trade in these is effectively banned other than in the most exceptional circumstances. Appendix II species can be internationally transported and traded, but only if they are accompanied by the appropriate CITES documentation. Without this, both export (usually from the source country) and import (into transit or market countries) will not be allowed. Most of the species covered by CITES are Appendix II species. An export certificate under CITES will only be granted for Appendix II species where the experts in the source country are satisfied that it will not be detrimental to the survival of the species, since protecting the conservation of species in the wild is stated to be the main aim of the convention. As such, quotas can be set up by source countries for Appendix II species. Appendix III species are subject to the lowest level of protection, and trade in these is regulated only because at least one CITES state party has asked the other CITES countries to help it protect wildlife which it feels is being unsustainably exploited.

CITES presently has 183 state parties. The convention requires its member states to designate authorities for managing its terms, at the centre of which is the permitting system that supports the administration of the Appendices, which together now cover in the region of 35,000 species of animals and plants. There is nothing to stop individual countries or blocks of countries introducing laws which are stricter than the permitting system CITES requires and many, such as the EU, have done this. Countries can choose to implement CITES with criminal penalties, as many have done, or civil or administrative sanctions (Nurse 2015; Wyatt 2013).

The CITES mechanism has been criticized as allowing opportunities for laundering. It is sometimes hard for non-experts to easily distinguish between species listed in the Appendices and even in some cases between species that are regulated and those that are not, which presents opportunities for traffickers to mis-declare one type of animal or plant as another (Hutton and Dickson 2000; Warchol et al 2003). The convention and its mechanisms have also been criticized as products of a colonial and paternalistic ideology, not giving sufficient weight to the concerns of local populations and their traditional use of wildlife which may conflict with stiff regulations on trade or outright bans (Hübschle 2017; Peterson et al 2016).

This critique of CITES maps on to a more generalized critique of many of the features of the international framework of regulation for protected wildlife as being too blind to the perspective of local users of plants and animals. The CITES framework of listed species protections and trade bans has been argued to be a product of a colonial mindset (Garland 2008) that looks at matters from the western perspective of market states and gives insufficient consideration to the lives, livelihoods and alternative viewpoints of local populations at the source end of the market in developing countries (Dickson 2003; Hübschle 2017). This western market perspective is said to only see the problem and its solutions in terms of enhancing protection measures at source rather than energetically regulating the rich countries' own markets in wildlife. This is a critique that we also saw in relation to the war on drugs, and we will come to see it repeated also in relation to other types of trafficking considered in this book. As with the war on drugs, this western interventionism is seen as sometimes patronizing and coercive, and therefore unwelcome. Approaches that criminalize local relations with wildlife which have in some cases become deeply historically and culturally entrenched polarize communities and officials in wildlife-rich regions and strip of their perceived legitimacy policies that are seen as interfering based on western self-interest (Duffy 2010).

Wildlife trafficking is peculiar among the forms of trafficking discussed in this book in that it has attracted reasonably extensive comment from rational choice and opportunity theorists who use a situational crime prevention approach (Lemieux and Clarke 2009;

Pires and Clarke 2011b; Kurland and Pires 2017; Kurland et al 2017; Lavorgna et al 2018). This approach in its contemporary form asks regulators to consider reducing the rewards of wildlife trafficking, raising the risks and effort for traffickers, and reducing provocations and excuses. Other cognate approaches in terms of situation- and opportunity-based analysis of wildlife trafficking include routine activities theory (Warchol and Harrington 2016). This helps conceptualize findings such as that:

> local residents of lower socio-economic status preferred to poach the readily available and accessible species that bring in less profit, over the rare and more valuable species sold in open markets. Moreover this type of opportunity poaching occurred more often where the parrot, poacher and market converged in a manner that allows for an efficient and inexpensive process for capture and sale. (Warchol and Harrington 2016: 26, referring to Pires and Clarke 2011a, 2011b)

The situational approach highlights some of the key features of the economic opportunity structure of wildlife trafficking, which is similar to other trafficking markets. In particular, at source, the benefits of wildlife trafficking are clear, with an abundance of a valuable commodity at source and a low likelihood of apprehension for criminals. Some forms of wildlife are highly valuable; for example rhino horn is regularly cited as being more valuable, ounce for ounce, than gold or class A drugs (Elliott 2009: 61; van Uhm 2016). We have noted that the risk of detection for poachers is low because of the remote location of much targeted wildlife, and this is compounded by the low level of resource devoted to law enforcement engaging with wildlife crimes in many of the developing countries which are the rich sources of biodiversity (Pires and Moreto 2011). Under-resourcing and marginalization of specialist policing of wildlife crime is a problem experienced in market countries as well as source countries and this is related to wildlife crime sometimes being perceived as less serious than other types of crime (Wellsmith 2011).

In addition to a situational crime prevention perspective, scholars who see wildlife trafficking as driven by demand have considered the value of developing a 'market reduction approach' to regulation in this area (Schneider 2008). This follows theoretical developments in relation to more mundane stolen goods markets (Sutton 1998), involving policies such as targeted police crackdowns in the marketplace aimed at instilling a sense of riskiness for market buyers who may otherwise be tempted to engage in what they perceived as an unregulated illicit trade.

Wildlife trafficking as business enterprise

In wildlife trafficking we see a theme introduced which has not emerged to a great extent in the literature on drug and human trafficking but which will resurface in the consideration of diamond and antiquities trafficking to come. This is the theme of consumerism in relation to luxury goods, the binding of conspicuous consumption to social status in western and westernized societies and the globally destructive consequences of what has become an expectation in these consumer capitalist societies that access to symbolic status goods is an entitlement.

Animal species are prized by collectors and consumers for their rarity and perceived wildness, combined with an impression of the prestige of the species or the medicinal properties. So common animals and those in captivity, and products made from them, are less desirable and less expensive:

> The idea has taken hold that wildlife products from wild animals are more 'pure and natural' than products from captive-bred species. Therefore the value of rhino horn, tiger bones and caviar from species from the wild is higher due to the belief that the taste would be more exquisite or the healing qualities more profound. Consequently, tiger bones from Chinese farms are of a lower value than the tiger bones of real wild tigers, rhino horns from farmed rhinos are believed to have lower medicinal values and caviar from cultivated caviar is being sold as 'illegal' wild caviar to increase its monetary value. (van Uhm 2016: 256)

Being less desirable and less expensive, the demand for illegal supplies of common or farmed animals is less, leading poachers and traffickers to focus more on rare, protected, wild species. The economics of supply and demand in wildlife trafficking is therefore, as with the other markets covered in this book, the key driver of the problem. This economic driver is clearly linked, though, to the social construction of meaning in relation to collection or consumption of different types of wildlife, just as other consumer markets in more mundane goods function for many products in part on the basis of the symbolic value of the object as well as its functional value (Appadurai 1986).

Veblen coined the term 'conspicuous consumption' in his theory of the leisure class (Veblen 1994 [1899]) – the nouveau riche that emerged in the late nineteenth and early twentieth centuries – and who had the wherewithal to buy consumer goods as an exercise in distinction (Bourdieu 1984). These goods symbolized that the purchasers had the economic power to engage in discretionary spending on non-necessary items and in this way, to read the proposition in Bourdieuan terms, economic capital was transformed into symbolic capital. At the extremes of wildlife collection, the symbolic meaning of certain animals and the status their possession gives you among other collectors (because they give the impression you are knowledgeable) takes on the lived experience of a craving, hard to sate, constantly looking for the next rarity:

> Reptile people are on a trajectory ... bigger, meaner, rarer, hot ... A desire for rarer animals reflects the hobbyist's deepening interest and the addictive quality of any hard-earned knowledge. (Christy 2008: 3–4)

We can find another example from a dealer operating in the market for dinosaur bones and fossils:

> Gosh, I have a client right now that wants a five-inch T Rex tooth, you know, he's been waiting for four years now. He goes 'What's the largest size you've ever seen?' you know, on the market that is. I said, 'Well, usually they get as big as like maybe four, four-and-a-quarter, and that's pretty big'. 'Well, I want larger. Anything five or bigger. You come across something good five or bigger, I want it'. (Long 2002: 163)

Susan Orlean's coverage of the trial of orchid collector John Laroche plays on similar themes, in this case the obsession with variants of the rare flower that has been called 'sexually suggestive' and the desire for which appeared close enough to a compulsive madness that the Victorians coined the term 'orchidelerium' (Mackenzie and Yates 2016). Orlean sees Laroche, in his criminal desire to obtain rare plants, as 'the end point in a continuum. He was the oddball ultimate of those people who are enthralled by nonhuman living things and who pursue them like lovers' (Orlean 1998).

As with the other markets presented in this book, the overall high-level picture of wildlife trafficking (that is, lifting the viewpoint to the general level so as to acknowledge differences in local markets and other variations but assessing the major pattern overall) as flowing from poor to rich countries, from abundant sources of biodiversity to consumer markets where the demand lies, has been considered as part of a world map of global asymmetries. Van Uhm, for example, has applied Passas's (1999) perspective to his analysis of wildlife trafficking, seeing the ultimate driver of this phenomenon as resting in the imbalance between global sources of supply and demand for protected wildlife (van Uhm 2016: 258 et seq). The observation that wealth in developed countries exerts a pull on natural resources of all kinds, including wildlife, from poorer countries is a common feature across a range of disciplinary orientations including green criminologists (Lynch and Stretesky 2014), white-collar criminologists (Passas and Goodwin 2004), development scholars (Collier 2008) and political scientists (Andreas 2011). Where these commentaries have recognized that illegal trade is part of the 'resource curse' for developing countries that are rich in natural resource but poor in terms of local wealth and good governance, it can be tied to conflict, corruption (van Uhm and Moreto 2018) and resource exploitation at source and to perpetuating global asymmetries rather than resolving them.

This high-level view needs to be complemented by an appreciation of the reality 'lower down', on the ground as it were – in other words the deep ethnographic and interview data that are available on the local traditions of use and interaction with wildlife in source countries and how this interfaces with the commoditization and movement undertaken by international trafficking. There are many ways in which local rational and cultural interactions with wildlife exist in tension with the idea of conservation and sustainable use, especially when these are combined with a market context. For example, certain animals, such as leopards and cheetahs, are seen as pests to local ranchers or farmers and have been traditionally eliminated as such. When the neoliberal market creates a financially rewarding outlet for the products of normal or traditional local wildlife use and killing, however, wildlife trafficking researchers consider that 'need turns into greed' (Warchol et al 2003: 17–18). Similarly, the tourist industry based on exotic game hunting, while clearly having an interest in sustainability of the resource its income is based on, is driven financially by the desire of tourists to kill exotic species in numbers, and that business orientation can incentivize abuses of the ecosystem. In some analyses, local actors in source countries are thought to be simply continuing traditional practices of hunting and gathering throughout a period where new wildlife laws and global market sensibilities have criminalized these long-standing patterns of behaviour, which have continued regardless. On that view, deviance has not been driven by any particular trafficking-oriented mentality, it is just a new criminal label that has been applied to ongoing community routines in developing countries (Peterson et al 2016).

Hübschle's ethnography of rhino horn poaching in South Africa's national parks is instructive here. She found a clear causal connection between the international market for rhino horn and poaching: 'the most obvious answer would be the high price tag paid at the source and rising demand for rhino horn in consumer markets … the rhino has a bounty on its horn that far outweighs the average annual income of rural communities …' (Hübschle 2017: 433). However, the rational profit motive as a driver of poaching needs to be understood, she thinks, 'in the context of historical marginalisation of rural communities and their continued sense of alienation' (Hübschle 2017: 434). This marginalization has occurred through 'green land grabs', where villagers have been evicted from national park land and relocated in a process of 'displacement and dispossession', resulting in anger and resentment which has in turn been channelled in some cases into poaching (Hübschle 2017). The sense these displaced locals feel – that wildlife and tourism are more politically important than local people – has led to the white rhino becoming symbolic for them of their political, geographic and economic exclusion. The reaction to this exclusion is to target the rhino as a source of the solution to the 'emasculation, stress, disempowerment and anger' that the poachers feel (Hübschle 2017: 436) and to overcome the shame of economic exclusion and not being able to provide for their families. One of the Mozambican rhino horn poaching kingpins in Hübschle's study puts it eloquently: 'we are using rhino horn to free ourselves' (Hübschle 2017: 436). This is, however, a freedom the dimensions of which are constituted by the market – economically rewarding resource trading as a form of social emancipation from the structural violence and insecurity of being systemically abandoned by the state and the elites who run the national parks. In short, then, in resisting conservation governmentalities (Holmes 2007), the framework for that resistance is conceived by the poachers and traffickers in terms of neoliberal market activity, and actualized as such.

Many other case studies are available, both in the scholarly and the journalistic literature, of wildlife poachers and traffickers who engage in these criminal activities either as a full time job or as a part-time supplementary source of income. Rachel Nuwer (2018b) met a pangolin poacher, Tám Hô, in Vietnam who trapped animals as his main profession, initially to pay his disabled son's medical bills and then to save for his education. For people like Hô, who live in poverty near forests that hold wildlife that he says 'carry a price like gold', illegal trapping is entirely rational: the chances of apprehension by rangers are minimal, as he says they are easily avoided, and the profits to be made are significant. In a region where the average household earns just $1,000 per year, and a single pangolin can sell for $450, the economics of illegal enterprise are compelling. Moral or emotional considerations about the value of animal lives do not really come into it where economic strain and payoff converge. As Nuwer puts it: 'the ethics of poaching seem pretty clear – there are none, right?' (Nuwer 2018a).

Bryan Christy pursues similar themes of low risk, high reward, calculated economic thinking in his true crime story about reptile trafficker Mike Van Nostrand, who owned *Strictly Reptiles*, the largest reptile import–export business in the US at the time:

> Nobody got caught; and then even if you did, the penalty was not jail, it was a parking ticket ... you didn't go to prison for what he carried in his suitcase ... He had tried birds, but birds died. Reptiles were as durable and easy to pack as precious stones, without the up-front costs. And the profit margins were as good as cocaine without the machine guns or the felony drug charges ... Really, you would be stupid not to do it. (Christy 2008: 1)

In fact the mule in the above quote, one of Van Nostrand's carriers, does eventually get apprehended by customs on entry to the US, which is why his story is known. The – reasonably accurate – perception that on each journey the risk of getting caught is low turns into an accumulated higher risk the more trips are made, but traffickers are often not so rational as to recognize this. Instead, they work with a sense that past performance is a good predictor of future events: so they think that as they have made many clean runs in the past, this demonstrates that the risk of apprehension this time is low. Like Russian Roulette though, although the probability may remain the same each time, the longer you play the more likely you are to experience a bad result.

So, to summarize, in wildlife trafficking we see an intriguing alloy of rationality and emotion. An economic, business-oriented approach to the pecuniary rewards of illicit enterprise, founded in many source locations in the same deep and persistent structural socio-economic exclusion we saw at the sources of drug and human trafficking networks, meet with an emotional drive to acquire, collect, breed and deal in rare species of wildlife. It is an intriguing alloy because the emotional drive to commit crimes in this case seems to approach forms of craving and desire that are reported – with all due artistic licence by many of the works in question which are written by journalists looking for a bestseller – as approaching a state of losing one's mind. That, of course, would be the opposite of rationality. How then do these two seemingly opposing states – a clear-headed profit motive and a foggy-minded acquisitive delirium – come together to constitute the social psychology of wildlife trafficking? The answer is surely that, as we have explored above in relation to the phenomenon of contemporary consumer capitalism, extreme desire for a product which encapsulates a symbolic value with a power that reaches out well beyond its physical form is the perfect fertile meeting point of ideology and the market. In most of the available stories of apparently 'mad' collectors of the rare and precious things we are looking at here, there have been significant profits to be made from dealing since there always seems to be another buyer down the line who is even more mad for the rarity in question than you are. The bottom line is that a borderline-delirious desire for rarity among pockets of dealers and collectors, combined with a global marketplace that can service that desire by providing relatively untrammelled access to the sources of supply of that rarity, makes for good business for all involved.

5

Diamond Trafficking

The nature and extent of the harm

Conflict, or 'blood', diamonds from regions such as Sierra Leone, Angola, Liberia and the Democratic Republic of the Congo are a small fraction of the overall diamond supply chain. In 2002, the World Peace Foundation estimated that rebels controlled between 3 and 4 per cent of the world's total rough diamond supply (Tamm 2002: 7). Although this makes conflict diamonds seem like a relatively small problem, in real terms these diamonds can fund significant conflict and death. The same report notes that 'if an automatic weapon costs as little as ten dollars, then UNITA rebels, in control of perhaps $100 million per year income from sale of rough Angolan diamonds, can buy 100,000 weapons' (Tamm 2002: 7). Other estimates have speculated that the proportion of blood diamonds on the market could be substantially higher than this; in one example that caused much dispute and debate, a journalist who has done ethnographic research into the illegal diamond supply chain speculated that 'up to 25% of the 50 billion dollars in diamonds sold across the world today might be laundered' (Miklian 2013a; Beck 2013). Since misdeclaration and under-reporting of exports is rampant, estimating the true size of the problem is a challenge, as indeed it is with other types of trafficking. However, it can be done by comparing imports and sales in market countries to known legal and illegal mining activities and declared exports from source countries. These figures show major discrepancies, revealing a sizable global illicit marketplace. For example:

> In 1999, Sierra Leone officially exported $1.5 million worth of diamonds; the diamond industry estimated the real commercial value at $70 million. In addition to the official trade, tens of millions of dollars worth of diamonds were illicitly exported by the RUF, foreign troops, domestic and foreign smugglers. Much of the illicit diamond revenue was used to purchase small arms. (Montague 2002: 229)

The human rights implications of conflict diamonds are therefore significant and have captured the attention of the media since the issue first came to attention in the 1990s. As well as funding conflict, diamond mining and the desire to control it has been identified as a contributing reason for conflict in the first place as rebel groups compete with national governments for control of natural resources that can profitably be extracted (Kaplan 2003). In the context of such diamond-fuelled and diamond-oriented violence, associated harms that have been observed include land confiscations, rapes, killings, other serious physical injuries and of course the political destabilization, corruption and autocratic despotism that goes along with diamond mining. For an example of this, we can look to Sierra Leone, where rebels from the Revolutionary United Front were supported by Charles Taylor in neighbouring Liberia through arms-for-diamonds deals that we will revisit in the chapter on arms trafficking.

Unlicensed diamond mining is dirty and dangerous work, and miners suffer a range of acute and chronic illnesses and injuries. In under-regulated centres for diamond processing like Surat in India, teenage labour is cheap (Miklian 2013b). Long days working in poor conditions polishing and examining stones in microfactories leads to early onset vision impairment for these young aspiring diamantairs. Tuberculosis from inhaling microscopic particles of diamond released into the air by polishing is frequent enough to have earned the nickname 'diamond lung' (Miklian 2013b).

The structure of diamond trafficking: source, transit, demand

Diamonds travel international routes from source to market, just like other commodities discussed in this book. In the case of diamonds, the source is mining in countries where rough diamonds can be found under the ground, and the ultimate market destination is retail jewellery shops and other similar types of dealer-to-customer sales. Diamond mining happens to some extent in a lot of countries but the main sources of mining output by serious volume are fairly limited: Botswana, South Africa, Angola, Namibia, the Democratic Republic of Congo (DRC), Russia and Australia (Siegel 2011). Diamonds can be stolen from mining operations or at other points in the supply chain. In the market, for example, diamonds make attractive targets for theft due to the difficulty in subsequently discerning those that have been stolen from those that have not, and the high value for their relatively small size. Trafficking can follow such thefts, before the sale of the stolen diamonds in a different country (Siegel 2008). The most controversial type of trafficking, however, is in conflict diamonds. These are rough diamonds that are excavated in regions experiencing civil wars and other kinds of armed rebellions, and where the diamonds are being used to finance the warfare, usually aimed at undermining legitimate governments.

De Beers grew to be the predominant corporate operator in the international diamond trade from its inception in 1880. It owns and operates diamond mines in source countries and has interests throughout the chain of supply. In 1987 it controlled 80 per cent of the world's annual supply of rough diamonds, but by 2018 this had shrunk to 37 per cent as new companies opened mines in countries such as Russia, Australia and Canada and existing mines broke away from the De Beers cartel and began selling direct to market themselves. In its heyday De Beers sent its rough diamonds, mined and bought, to the Diamond Trading Company in London, which is its global sorting headquarters. From here it would sell them to wholesalers called 'sightholders', who took the rough diamonds to the cutting and polishing hubs in Antwerp, Tel Aviv, New York, Johannesburg and other such diamond refining locations.

Once cut and polished, diamonds are sold wholesale from dealer to dealer, and can pass through many hands before reaching a retail sale in the consumer marketplace. At each transaction they are mixed in the hands of the new owner with existing stock, making what is usually referred to as the 'diamond pipeline' less like a straight line from source to market than the term implies (Tamm 2002).

De Beers controlled the diamond market by setting the prices of the boxes of rough diamonds it sold – on a non-negotiable basis and only to its authorized sightholders – and deciding how much it would supply at a time. Combined with its overall huge share of ownership of rough diamonds, this meant it was effectively setting the base limit of prices for the world's diamond supply, taking care to make sure that the market was not flooded, which would lower prices. Since its power in the market is now eroded, what was once more or less a monopoly has given way to a market in which prices are dictated by the usual forces of supply and demand.

An hourglass shape is seen in the diamond trade, as with many other trafficking markets: various sources of supply and a wide distribution of demand, with a pinch-point in the middle of the supply chain where we see only a relatively small number of dealers or intermediaries compared to the numbers of producers and consumers at each end of the chain. For diamonds, the middleman phase of the trade happens in polishing factories and bourses, which are diamond trading exchanges. Here, rough diamonds are bought and worked by experts to produce the cut diamonds we buy in the shops, and diamond supplies are mixed, appraised and sold wholesale to the retail markets. The main locations of these bourses have traditionally been in Antwerp and Tel Aviv, providing a global market that is unusual in having such a concentration of middle-market dealers geographically, although this is now changing somewhat (see below). The trade in Antwerp and Tel Aviv has for generations been dominated by Jewish families who have cultivated a reputation for expertise in diamonds, handing the skills and knowledge down from grandparents to parents to children, although more recently the presence of the Jewish community in the 'diamankwartier' in Antwerp has been diluted with the entry of Indian, Armenian and Lebanese dealers into the trade there (de Carlos Sola 2019).

Anthropologist and criminologist Dina Siegel has studied trafficking in diamonds for many years. She has identified three main types of diamond smuggling. The first is 'smuggling for survival, when extreme poverty pushes miners and diggers to steal diamonds from the mines and sell them to local dealers'. Second is 'smuggling by organized crime groups, when false certificates are used so that the origin of diamonds is provided with a legal cover'. Third, 'the diamonds laundry, where diamonds from conflict regions are smuggled to neighbouring non-conflict countries to enter the legal trade' (Siegel 2011: 224).

Each of these types of trafficking amount to different ways in which the same end result is achieved: the mixing of illicit diamonds into the licit supply chain so that as they continue their journey through further deals and retail purchases they are indistinguishable from legal diamonds. Diamonds cannot be discerned by physical inspection or scientific analysis as coming from one source or another, making it relatively straightforward to misrepresent their point of discovery or to lose them among the legitimate supply.

Unlicensed diamond mining is widely practised and condoned in some source countries where, like the sources of antiquities, diamonds are often found in remote locations. Unlicensed diamond mining often happens alongside and interfaces with licensed diamond mines. Where a diamond is found, its value will normally be split among the participants in the enterprise, and there is therefore strong incentive for finders to hide diamonds when they find them and later sell them to a local dealer, keeping the whole price for themselves. This makes for an atmosphere of constant suspicion at licensed and unlicensed diamond mines, and violent repercussions where the system has been abused in such a way. At licensed mines, armed guards keep watch on behalf of the licensee running the mine, and they search the diggers at the end of their shift manually and using x-ray scanners, looking for diamonds concealed about them (Hart 2003).

Farah (2013) uses the case of the market in conflict diamonds to illustrate his idea of illicit trade networks consisting of 'fixers', 'super fixers' and 'shadow facilitators'. In this scheme, the fixers are the local agents with know-how in relation to managing the initial transition of diamonds from natural resource to commodity. Local fixers have the financial and trade networks required to effectively move diamonds out of the region of production. They do not, however, have the higher level international financial and trade contacts and skills required to move the diamonds into the global market. Therefore, the local fixers connect with so-called super fixers and shadow facilitators to achieve this next phase of the trade network. Although Farah's language of the fix is particular to his analysis of brokers and facilitators in illicit trade, the basic concepts in this framework are observable in similar terms in the work of analysts of illicit markets. The idea is a well-explored one in the literature, that local or regional actors link up with more international-facing traders, forming a network that through sale and purchase, in steps, moves illicit commodities out of source countries and into the global market.

In the case of diamonds, Farah makes the point with a case study of Charles Taylor, who 'had a small core of trusted super fixers who could move in the broader world, operate bank accounts, and seek out connections *but did not have the capacity to actually provide and move the products he wanted*' (Farah 2013: 78, my emphasis). These international brokers are therefore an essential part of the network, connecting the illicit supply to later stage trade that moves the diamonds closer to the end consumer in a geographically distant market. As the emphasis in the quote highlights, they are facilitators in the purest sense, not having access to – or any control over – the sources of production of the raw materials themselves or the means by which they are moved; these latter are the remit of the 'shadow facilitators'.

The picture of shadow facilitators is therefore one of experts in the illicit traffic of goods, plus associated skills including faking documents, bribing border agents, dealing with shipping agents and perhaps laundering money (Farah 2013). It is not clear, however, that such a role exists or is necessary in all illicit markets, and in some markets where international transit is less well regulated and therefore more straightforward, such as antiquities, we find that the super fixer and shadow facilitator roles are combined in practice.

Charles Taylor, the rebel warlord who through insurgency became President of Liberia, funded his militias through a commodities-for-arms exchange network. Taylor had effective control of timber through logging operations in Liberia and diamonds in neighbouring Sierra Leone, where he also fomented conflict. Selling illegally plundered timber and conflict diamonds, he would then divert the financial proceeds to arms dealers in payment for weapons: 'In this circular pipeline, the timber [and the diamonds] flowed out and the cash flowed in, then the cash flowed out as the weapons flowed in' (Farah 2013: 85). This pattern of resource-out, arms-in has been observed elsewhere too:

> Many arms traffickers are either directly involved in smuggling both arms and minerals for their clients or are paid in funds raised by militias who have seized control over such resources. In the Democratic Republic of Congo, for example, nongovernment forces have used their access to arms to seize control over lucrative diamond mines. The militias use forced labour to extract the diamonds which are then sold on the international black market. The funds that are raised in this way are used to purchase additional arms to carry on their part of the war. Arms trafficking and mineral smuggling thus become part of a self-supporting system: a criminal and devastating vicious circle. (Feinstein and Holden 2014: 452)

Governments too, as well as regionally dominant warlords, can be complicit in the illicit export of diamonds. Many countries experiencing conflict have what is essentially a mixed export stream, where a certain proportion of legal and certified diamonds are exported and declared to international recording agencies, while illegal and undeclared export streams run in parallel. This gives these countries the appearance of compliance with international regulations, while a parallel black market achieves the money-in/diamonds-out processes necessary to provide funds for arms or payouts for corrupt officials. In addition to these corrupt official flows, lower level trafficking is practised in the same way we have seen it in other transnational criminal trades. So, for diamonds: 'You can wear them, hide them in a bag, put them in your boots', according to one informant (Miklian 2013a).

We can therefore construct a picture of international diamond trafficking as an illicit market that individuals, officials and governments take part in; but another piece of the puzzle is the corporate–military complex, in which private security companies and corporatized armies have inserted themselves into conflicts in diamond-rich regions. For example, when the RUF occupied diamond mines in Sierra Leone, cutting off the government's access to those diamonds and thus constricting its capacity to buy weapons, a private military company euphemistically named Executive Outcomes offered its services. It was contracted by the government of Sierra Leone to conduct a war to drive the RUF out of the mines, and it partnered with a company called Branch Energy Limited, which required access to conduct diamond mining. The deal was essentially that the government would in due course take a cut of the proceeds of the diamond mining from Branch, from which it would retrospectively pay Executive Outcomes for its military interventions (Montague 2002). This has been called a Faustian bargain, with a weak government left with little choice but to deal with private mercenaries connected to foreign mining interests that aim to secure and extract the country's precious natural gemstone resources (Smillie et al 2000). Where international capital markets, spearheaded by private armies, reach into fragile developing countries in conflict in order to access commodities destined for affluent western consumers, the uneasily close ties between consumer markets and the exploitation of global instability become clearer. In white-collar crime commentary, they say the best way to rob a bank is to own one (Black 2005). Similarly, if you steal and smuggle a diamond as a private individual, you are a trafficker; but if you strongarm a weak government into allowing you and your mercenaries to take thousands of diamonds, you are at the cutting edge of global commercial entrepreneurialism in the mining industry.

Similar to other transnational markets, the dynamics of the illicit diamond trade do not remain static. In the context of the rising global commercial power and importance of Asia and some centres in the Middle East, and the break-up of the De Beers monopoly, the 'old guard' of Antwerp and Tel Aviv have increasingly come to be challenged as predominant centres of rough diamond polishing and processing by places such as Hong Kong, Dubai and the Indian city of Surat. In these transit portals, rough diamonds arrive from Africa and Asia and the mixing of licit and illicit stones happens on an industrial scale, condoned and in some cases facilitated by the regional administration (Miklian 2013b). The world's largest diamond bourse is now BDB (Bharat Diamond Bourse), which is a 20-acre complex in Mumbai and accommodates around 2,500 diamond traders.

Regulation and control of diamond trafficking

The Kimberley Process Certification Scheme is an international agreement that sets up a system of standardized certificates which vouch for shipments of rough diamonds when they are in international transit. The aim of the system is to prevent conflict diamonds from entering the global supply chain. In practical terms, it is an import–export chain-of-custody certification scheme which requires the governments of participating countries to certify the clean status of each shipment of diamonds as they move through the process of leaving one country and entering another. Participating countries are required to ensure that they do not export to, or import from, non-participating countries, and so the Kimberley Process aims to set up a verifiably clean global market that excludes countries not prepared to sign up. The Kimberley Process controls around nine-tenths of the world's legal trade in rough diamonds, and so the ultimate threat behind the system is effectively the exclusion of countries from world diamond markets where they are found to be in breach of the scheme's commitments to ban the trade in conflict diamonds.

The import–export aspects of the Kimberley Process are similar to the idea of CITES licences to prevent wildlife trafficking. Where an exporting country releases a shipment of rough diamonds, they must be packed in a tamperproof security container and have a suitable Kimberley Process certificate. The certificate verifies they have been authorized for export and are not conflict diamonds. It also contains some standard information like the identity of the exporter, the identity of the importer to whom the shipment is bound and the value of the diamonds. In turn, the importing country will not accept the shipment unless they see the certificate, and they confirm receipt by sending a confirmation to the exporting authority. Shipments in transit are not to be opened or tampered with. In theory, this prevents illicit shipments containing conflict diamonds from entering the supply chain, as they should be unable to obtain the appropriate certification and therefore will not be accepted by the customs authorities of the importing country.

The Kimberley Process is a tripartite conference, consisting of governments who make and implement the laws regulating the trade, the NGOs agitating for a less abusive and harmful international diamond trading process, and the World Diamond Council (WDC), which is an umbrella organization representing the trade's interests, comprised of the most powerful diamond producers, jewellers and exchanges.

The Kimberley Process has been the subject of serious criticism, but at the same time it is often held up, alongside the CITES process for wildlife, as a model of global regulation that could be followed in the effort to exert controls over other types of trafficking (Mackenzie 2015). The problems the Kimberley Process suffers are not altogether surprising given what is already well known about the usual role of the UN as diplomatic standard-setter and promoter of good practice rather than enforcer of universal legal norms, and also the contexts of widespread corruption with which many attempts at international governance have to engage. The agreement is not a treaty or other legislative instrument and so its terms only have the status of agreed principles, and its provisions are put to member states as recommendations. The force of law supporting the Kimberley Process comes only through the adoption and implementation of its provisions in domestic legislation, which is similar to many of the other international regulatory processes we observe in this book.

Many of the ongoing criticisms of the Kimberley Process stem from this status as a set of principles that are, when push comes to shove, effectively unenforceable, combined with the powerful role of the WDC as influencer in decisions about the Process. Participants in the Process are required in practice to police themselves, as they can only police each other through a consensus-oriented voting mechanism that makes it too easy for defaulting countries to escape penalties if they have sympathetic strategic partners willing to protect them. The obvious susceptibility to corruption of the packaging and certification-based import–export system has been largely ignored, so the system cannot vouch:

> that no government inspector at the mining site was bribed to deny that guerrilla forces controlled the mines, that no customs official was bribed to issue a certificate that the package of stones was conflict-free, and that no diamond merchant on 47th St. in Manhattan slipped a gem into the package bought cheap from someone who had smuggled it in under his tongue. (Feldman 2003)

Where the countries conflict diamonds come from are, by definition, experiencing civil unrest that makes security and governance challenging for governments, the corruption of a supply chain certification process is hardly unexpected. Fake paperwork can launder illicit diamonds under such a formal certification system, making it look like a shipment of conflict diamonds has as its point of origin a neighbouring country where there is no conflict (Siegel 2008).

Embargoed Sierra Leonian diamonds, labelled as 'Guinean', 'Gambian' or 'Liberian', have been exported to finance weapons (Montague 2002). This type of 'neighbourhood dissembling' is a tactic used by traffickers in other transnational criminal markets too – for example antiquities (Gilgan 2001). An early study of the Kimberley Process found this type of misdeclaration of origin to be clearly discernible in the diamond trading import–export statistics, noting that the origin of millions of carats of diamonds must have been misrepresented on Kimberley Process certificates, as the sum total declared as coming from diamond-producing countries substantially exceeded their domestic production (Weyzig 2004).

In fact, while one might think that conflict diamonds emerge from situations that are relatively anomic, alternative systems of quasi-regulation can sometimes develop, calculated to exploit local diamond markets by extracting 'taxes'. Military generals in various regions have been said to set up systems where they make money by issuing 'permits' to mine diamonds in the areas under their control, in at least one case, in the Central African Republic (CAR), developing:

> a parallel administration system to monitor and exploit the mining sector. Through this structure they [rebel soldiers occupying the region] issued mining authorisations, collected illegal taxes, and ran protection rackets that targeted miners and those operating around mining sites. (Global Witness 2017: 5–6)

Even outside conflict zones, informal types of regulation can develop which take advantage of, and undermine, the formal Kimberley Process. In many of the developing diamond mining countries as we have noted so-called artisanal miners operate alongside legitimate mining operations. These artisans are unlicensed but tolerated by local government inspectors and the easiest mode of disposal of the diamonds they find is simply to sell them to the licensed operators working out of the same region. The inspectors take a cut to overlook these trades, and the Kimberley Process controls are derailed at the very start of the supply chain as stones that are not the product of authorized finds are included at source in this way (Malamut 2005; Kaplan 2003). In Sierra Leone, artisanal mining is a source of labour for upwards of half a million workers, making it the second largest source of employment after farming (Samboma 2019).

Throughout the development of the Kimberley Process, the NGOs that are the third pillar of the regulatory framework, applying pressure and monitoring what would otherwise only be an agreement between government and industry, have consistently voiced strong disappointment with the results. While acknowledging that there have been some positive aspects to the Process, the lead NGO, Global Witness, has labelled it 'a cynical corporate accreditation scheme' and 'an accomplice to diamond laundering' (Gooch 2011). The main problem from the NGOs' perspective has consistently been seen as the voluntary nature of the scheme in respect of the system of intra-national warranties that industry undertakes in source countries, verifying that diamonds entering the supply chain comply with the requirements of the Kimberley Process. With no methodical system of external auditing of these warranties, such a self-regulation system is open to abuse where the industry bodies giving the warranties have clear profitable interests in selling the diamonds (Wexler 2010). From the perspective of criminologists concerned with trafficking, however, there is an even more obvious issue with the Kimberley Process. It cannot engage with straightforward cases of trafficking, where conflict or otherwise illegal diamonds are smuggled out of their source countries, brought into transit or market countries and mixed into the chain of legal supply there. Traffickers in the CAR use this kind of transit and mixing of supplies to achieve the 'neighbourhood dissembling' technique we noted above. They move illicit diamonds to Cameroon, where they mix them in with other diamonds and say they are all from elsewhere. They arrange official paperwork and pay the relevant export tax from Cameroon, and thereafter the stones are in the legitimate supply chain. Traffickers call this process 'naturalization': like obtaining citizenship for a person, 'they give CAR diamonds Cameroonian nationality' (Global Witness 2017: 8).

Recently, in 2018, some movement towards addressing known issues with the Kimberley Process began to take hold, resulting in a UN General Assembly resolution that sets out to tackle problems including the narrow definition of conflict diamonds that has previously only included rough diamonds used to finance wars against governments. This excluded stones linked to human rights abuses by governments rather than rebellious anti-government forces. Several such abuses have been recorded, for example by the Mugabe regime in Zimbabwe (Human Rights Watch 2009). The argument that conflict diamonds should include all forms of systemic violence in the diamond-producing regions now seems to be moving towards being accepted, albeit not without some concerns being expressed by governments with tainted human rights records in the mining sector.

There remain some very serious practical problems with the Kimberley Process though. Miklian's investigative work in the DRC and India has pointed out some of the most basic issues:

> [The Kimberley certificate] is shamefully basic ... It's about as easy to fake as an old driver's license. Because certificates only note the total amount of rough carats, it's also easy to add or subtract polished merchandise to the bags as needed because polishing can carve away up to 50 percent of the original rough carat weight. As India is now the world's third-largest diamond consumer (after the United States and China), leftover certificates from shipments intended for domestic sales are reused to smuggle conflict stones out of the country, providing another laundering avenue. (Miklian 2013b)

The Indian Directorate of Revenue Intelligence seizes some illegal diamonds entering India, but these are then sold at auction to support the Indian treasury: 'Local and international diamond firms are then free to bid on the lots. Stamped with a new origin in a Kimberley-approved country, these blood diamonds are handed right back to the global market – now totally untraceable and indistinguishable from legitimately sourced stones' (Miklian 2013b).

Diamond trafficking as illicit business enterprise

The international diamond industry is a classic study of the social construction of an ideology that transforms, on the level of symbolism, a gemstone into a highly desirable consumer commodity. The industry continues to be criticized for human rights abuses in the supply chain including child labour, forced labour, funding conflict, environmental damage and corruption (Pickles 2018). Yet the diamond sparkles and speaks not of these violations but of affluence, purity and love. This is in large part due to the inventive public relations work done by the major corporate interests that have shaped the international market for diamonds over the years. De Beers undertook significant social constructionist work, through advertisements and sponsorship, establishing the diamond as symbolic of wealth, power, emotion and relationship commitment (Hart 2003; Bergenstock and Maskulka 2001; Epstein 1982). It's *a diamond is forever* advertising campaign, 'the number one rated ad slogan of the twentieth century' (Bergenstock and Maskulka 2001: 37; citing Advertising Age 1999), has been credited with nothing less than inventing the modern day engagement ring (Friedman 2015).

This market-making ideological work has been important in framing public and policy interpretations of the illegal market in diamonds too, since the imagery of purity and elegance of cut and polished diamonds for sale in the marketplace makes for an attractive veil behind which the dirty dealings of the means of production and transit are rendered somewhat opaque and of diminished relevance. This type of consumer mystification is common practice in the transnational supply chains of the new global economy, where corporate interests in the major world markets have outsourced production to regions where it is cheaper, resulting in a variety of moral and legal threats to the integrity and legitimacy of the commodity supply in question. These include child labour, unfit working conditions and low pay for workers (Bakan 2004), as well as the difficulties in detecting and excising illicit supply chains from international legal markets where the outsourcing of production has also given rise to fragmented and complex parallel markets, comprising decentralized supply chain networks made up of a multitude of actors rather than subject to one system of overall ownership of the goods from source to market (Mackenzie 2010a). So yet again, we see that the problems of trafficking – in this case, of diamonds – are most appropriately situated for analysis in the context of the circuits of commerce of the post-industrial and globalized neoliberal economic regime.

The diamond traders in hubs such as Antwerp do business on the basis of their reputation (they are similar to antiquities dealers in this respect) and so the sense one gets from these legitimate traders is that the above-board diamond trading scene is a clean market into which illegitimate dealers sometimes try to enter. This is the 'bad apples' or 'black market' version of the story of diamond dealing: the impression of the clean 'white' trade existing alongside a small and relatively unimportant number of bad apples or black market traders, with little to no intersection between these two worlds. Just as is the case with other transnational criminal markets such as antiquities and wildlife, however, the reality is not a black and a white market running parallel, but a grey market with regular intersections and trades between officially registered diamond traders and what Siegel has referred to as the 'so-called pseudo-diamantairs', who are self-appointed diamond dealers engaged in disreputable business. But still 'business remains business and brokers connect not only among the respectable diamond dealers, but also among the diamantairs and those who offer a good price for stones' (Siegel 2011: 225).

Reaching back down the chain of supply, looking behind these diamantairs who Siegel sees as disreputable dealers in illicit stones, we can find some studies and journalistic reports that give an insight into the world of the source-end brokers and finders of the illegal diamonds that are circumventing the Kimberley Process. These reports confirm the impression we have been forming throughout this book of traffickers in illegal commodities thinking about what they are doing in terms of illicit or grey enterprise and talking about these criminal activities in terms that show that their framework of understanding – and explaining – what they are doing is a business one. In an interview with a Congolese 'diamond bootlegger' in Kinshasa – an intermediary buying stones from the DRC, Angola and Zimbabwe and then selling them to Indian buying offices – the respondent says simply: 'I'm a businessman, I'm interested only in making good business … It's an exciting business, there's a lot of money to be made! … Let's deal' (Miklian 2013a). A diamond trafficking 'middleman' interviewed by the Global Witness team, moving stones out of the CAR to trading centres across the world says, 'It is business. With or without Kimberley, we carry the products to wherever we want' (Global Witness 2017: 9).

Miklian's conversations with participants in the diamond trafficking supply chain in India reveals business mentality at all levels. The owners of polishing 'chop shops' in Surat acknowledge that 'our entire business is black market', as they pay their teenage workers one dollar for each stone they polish (Miklian 2013b). Surat, as a massive diamond processing centre, operates on a rough-diamonds-in/polished-diamonds-out basis, and the processed stones are transported to Mumbai for worldwide sale by a network of mules who ride the train to get there, again paid minimally for their service. The stones are sold in Mumbai to international buyers in a culture of trading ignorance about origins that is highly reminiscent of the circuits of consumption in other illicit commodity markets:

> As one major dealer told me, buyers don't ask about working conditions in Surat because they don't care; they don't ask about the Kimberley Process in Mumbai because they know it's useless. (Miklian 2013b)

Conflict diamonds polished in Surat and sold in this way in Mumbai generally pass through the customs barrier on export from India unhindered:

> 'For us, the Kimberley Process has no relevance' explained a frustrated senior official [at customs] … the law requires

> they let even the most suspicious shipments go if they pass the minimal Kimberley bar. (Miklian 2013b)

Since each export shipment will come with a Kimberley certificate, faked, reused or used to cover illicit stones mixed with licit ones, the final export process of trafficking these illegal diamonds internationally is exactly the same as the routine of exporting a legal shipment of diamonds. The books are stamped by the officials, the diamonds are released and the laundering process is complete.

In the chapter on human trafficking above, we closed by identifying layered macro-, meso- and micro-level interpretations of the context and motivations for that type of illicit enterprise. These layered explanations apply equally to diamond trafficking. The macro-context is of regional economic inequality and local exclusion from sources of legitimate labour, combined with a micro-context of individual decision-making in which opportunistic diggers and traffickers engage with the wealth of natural resource they have easy access to. They exploit it for their own benefit using the same routines and rhythms that the legal market employs, and indeed they interface with that legal market at various points. Conflict and political instability adds various openings and imperatives to this fertile landscape for the growth of illicit economic enterprise, and western companies and private security entrepreneurs muscle in too. The meso-level is the layer of social analysis in which we have identified the organizational features of the transnational market in question and the justificatory or denial narratives that are propagated among international dealers/traffickers in the marketplace at this level. In the diamond trade we have seen these as present in similar measure and form to other trafficking markets: dealers and consumers who do not ask questions about the sources of diamonds; the dominant idea that the market is generally clean and that illegal gems are only traded by 'bad apples' rather than being prevalent throughout the chain of supply; and a socially constructed and commercially quite deliberate ideology of purity and positive emotion self-servingly invented and then celebrated by big corporate players.

As with the wildlife trade, where we observed the phenomenon of craving rarity at the consumer end of the supply chain, the business of diamond trafficking is sustained by consumer desire that is orchestrated by the vested interests of the trade to manifest as an acquisitive emotion: a desire to *have things*, largely because of their symbolic meaning to the owner and to others. Ideas of rarity and preciousness are key to the consumer drive to buy diamonds, in comparable ways to the expression we have seen of this consumptive desire in the market for exotic wildlife. The meanings of these consumer goods may be different in many ways, but for analysts of trafficking the overall pattern is similar: of illicit business serving a system of consumptive desire that is keenly felt as an acquisitive and possessive emotion by the buyers but which may seem rather artificial, contingent or even weird to observers who are not part of the target consumer market. We will see similar themes emerging in relation to collectors of rare and precious antiquities when we come to study that market in a later chapter.

Finally, following our observations about wildlife trafficking being part of the neo-colonial hegemonic power of global neoliberal markets, we can reiterate as we have pointed out above that similar points have of course been made in relation to diamonds. We will begin the next chapter, on arms trafficking, with a reflection on Anthony Sampson's book *The Arms Bazaar* (1977), and we can close this chapter with reference to another of his works, in this case, his review of Matthew Hart's book, *Diamond: The History of a Cold-Blooded Love Affair* (2003). In that piece, he says of the diamond trade:

> It is a new version of the 19th-century 'scramble for Africa', with black leaders now joined with western corporations to take out the mineral wealth of the continent without interference from the African people. The trade in 'blood diamonds' or 'conflict diamonds' provides an extreme case of the ruination of developing countries by the depredations of commerce and greed. No search for peace in Africa will succeed without effectively controlling the commercial interests which have helped to tear its young nations apart. (Sampson 2002)

The depredations of commerce and greed referred to are the routines of the spectrum of enterprise that incorporates legal and illegal business and which, in the case of the global diamond trade, ties these systems of legal and illegal enterprise together like the strands in a rope, interlaced so that wrongdoing and harmful enterprise is hidden in plain sight. My argument in this book is that traffickers compartmentalize their criminal and harmful behaviour as the routine performance of illicit, informal or grey business and that by framing their behaviour in this way, as 'just business', they draw some neutralizing insulation from having to come to terms with the harm they cause. In some types of trafficking, for example human trafficking, this effort at framing harmful behaviour as something else may seem to require quite some mental work on the part of the trafficker, and we have discussed how it can be accomplished in that chapter above. In other markets like diamonds, however, the nexus between the legal and illegal trade, and the historical norm of resource extraction from the developing world, is so deeply entrenched that it may be hard to imagine how else could traffickers define their enterprise besides doing business.

6

Arms Trafficking

The nature and extent of the harm

Arms trafficking is the transfer of weapons in breach of national or international laws and conventions where they prohibit such transfer. Arms trafficking supplies weapons to criminals and to regions in conflict. The economic value of the illicit trade in arms has been estimated as somewhere between $170 million and $320 million (Leggett 2019, using 2006 figures), making the market for illegal guns many shades less valuable than the other criminal trades covered in this book. However, while the types and levels of non-economic harms in markets for consumer or collector commodities such as drugs or antiquities can be argued about, the direct and violent harms caused by the global movement of illegal arms is clear enough. Anthony Sampson, author of the major journalistic account of what he called *The Arms Bazaar*, summarizes in the introduction to the book the underpinning reality of a commercial arms fair he visited: 'there was no room for misunderstanding: the real point is to kill' (Sampson 1977: 13).

To the extent that arms trafficking facilitates the militarization of undemocratic political regimes it supports authoritarianism and dictatorship, and arms trafficking is therefore directly responsible when civilian populations are persecuted by the iron fists of the generals implementing the direction of a hard-line administration (Myrdal 1977). We begin to see, then, that arms trafficking and the violence it supports can have consequential effects that reach far beyond just the deaths and injuries directly caused by the weapons that have been traded. Efrat summarizes some of the relevant harms in the literature:

> Widespread gun violence inflicts various social and economic costs, including medical treatment, refugee flows, destruction of physical infrastructure, losses in productivity and foreign investment, political instability, trade obstruction, as well as disruption of health care and education. Small arms are widely used for terrorism,

> organized crime and gang warfare. They also facilitate a large spectrum of human rights violations including killing, rape, and torture. (Efrat 2010: 98)

It has been noted that among the panoply of illegal markets, including those few that are covered in this book, firearms have a 'transcending quality' (Morselli 2012: 130; Koper and Reuter 1996). That is to say, the use of guns is ancillary to many illegal trades, as threat, as personal protection and in some case as a tool for doing the particular type of illegal business in question. Arms are present throughout drug trafficking and trade, in human trafficking, in the conflict that generates conflict diamonds, in the poaching stage of the wildlife trade and in a few cases, although it is not the norm, in antiquities looting such as the recent depredations in Iraq and Syria by ISIS. In this way then, firearms are a separate stream of trafficked commodity – to be analysed as a global trafficking problem in their own right – while also being an illegal trade that interfaces with all of the others we have discussed. In that sense, the breadth of the harm footprint of weapons trafficking grows to include the facilitation of the various harms attributed to these other types of trafficking, which we have elucidated in each individual chapter.

The structure of arms trafficking: source, transit, demand

The arms trade is a good case study of the spectrum of enterprise. Arms trading can happen legally, as is the case where governments sell arms to other governments. These types of trade are not infrequently caught up in allegations of bribery and corruption, and it has been a long-standing practice in international arms deals for sellers to grease the wheels of commerce by making payments on the side to buyers in the name of securing the contract, to make their bid competitive against other countries who might also want to sell to the buyer. So bribery and corruption may be thought to 'grey' legitimate international arms trading, pulling it down the spectrum of enterprise towards the murky middle.

Further down the spectrum, in the criminal zone, is arms trafficking by groups and individuals not operating on behalf of states but for their own benefit. This too is not so black and white as it may appear though, as states have been known to use independent criminal brokers as arms traffickers to assist them in moving weapons around the world, where they would otherwise not be able to do so. Overall then:

> While arms industry executives are often keen to emphasise the difference between the two realities, there is substantial evidence to suggest the existence of a continuum of unethical behaviour and illegality that characterises the arms trade in all its manifestations to varying degrees. There are, in effect, two worlds, each interlinked and involving players that move from one reality to another ... the 'respectable' world of state-sanctioned government-to-government contracts ... [and] ... the 'shadow world' constituted by deals conducted in the 'grey' and 'black markets'. (Feinstein and Holden 2014: 445)

In this 'shadow world', the grey market is off-the-books transfers of arms by state officials, who are usually aiming to achieve political ends without the scandal that might be attached were the trafficking publicly known, such as where the transfer is illegal or in breach of an international embargo. The black market is the realm of illegal arms dealers who are independent business-oriented traffickers. As intimated above, the black and the grey can overlap, and the 'respectable' world clearly interacts with both, so in that respect the language of the 'shadow world' is not uniformly helpful and the spectrum of enterprise is a better heuristic where arms trade and arms trafficking exist on the same dimension of international political economy.

At the high end of arms trafficking markets (that is, large shipments, not small-time independent trafficking of single weapons or small caches), used arms move in sporadic flows rather than the constant stream that is seen for goods designed for consumption (for example, drugs) or markets where newly emerging objects are prized over recirculating ones (for example, antiquities). Neither of these is the case for arms, where old weapons usually function as well as new ones and last for a long time. As such, the patterns of trafficking in arms are more 'episodic' (Leggett 2019: 37) than in other trafficking markets, essentially moving stockpiles of weapons to sites of major conflict from regions where they are now surplus to requirement. The end of the Cold War resulted in stockpiles that were surplus to requirement in this way, and these stockpiles have supported local and regional conflict, for example in Ukraine and the Balkans, as well as being trafficked further afield. While during the 1990s post-Soviet era, private individuals operating in states with fractured and weak controls were able to access and negotiate the sale of government military paraphernalia, more recently state controls have been re-exerted and it is now said to be the governments themselves in this region that are behind the significant weapons exports that fuel conflict abroad. An illustration of this can be found in an investigation of Russian and Ukrainian logistics companies linked to the governments of those countries, which suggested they were transporting weapons out of Russia and Ukraine to, among other buyers, the Assad regime in Syria (Wallace and Mesko 2013). There are many other examples of this phenomenon that has been called 'the wandering weapons' (Sampson 1977), as stocks move from one conflict to another and as historically both parties to the Cold War were funnelling arms to one or the other side in regional conflicts in an attempt to shore up their political interests overseas. Almost all guns that are stolen or otherwise diverted from stockpiles to be trafficked and illicitly traded will have begun their lives as legally produced and traded items in the commercial arms producing nations (Goldring 2006).

There are two types of flows in global arms supply: the recycling and reuse type of flow described above for existing arms, which is the predominant concern, and the flow of newly manufactured arms which continually feeds the overall supply (Brauer and Muggah 2006). Notable in arms trafficking, as different from many of the other forms of trafficking discussed in this book, is that guns are mostly produced in the industrial nations of the world. Production of small arms is worldwide – produced by over 1,200 companies operating in more than 90 countries (Hill 2007: 5) – but in volume terms the centres of arms production are the developed industrial economies. When they are trafficked from these developed industrial economies to the developing world to fuel crime, insecurity and conflict, we see a direction of flow which is the reverse of the usual pattern we have observed where illicit goods move from the developing world to an affluent consumer base in the global north and west. Episodic, and based also on the warehousing of arsenals outside the countries of production, the flows of trafficking in arms deals are not always in this rich-to-poor direction, but in the cases where that does happen it is an interesting point of analytical difference from the norm in global trafficking.

Arms trafficking to regions experiencing violent political upheaval, in other words armed militancy and rebellion, is organized to meet the needs of rebel forces who do not have access to guns and/or governments that are the subject of international arms embargo. For a famous example of the latter, President Reagan and elements of his administration and military broke the arms embargo on Iran, illicitly selling weapons to Iran in exchange for the release of hostages and then channelling some of those illicit funds, against the orders of Congress, to the Nicaraguan Contras (Walsh 1997).

Guns bought in the US, often by 'straw purchasers', are trafficked to Mexico to support the illegal drug trade there. Controls on gun purchases in Mexico are tighter than in the US, and so the demand pulls the supply southwards (McDougal et al 2014). This trafficking route appears to be more regular than the episodic template given above, and we see the same structural picture as has been presented in relation to other markets covered so far in this book – opportunistic trafficking to connect supply and demand which does not amount to an impression of large stable networks or organized crime group market or transit dominance. Rather: 'all the available evidence suggests most of the firearms trafficking is done by small groups moving small amounts of weapons very frequently' (Leggett 2019: 38).

Leggett (2019) points out that there is not much of a market for military-grade weapons among gun-using criminals, who prefer handguns which are easily concealable, suitably effective and easier to obtain, especially in countries such as the US where there is a legal consumer market for them. Straw purchases from legal commercial stores and thefts from legal owners provide the ability for criminals to access guns for domestic criminal use registered in someone else's name, and so trafficking in the international sense is not really necessary for this type of demand. Morselli's interview study of illegal gun acquisition in Canada confirmed that the purchase of illegal guns for personal use in criminal enterprise is normally a case of trades 'triggered by serendipitous offers that required little effort' in the context of family, friends and acquaintances who can connect those looking for guns to suppliers or to intermediaries who can broker the deal, having access to suppliers (Morselli 2012: 142). The arrangement of illegal gun purchases through these informal channels – that is, opportunistic trades among existing acquaintances rather than the sourcing of guns through the usual retail method of fixed channels of supply with 'key point sources' – is a common finding in the research literature on the retail end of private illegal gun deals (Wright and Rossi 1986; Morselli 2002; Koper and Reuter 1996).

The Mexican drug cartels are not the only customers for weapons trafficked out of the US: guns travel from there to Africa, Asia, Europe, the Middle East, and Central and South America. Gun parts can be ordered over the internet, shipped and then assembled into functioning weapons at the destination or repackaged by traffickers and shipped onwards to other destinations (Schroeder 2016). Unfinished parts of weapons, such as machined bodies that can be fashioned into functioning guns with little effort at the destination, do not qualify as firearms in US law and therefore are not subject to the relevant production and export controls – for example they can be shipped overseas easily and without serial numbers (Schroeder 2016: 5). Like drugs and wildlife, illicit arms can be couriered in person on commercial airliners or in the postal service, hidden in secret compartments in motor vehicles or shipped in maritime shipping containers along with the normal trade in commercial goods that travel in this way. As with the trafficking routes and techniques for other illicit goods, trafficking in arms may involve clandestine border crossing in which items are concealed in transit; or isolated and unprotected border crossing routes are selected because they avoid the usual customs check-points; or the 'merchants of death' organize larger shipments to armed groups and organized criminals in privately acquired decommissioned military cargo planes.

The most common and mundane type of arms trafficking, though, involves mimicking conventional legal supply chains for arms by using false – or genuine but fraudulently obtained – documentation and misrepresenting the source and nature of the weapons in transit. As with antiquities, diamonds, wildlife and humans, things which by their looks are relatively hard to distinguish from legal goods in transit offer the opportunity for border crossing in the form of what we might call 'trafficking in plain sight'.

Studies of 'supply chain security' by the Government Accountability Office in the US regularly note the tens of thousands of shipping containers that pass through major seaports in a day and the difficulty of identifying contraband goods hidden among conventional shipments in containers, even with the use of new scanning technology (Caldwell 2012; Grover 2015). In his summary of the Small Arms Survey research on trafficking weapons from the US, Schroeder sums this up:

> They arrive in dribs and drabs, hidden under clothing and toys in 20-foot shipping containers owned by legitimate companies. This side of the illicit arms trade is more mundane and, in some ways, more challenging to stop than the multi-ton shipments arranged by the merchants of death. Even governments with mature and well-funded export control systems struggle to intercept the thousands of small arms, parts, accessories, and rounds of ammunition that are illegally exported abroad every year. (Schroeder 2016: 14)

Weapons and parts are frequently misdeclared on customs forms as things like 'metal hunting tools, steel blocks and toy parts' (Schroeder 2016: 11). This kind of misrepresentation on shipping forms is something we have seen in other kinds of trafficking so far covered, and we will revisit it again when we look at antiquities trafficking, where artefacts are sometimes misdeclared as 'handicrafts' and other euphemistically obfuscating terms. As with other trafficking markets, shipping companies may be provided with a false identity and address by the consignor, making the sender harder to trace if the shipment is intercepted by law enforcement.

The organized crime literature has only fairly recently acknowledged the importance of facilitators to the overall functioning of successful networks (for example, Klerks 2003; Morselli 2009). These facilitators are specialists, like accountants, solicitors, estate agents, haulage companies and other transporters. They may also be other people with special skills, or in a special position in any given network, such as brokers who connect people for trades or the various types of 'fixers' we found in Farah's work, discussed in the preceding chapter on diamond trafficking. Farah charts one such example of his schema of 'fixers, super fixers and shadow facilitators' in his study of the infamous Russian arms trafficker Viktor Bout, known as the merchant of death. Bout traded his weapons with Charles Taylor in Liberia and is alleged to have sometimes taken payment in conflict diamonds, a trade which, as we have seen, supported the conflicts in Liberia and Sierra Leone (Farah 2013). Bout sourced the majority of his weapons from the Ukraine, a region which, after the Cold War, in 1992 had an estimated $89 billion stockpile of weapons, $32 billion of which were stolen over the following 6 years (Feinstein and Holden 2014). Bout established a complex network of front companies and registered his aircraft in pliant countries like Liberia which benefitted from his trafficking. He was not averse to servicing both sides of a conflict, doing so, for example, in the Angolan conflict of the late 1990s, supplying $325 million in contracts to the Angolan government while also supplying UNITA, the government's main opponent (Feinstein and Holden 2014). After the collapse of the Soviet Union, military personnel sold off decommissioned aircraft at a fraction of their real value, often pocketing the proceeds personally. Bout was one beneficiary of this, buying up old Red Army aeroplane stock cheaply and therefore, like some other transport specialists in international commodity trafficking networks, giving himself the capacity to extract his product using remote airfields in unstable countries and take it directly to the regions of international demand.

Regulation and control of arms trafficking

As with human trafficking, arms trafficking is the subject of a protocol to the UNTOC convention (United Nations 2000). The relevant protocol is titled *Protocol against the Illicit Manufacturing of and Trafficking in Firearms, their Parts and Components and Ammunition* ('the Firearms Protocol'). The protocol came into force in April 2005 and aims, ambitiously, to end illicit production and trafficking of arms. The protocol has become somewhat marginalized in relation to small arms compared to the UN's 'Program of Action to Prevent, Combat and Eradicate the Illicit Trade in Small Arms and Light Weapons in All its Aspects', adopted in July 2001 and known as the Program of Action, or PoA for short. The PoA is not legally binding and has no meaningful enforcement mechanism. It is a political declaration setting up a loose framework of engagement with the proliferation of small arms. Major arms-exporting countries like China and the US prefer the PoA's significantly lower levels of control over their enterprise activities in arms production and sale, compared with the more stringent requirements of the Firearms Protocol, which neither have ratified (Efrat 2010).

For African governments, for example, who suffer the effects of the international movement of small arms and light weapons (SALW), political declarative texts are as frustrating as they are helpful. Efrat quotes an interview he conducted with a respondent from Tanzania who said of the PoA that it 'does not force anyone to do anything' (Efrat 2010: 125). There is a discernible pressure in the negotiation of international treaties and prospective regulatory agreements to develop, through rounds of discussion and amendment, governing texts that in the end are so broad as to have wide appeal but little bite. In the governance of antiquities trafficking we find similar critiques of instruments that it is only a little bit of an exaggeration to say have been developed to suit everyone while pleasing no one. Where the world is split in terms of interest between the financial interests of the wealthy and powerful countries and the social, cultural or safety interests of the poorer and less powerful countries, there is little common ground for the creation of and accession to international agreements that would seriously curtail global trade flows, even where those flows are well known to be significantly compromised by crime.

As with the human trafficking protocol to UNTOC, the implementation of the convention's principles is left to domestic legislation in the member states. In the US, for example, a long-standing piece of legislation, the Arms Export Controls Act 1976, together with the current version from time to time of the International Traffic in Arms Regulations, requires a prospective exporter of arms to apply for a licence to do so. A licence would not be granted where the export was destined for a prohibited recipient, such as where an arms embargo was in place relating to a particular country, and if the exporter tried to continue without a licence this would be unlawful and therefore constitute arms trafficking, punishable by a considerable term of imprisonment or a large fine (Feinstein 2011). The UN, through the Security Council, and the EU issue their own lists of arms embargoed countries, and member states are required to implement domestic legal measures to observe and enforce these (Feinstein and Holden 2014).

Breaches of arms embargoes are very rarely successfully prosecuted, and arms traffickers operate in an environment where law enforcement is frequently frustrated by structural impediments. Jurisdictional issues plague arms trafficking prosecutions, where often the charges relate to crimes committed in another country and to individual offenders who are domiciled outside the jurisdiction of the court hearing the case. This makes it hard for individual states, which are naturally concerned first and foremost with their own laws and crimes committed in their own jurisdictions, to take the requisite steps to dismantle a global illicit business enterprise. The limits of individual state capacity to 'see' and acknowledge criminal trafficking that extends worldwide is compounded in some cases by their complicity in that trafficking. For example, Viktor Bout, discussed above, was protected first by US intelligence services and then by Russia, in a career that included weapons deals tied to the US Department of Defense (Farah and Braun 2007). Even without the problems of state complicity, where genuine prosecutions do take place the gathering of sufficient evidence is a major challenge considering that much arms trafficking takes place into and out of regions experiencing things like social and political upheaval, violent conflict, authoritarian or despotic dictatorship, corruption of local law enforcement, and catastrophic failure of the institutions that would normally promote social order in less anomic times. These are not contexts conducive to offering up clear evidence trails of illegal entrepreneurial behaviour, including arms trafficking (Feinstein and Holden 2014).

The legacy of more or less untrammelled arms trafficking around the world to date has left large numbers of weapons in stockpiles in fragile states and in the hands of various brands of revolutionaries, freedom fighters and terrorists. Even as we see the slow movement towards regulation of exports from the industrial producers of guns then, the raw materials for arms traffickers are still readily available elsewhere and this 'massive surplus of easily available arms means that setting up in business as an arms trafficker takes little more than motivation and a sense of moral ambiguity' (Feinstein and Holden 2014: 456).

Other approaches to control that have been suggested ring a familiar bell for observers of the variety of ongoing international debates about the different types of trafficking covered in this book. Advocates have argued for enhanced record keeping for arms while in stockpiles and in transfers. Marking or otherwise tracing the movement of arms through the use of technical or technological tracking mechanisms has also been put forward as a route to improved monitoring and control (Goldring 2006). These propositions are similar to tracking and tracing ideas that have been suggested for other internationally illicitly traded commodities and things, like wildlife and antiquities. There are difficulties in implementing such measures though. While tagging newly produced weapons may be possible, it would be harder for those already in circulation.

Most of the regulations and discussions about control in relation to arms trafficking have been about supply-side controls. As we have noted already in this book, supply-side controls are a common proposition in global trafficking markets, but are just as commonly criticized in the academic literature as likely to be ineffective without appropriate attention to the demand for the relevant illicit goods. Where there is a force drawing things out of source countries – a strong 'pull' factor – stemming the tide with attempts at supply interdiction has been a historical failure across black markets, whatever the commodity in question has been (Naylor 2004). In arms trafficking this problem is reified by the fact that the trade is characterized not only by willing buyers and willing sellers, which of course is the nature of all the illicit economies we discuss in this book, but also that it is supported by state-level interests both at the supply and at the demand ends. Where the very governments that are vested with the power to stop arms trafficking are sometimes complicit in the illegal trade, and even if not always complicit are still compromised and conflicted in their engagement with it as a criminal issue, the scene is hardly set for effective governance or full-throated regulation.

Added to this self-interest of states is the strong lobbying pressure from corporate producers of weapons, who have no interest in reducing the supply of arms to the world. Nonetheless, some types of supply reduction have been achieved – notably in relation to anti-personnel landmines. The Ottawa Convention of 1997 banned the production, stockpiling, transfer and use of these mines, and the Convention has been reasonably widely adopted, achieving good inroads into what was commonly agreed to be a pernicious issue.

While demand-end interventions have been argued to be a more productive avenue than supply-side interdiction for arms trafficking, precisely what these demand-end interventions might look like is often not specified in international instruments like the PoA. Strategies tend to be quite general, such as 'that the promotion of security, conflict prevention and resolution, crime prevention, and the promotion of health and development can reduce people's desire to acquire (and ultimately use) small arms' (Brauer and Muggah 2006: 138).

Arms trafficking as business enterprise

In human trafficking, we saw a debate on what perspective should be applied to the issue – whether it was best considered an issue for criminal justice or for human rights – and the proliferation of SALW has raised the same ontological dispute:

> [T]here is little agreement as to what the specific SALW 'problem' actually is. For some it is a humanitarian or human rights issue, for others a public health or development issue, and for still more a post-conflict disarmament, terrorism or criminality issue. As each approach focuses on different aspects of the SALW problem, they each subsequently advocate different solutions. (Hill 2007: 2)

This kind of ontological uncertainty is therefore a common theme across various trafficking debates. We can see it also in relation to drug trafficking (is it a criminal justice or a public health issue?), wildlife (crime, a sustainability issue, an animal rights issue, or an issue of local development?) and we will see it in relation to antiquities trafficking (crime, an issue of cultural appropriation/appreciation, or an archaeological concern?). Of course, every phenomenon can be viewed from different perspectives, and a healthy debate about which is the more appropriate is quite normal. But the result for trafficking, in policy terms, is often a mixed bag of measures revolving around the principled declarations of international conventions, the often half-hearted or otherwise incomplete implementation of those principles into practice by nation states, and the suspicion by many actors both in the criminal justice enforcement machinery and beyond that the real answer may lie elsewhere, in social reform, health or development-based programmes and so on. The existential anxiety about the appropriate role of criminal justice in reducing global trafficking problems is therefore not just a question of ideology or viewpoint, it cuts in practical terms to the effectiveness and energetic implementation of the legal approach itself. This is seen in relation to arms trafficking just as it is in other types of traffic.

Sampson, in his early work, identified 'the colonialism of weapons' (1977: 315) in which the industrial producers of arms sold them to the developing world legally and, through underworld arms brokers such as Viktor Bout and Leonid Minin, illegally – and the result of these arms transfers would undoubtedly be civil war and other forms of regional insecurity and destabilizing violence. Arms trafficking has therefore been a form of global soft power and neo-colonial interventionism for the powerful nations, loading the dice in far-flung conflicts and, through this interference, shoring up their own positions of global hegemony.

As with other trafficking markets, we have seen that arms traffickers range from small to large operations. The small-time and occasional gun runners are equivalent perhaps to the 'armpit' drugs smugglers who move a little of the commodity without a large supporting infrastructure, with a view to making some money. Also sometimes referred to as 'ants' in the trafficking literature, these are people taking small quantities of illicit goods across borders, concealed on the person, in luggage, or in modest shipments of legitimate goods (Cooper 2006). Researchers have found this pattern of smuggling by 'ants' in studies of, for example, the arms trade into Colombia (Cragin and Hoffman 2003) and the cross-border drug trade in the Golden Triangle (Zhang and Chin 2011). At the other end of the spectrum are major players like Bout and Minid who ran significant and seriously organized global transport networks, making millions of dollars, backed both by undemocratic regimes and sometimes also by the security services of the liberal democracies. This diversity of scale and embeddedness in the trade makes it difficult to talk of arms traffickers as if they represent only one phenomenon. On the other hand, we regularly do exactly this for businesses, talking of 'business organization' and 'business interests' while of course implicitly acknowledging that small businesses may be somewhat different in many respects from large multinational corporations. Despite the obvious and recognized differences there are some things that most businesses have in common: a desire to make money and the creation of a rational structure of enterprise in order to do this.

One element of this rational structure of enterprise in the pursuit of profit in the organization of conventional business activities that has attracted much critical comment lately is the aim to pay as little tax as necessary. This is also the case for large criminal enterprises and the use of tax havens goes hand in hand with money laundering. So arms traffickers use offshore financial jurisdictions to launder their funds and at the same time to avoid paying the tax that would be due on them were they considered legitimate business by the tax authorities of a country with an interest. These offshore financial centres are places like the Cayman Islands and the British Virgin Islands, where banks offer confidential accounts and accept instructions for payments in and out with minimal scrutiny. The same offshore financial centres are used by conventional businesses to avoid tax in the jurisdictions they operate in, as well as wealthy individuals including politicians. The Panama Papers and similar leaks have revealed scandalous amounts of money being funnelled into these secretive bank accounts by a surprising number of powerful and well-known companies and individuals (Evertsson 2019). This is a global asymmetry that is the very definition of a moral and legal grey area: a tax-and-scrutiny avoidance mechanism, in many cases tending towards evasion rather than avoidance, and used by conventional and illegal entrepreneurs alike.

The global financial system can be seen, therefore, to be a spectrum of financial enterprise, far from the impression that economics journals usually give of conventional banking and shadow or underground banking. Just as with the melding of the upperworld of legitimate business and the underworld of illegal enterprise, which we have argued to be more intimately connected than is usually recognized, so too is the lie revealed of the separation of the upperworld of the global financial system from the underworld of money laundering and criminal finance. Writers such as Keith Hart (Hart 1985; Schouten 2013) have taken an instructive line here, in questioning the extent to which the old imagery of formal and informal economy survives the new global neoliberal corporate capitalism. To paraphrase and expand: if the conventional image of the world is of an above-board regulated 'clean', tax-paying dominant formal economy, shadowed by various underground unregulated 'dirty', untaxed subservient informal economies, can that image survive in light of current evidence? Is it not more accurate to say that the dominant norm in global commerce and finance has become informal, where the multinational corporations have accrued power and mobility such that they can minimize and avoid tax, escape regulation by moving to low-control jurisdictions and move their money through the same secretive offshore financial centres that shelter the funds of traffickers and terrorists? If what many economists and other commentators have characterized as the formal economy is to this extent more empirically informal – if the context for the rhythms of global financial flows is more anomic than is usually imagined – then clear-sounding distinctions like dirty and clean financial streams begin to lose their meaning.

Guns and other weapons may seem on the face of it to be the epitome of function: they are made to do one thing and the motivation of a buyer at the demand end of the chain of supply is therefore surely clear enough. That impression would be wrong though. As well as the clear functional attractions of arms to prospective users, they are cultural artefacts. Several studies have shown the various seductions of guns and other weapons across a diversity of geographical backgrounds and use cases. Harcourt recorded, through interviews, the meaning of guns to disempowered young people in Arizona, who were able to recite in some detail the technical prowess of different weapons and talk about the relative street cred and lure of each (Harcourt 2006). Cock explains guns as symbolic items in post-apartheid South Africa, recalling and embodying repression and resistance (Cock 1997), becoming 'socially sanctioned and normalised symbols of liberation [and a] substitute for other status symbols – the cell phone, glamorous woman, and gold chains – as a means of displaying (male) status and power' (Brauer and Muggah 2006: 141). Arsovska and Kostakos recall that in the Balkans, guns are infused with the impression of masculinity, honour and courage, citing cultural proverbs such as that 'you can kill an Albanian but you cannot make him give up his gun' and 'an Albanian loves his rifle as much as [he loves] his wife' (Arsovska and Kostakos 2008). Morselli conducted an interview study of illegal firearms acquirers and found that some of his sample were not criminals who had bought the guns for functional reasons but were 'passionate firearm collectors who were ready to acquire through illegal channels if it meant getting a gun that was difficult or impossible to obtain through legal means' (Morselli 2012: 147). Objects – things – have socially constructed meanings (Appadurai 1986) and in this respect even highly function-oriented items such as arms share some common ground with apparently less functionally designed objects like art and diamonds. Each type of commodity is wrapped in layers of social and cultural meaning for their collectors, users and consumers, and as such each trafficking market must be understood as fulfilling a demand for meaning in terms of these quite complex motivations among buyers.

Another cultural meaning of arms use, which trafficking feeds, is the gun as business tool. In the favelas of Rio de Janeiro, the drug trade drives demand for, conspicuous display of, and use of guns: the gun 'is a corporate tool, a business expense' (Brauer and Muggah 2006: 151; Dreyfus et al 2008). These reflections, first of a consumer base infused with symbolic meaning and second of those aspects of that symbolism that are tied to impressions of effective business enterprise, have raised for some authors the question whether arms trafficking should be primarily considered a 'rationally organised illicit enterprise that thrives and forms the same way legitimate businesses do … based on the simple economic rule of demand and supply as well as on rational choice theory' (Arsovska and Kostakos 2008: 355). These writers have suggested that such a parsimonious view of rational business enterprise fails to acknowledge the complexity of the arms trafficking market, especially considering issues of cultures of consumption. The dichotomy between business and culture they put forward is a false one though, albeit one which is frequently made, as if business enterprise has no conception of the cultural preferences of its consumer base, as if cultural modes of consumption cannot be rational, emotional and symbolic all at once and as if those operating in business are never affected by the same cultural interpretations of the products they are selling as the consumers are.

We have seen each of these false presumptions disproved in previous chapters of this book, which have built a picture of trafficking as a rational business response to profitable opportunities presented in otherwise strained circumstances, and which are driven by a market need to satisfy demands for people and products that can be highly emotional and not infrequently culturally specific in a variety of ways. We have developed a picture of an economy of acquisition that is often impressively symbolic in its estimation of the value of its objects of desire, and it is instructive to see that such an economy of symbol exists to some extent in arms deals too.

While for consumers guns may have a variety of uses and meanings, for traffickers the situation seems more straightforward. As we have seen in previous chapters, traffickers frame their involvement in transnational crime in terms of business enterprise, and they deny, justify or excuse the harm that involvement causes. Arms traffickers appear also to fit that description. We can conclude this chapter with a typical quote from journalistic work on arms traffickers, in this case a writer for the *New York Times* who gained an audience with Viktor Bout:

> 'Look, killing isn't about weapons', Bout replied impatiently. 'It's about the humans who use them'. Bout fell silent. His wit and insider's perspective on international geopolitics

suddenly coalesced into the cynical visage of a drug dealer peddling crack in a schoolyard. He was just a businessman selling his wares. Who was he to be the arbiter of good and evil? (Landesman 2003)

7

Antiquities Trafficking

The nature and extent of the harm

We have seen that the globalization of trade in the world economy has accelerated a trend that existed previously and is now continuing at pace: the expeditious removal of wealth and natural resources from developing countries and the accretion of these in richer nations. The natural resources referred to include raw materials and precious things like the diamonds and wildlife we have discussed in previous chapters. The tangible cultural heritage of countries might also by analogy be considered as if it were a natural resource for the purposes of this analysis, since it consists of ancient temples, statues and other artefacts that were manufactured hundreds of years ago and much of it now exists undiscovered under the ground or in a variety of states of abandon in jungles, deserts and other secluded regions of developing countries. Just as with wildlife, diamonds and the drain of other natural resources from the developing to the developed world, so it is with antiquities.

The harm done by antiquities trafficking is mainly twofold: historical and economic. First, historical knowledge is lost when antiquities are looted. Even where the objects are well preserved in the process, which is far from always the case, the archaeological context of the artefact's discovery is usually destroyed. Looters dig up heritage sites, graves and other underground deposits, messing up the site in the process and thereby denying archaeologists the chance to study the way the artefacts were deposited in the ground. Archaeologists learn much from this 'context' in which cultural objects are found, and they cannot reconstruct this lost knowledge simply by studying the objects themselves 'out of context' in the marketplace or in museums or other collections (Brodie et al 2000). Additionally, many objects are damaged in the process of looting, inadvertently or deliberately. The deliberate damage often occurs when large items are broken down for ease of transport or to make smuggling less obvious and problematic – so heads are cut from statues, or whole statues are broken at the ankles to be removed from their feet and pedestal, or large stelae (engraved stone panels from temples) are broken into pieces to be reconstructed later at the destination and so on (Mackenzie and Davis 2014). So historical cultural heritage objects are damaged and destroyed by looting, and the process of looting itself destroys archaeological context and therefore the irrecoverable possibility of historical knowledge about previous civilizations. It is a very damaging pursuit.

Second, we can consider the economic loss involved in looting. Cultural heritage provides the basis of a significant source of tourist income for many of the relatively poor countries where major deposits of ancient temples and artefacts are found. The destruction and theft of these therefore directly impacts the economic wellbeing of source countries and consequently further impoverishes their citizens (Mackenzie and Yates 2017a). The income derived by some of those citizens by conducting the looting provides no real counterweight to that overall economic loss, as looters are generally quite poorly rewarded for their efforts and of course any funds they receive from their sales are only a private benefit, which arises at the expense of the general public good (Brodie 2010). It has been estimated that on average looters receive less than 1 per cent of the final sale price antiquities achieve once they have made the journey to a destination market (Brodie 1998). The serious money is made by the middlemen – the traffickers. There is no sustainability to the economic model of looting: once artefacts have been sold they are gone forever, and at some point the supply will run out (Mackenzie et al 2020).

The precise scale of antiquities looting and trafficking is a subject of constant debate among commentators. It is very difficult to estimate, for various reasons. For one, common to many cases of smuggling or trafficking, the illegal trade takes steps to avoid detection and this makes studying the volume of trade in illicit antiquities hard. What further compounds the issue in the particular case of antiquities, however, is that recorded data is often not very revealing. Police in many countries record cases of art and antiquities crime only under their category of general stolen goods, which makes disaggregating the cases of interest a prohibitively time-consuming effort for researchers. We do, however, know that there are recorded instances of looting happening in great volume in many countries around the world (Brodie et al 2001; Mackenzie et al 2019), and when we add to that a speculative amount of unrecorded looting events – which are clearly many in number – the question arises where all the loot is going. The answer provided by researchers to date has been twofold. First, it goes into the 'legitimate' market, which thereby becomes tainted with these stolen goods and is best identified as a grey market (Mackenzie and Yates 2017b). Second, some of it – an unknown proportion but probably much less than hits the open market – goes straight into the hands of dealers and collectors who engage with the loot in private. In that scenario, coming from an unrecorded source, being smuggled through customs without being recognized and then privately acquired by buyers in the destination region, the artefacts may well be unknown to the public market as well as to archaeology and art history, and from this hidden quality comes the name for this segment of the trade: the invisible market (Nørskov 2002).

The structure of antiquities trafficking: source, transit, demand

The source–transit–demand outline we have identified as a common frame of reference for many transnational criminal markets applies to antiquities just as it has done to the previous markets we have examined. Source countries for antiquities tend to be developing countries whereas the destination markets are in the richer countries where the buyers are. These buyers may be high-end collectors, public or private museums, or dealers who will then try in turn to sell an artefact on to one of their clients.

Countries that suffer looting are not confined to one geographic region. Significant cases of looting have been recorded in Central and South American countries such as Peru, Guatemala and Mexico (Coggins 1969), Southeast Asian countries such as Cambodia and Thailand (Thosarat 2001; Davis and Mackenzie 2015), European countries, in particular Italy and Greece (Renfrew 1999; Tsirogiannis 2013b), Asian countries including India, Pakistan, China and Nepal (Schick 1997; Murphy 1995; Fincham 2014) and others such as Egypt and Turkey (Gerstenblith 2009; Kaye and Main 1995). Recently the conflict in the Middle East has supported a flood of illicit antiquities out of Iraq and Syria, and while this is the latest crisis, looting has been a feature of the region for years, with nearby countries such as Jordan, Yemen and Libya suffering in relative media silence (Brodie 2015a, 2015b). Some market countries, like the UK and US, are also significant source countries for antiquities, which confuses the surface simplicity of the source–transit–demand model, but overall the trend of economic powerhouse countries sucking the cultural heritage out of under-resourced and economically stretched source countries is an accurate representation of the big picture.

The culture of the trade in antiquities is largely responsible for the facilitation of the insertion of looted artefacts into the public chain of supply. Harking back to the colonial roots of the collection and display of antiquities as a 'gentleman's pursuit', and a marker of class and distinction (Yates et al 2017), the idea of asking direct questions of a vendor about where precisely a particular item has come from is seen as vulgar. Dealers in the antiquities market report that traditionally deals have been done on a handshake, with the ecosystem of the antiquities trade premised largely on trust and insider knowledge (Mackenzie 2005b). Dubious offers will normally either be rebuffed or, if the temptation is great enough, accepted, but either way the police are unlikely to be called (Mackenzie 2005a).

The keystone of deciding whether an artefact has been looted or not is 'provenance', which is a story about the prior ownership history of the object ideally, but not normally, reaching back to the place and circumstances of its discovery. The cultural reluctance of market participants to ask searching questions about provenance is self-serving: it allows them to buy trafficked antiquities with a suitable measure of plausible deniability about the likely origins of the stolen goods. The circumstances in which most of the world's source countries would allow antiquities to be excavated and exported are so few as to mean that any newly surfacing cultural object ('surfacing' is the term the trade uses for objects appearing on the market for the first time) is likely to have been looted and trafficked. Provenances can be manufactured though, especially since there is no standard for what a provenance should look like: documentation is useful but not essential, and often dealers will accept stories backed up by a signature from the seller to warrant they are the legitimate owner (Mackenzie 2013). Clearly this is no deterrent to traffickers. There are famous examples in the antiquities trafficking literature of fictional collections being invented by entrepreneurial dealers in order to suggest a provenance for artefacts they are trying to sell. In one case this was done simply with a story backed up by labels artificially aged in tea, which were attached to looted Egyptian artefacts to make them appear to have been part of an old collection (Gerstenblith 2002, 2003, 2009).

To compound the difficulties, auction houses cite client confidentiality as a reason to publish only the barest bones of useful provenance information (Tsirogiannis 2013a), still referring to objects as coming 'from the collection of a Belgian gentleman' and other hopelessly opaque references to supposedly legitimate ownership. A buyer would be foolish to trust such references as providing evidence of a good provenance, but clearly many do. Another notorious reference which has been used over the years is to attribute an artefact for sale at auction as 'from a Swiss collection'. Given that one convicted dealer in illicit antiquities kept a warehouse of objects in the freeport in Geneva on their way from illegal origins to market insertion (Watson and Todeschini 2007), it is hardly reassuring for an unwitting buyer to be told that everything is okay because the artefact comes from a Swiss collection.

Regulation and control of antiquities trafficking

Most countries that are major sources of antiquities have passed laws taking ownership of undiscovered antiquities within their jurisdiction, so rather than 'finders keepers', this makes unauthorized excavation or other taking of antiquities (for example, cutting pieces off temples) a theft from the state (Prott and O'Keefe 1984). It also means that if the objects are subsequently trafficked overseas, the state from which they were stolen can take legal action in the destination country to ask for them to be returned. The other main tool used by source states to combat antiquities trafficking is export restrictions: for example, in most source countries export of antiquities is unlawful without a licence from the local authorities, often administered in practice by experts at the national museum (Prott and O'Keefe 1989). Due to issues of corruption and the legal and practical difficulty of enforcing export prohibitions internationally once the objects have escaped the customs barrier of the source state, these measures are not as effective as we might hope.

There are a number of international treaties governing antiquities trafficking. The two main ones are the UNESCO *Convention on the Means of Prohibiting and Preventing the Illicit Import, Export and Transfer of Ownership of Cultural Property* of 1970 and the UNIDROIT *Convention on Stolen or Illegally Exported Cultural Objects* of 1995. The former (UNESCO 1970) was established to set guidelines for repatriation of objects looted from inventoried public collections or sites in source countries, while the latter (UNIDROIT 1995) was introduced to cover the situation where the dispossessed owner was a private citizen, rather than the state. Most active source and market countries for antiquities have signed up to the UNESCO 1970 convention, while fewer have done so for UNIDROIT 1995. Those that have signed up to UNIDROIT 1995 are not the destination market countries. This represents a reluctance by countries that are major destination markets for antiquities to commit themselves to strong market regulation measures that would substantially diminish the volume of this branch of the art trade that passes through their jurisdictions.

In part this reluctance to implement strict regulation is a result of the powerful lobbying capacity of the antiquities dealing and collecting community, a sector with considerable cultural and economic capital as well as political connections and a reasonable argument, through museums and galleries, to be performing a valuable public service. In part though, it is also simply because there is little incentive for market countries to spend time, money and effort controlling an international problem where the main effects of the harm involved are perceived to be experienced elsewhere. International relations are seldom characterized by unrestrained altruism and where market countries have increased their levels of control over the problem in the past it has been in response to diplomatic pressure from source countries, often acting through the UN and activist lobbying groups. This pressure has yet to find the purchase to persuade the major world markets to implement the UNIDROIT 1995 convention.

This is a shame, because as well as being a useful complement to the UNESCO 1970 convention, the UNIDROIT 1995 convention sets up much tighter controls on antiquities trafficking. For example, it requires illegally exported (not only stolen) items of cultural property to be returned to the source state in certain circumstances, whereas the UNESCO 1970 convention does not apply to illegal export. It also applies to all cultural objects unlawfully taken from a source state, whereas the UNESCO 1970 convention requires stolen items to have been inventoried by the source state prior to their theft if they are to form the subject of a request for return from abroad. Additionally, UNIDROIT 1995 has preferential rules on limitation periods which tilt the balance in favour of successful claims by dispossessed owners over refutations by current possessors (Redmond-Cooper 1997, 2000). These provisions, and others, which we can broadly characterize as 'pro-return', are interpreted equally as 'anti-market' by the trade lobby (Pearlstein 1996) and consequently have not in the destination market countries been the subject of the wide implementation hoped for.

At the extreme end of policy interventions into antiquities trafficking are outright bans on acquiring objects from certain countries. This has been seen for Iraq and Syria, implemented by way of UN security resolutions (Brodie 2011c, 2015a). These resolutions can sometimes reverse the burden of proof in relation to the purchase of antiquities from these source regions. That is, rather than a prosecutor having to prove that an artefact has been looted and trafficked, while the dealer possessing the object is able to simply deny knowledge of that, the burden of proof is instead placed with the dealer who must be able to show that the item was capable of being legally acquired. In effect, this closes down much of the prospective market in stolen goods to dealers since while there will not usually be abundant or easily discernible evidence that an object has been looted and trafficked, neither will there be evidence that it has not (Gerstenblith 2007).

In order to try to evade interventions like these international bans on trade from particular regions, sellers can say the item originates in a neighbouring country to the embargoed one (Gilgan 2001). We saw this ploy previously in the chapter on diamond trafficking. Since the boundaries of ancient cultures and states do not accord with contemporary national borders, in many cases this can be a plausible ruse and absent direct evidence of the findspot it can be very hard to disprove. Another such ruse is to claim the item being offered for sale was out of the embargoed country prior to the date the trade ban came into force. Again this can be hard to disprove, given that export certificates are rare productions in the antiquities market, even though they should really be central to any such international market that aspires to clean and transparent trading. The benefit of the reversed burden of proof in such circumstances is that while the prosecutor would struggle to disprove these lies, where the burden lies with the dealer to prove their veracity, the invention of provenance details is substantially more difficult.

Transit ports have been a key intermediary point in the supply chain for antiquities over the years. These are receptive locations where significant amounts of trade are done and which may provide export papers for antiquities without inquiring into the circumstances of their import into the country. Hong Kong has been a transit portal for artefacts leaving China for many years (Murphy 1995; Polk 2000). Its proximity to the mainland has meant that it is reasonably easy to smuggle looted antiquities into Hong Kong, which has an active arts trading scene with major international auction houses present as well as dealers along the famous Hollywood Road. International buyers can visit, look and buy, and the dealers will arrange to transport the objects back to the buyers' home countries where they will enter with documents showing their authorized export from Hong Kong, covering up their looted origins. This is a mechanism of laundering for looted artefacts, and it happens because in this case trafficking is able to mimic legitimate international trade and shipment.

Not all laws facilitate the regulation of trafficking antiquities. Some laws, indeed, make it harder rather than easier to control this kind of trafficking. An example of such confounding laws is the statutes of limitation that in many countries set time limits on legal action over title claims to chattels after a theft. These limitation periods can be surprisingly short, so that a good faith buyer can acquire an unimpeachable title to stolen goods in some transit and market jurisdictions 3 to 5 years after a theft has occurred (Redmond-Cooper 2000; Kenyon and Mackenzie 2002). In that case, all a trafficker needs to do is warehouse the stolen loot, perhaps in a freeport such as Geneva, for the required period of time and thereafter sell it on to dealers or collectors in the market who will acquire good title to the antiquities as long as they are not demonstrably aware of their illicit origins. These limitation laws on the passing of title in goods, and the bar they impose to dispossessed owners suing for recovery of chattels after the expiry of the limitation period, are another strand in the web of legitimation and laundering that allows antiquities trafficking to interface with the public and ostensibly legitimate market in cultural objects.

The business of dealing in antiquities is therefore tightly interwoven with trafficking, which is in reality one of the major suppliers of goods in this particular market. The difficulty in discerning the legal from the illegal in this grey but public and generally socially accepted – indeed historically celebrated – marketplace means that antiquities trafficking is not just a supplier of goods to the business entrepreneurs who deal in ancient cultural objects, but it is better conceptualized as a core part of that business entrepreneurialism itself. In other words: trafficking is not an underlabourer to the upperworld of antiquities business, it *is* that business, and this is simply obscured by the opacity of the privacy and secrecy routines of the marketplace, which put a veneer of legitimacy and art appreciation over this long-standing historical process of stealing the cultural appurtenances of other countries and 'appreciating' them in the west.

As well as the legal interventions into the market – the international treaties and resolutions and the domestic laws – a supporting network of information and public education services exist. These services include databases of stolen objects, like the police art crime database held by Interpol and the database of stolen artworks held by the private company the Art Loss Register. The main challenge of these databases for researchers of antiquities trafficking is that the entry of an object onto such a register depends in the first instance on a dispossessed owner contacting the register with details of a theft. Where antiquities which have been clandestinely excavated enter the market, there is unlikely to be such a report and the dispossessed owner – usually the source state – may have no knowledge even that a theft has occurred.

Education campaigns aimed at the public include posters in airports warning tourists not to take antiquities home with them, and advertisements in magazines (O'Keefe 1997), but it has been a lot harder to galvanize public sympathy with the cause of looted antiquities than it has to tug the heartstrings in relation to wildlife trafficking. Antiquities trafficking researchers rue the fact that these artefacts, while beautiful, are often not as photogenic or impactful as the flora and fauna in the adverts of wildlife NGOs like TRAFFIC. The problem of course is that while a photo of a dead elephant with tusks removed speaks awful volumes, when the average member of the public sees a photo of a looted antiquity it may well seem to be still intact and without further explanation it is not always clear to the layperson what the problem is.

As with other transnational criminal markets, improving security at source is not really a viable policy solution. The sites of antiquities are so many, and often so remote, and the countries which are the targets of the most looting are so under-resourced in terms of the capacity to fund a specialized security force for antiquities protection, that heightened site security is not usually a practical option (Mackenzie et al 2019). As we saw with diamond trafficking, where we noted parallel systems of administration of mining regions by militia groups extracting taxes and issuing 'permits', where there is effective control over legal and illegal markets in a region it is not always in the form of governance that is conducive to the suppression of destructive and criminal resource extraction. Comparably, Daesh (ISIS) and Al Qaeda in Syria and Iraq (Felch 2014; Jones 2018), and the Taliban in Afghanistan (Hardy 2014; Peters 2010), have been said to have taxed antiquities looters based on the value of their finds, and there have been some reports that these systems may in some cases have been 'institutionalized' and fairly well-administered, comprising ledgers where the so-called *khums* taxes are recorded (Keller 2015; Paul 2016).

Antiquities trafficking as business enterprise

We have observed in the preceding sections that many of the routines of trafficking antiquities look the same as legitimate business. Dealers function in public view, from shops that anyone can walk into, and deal in some recirculating legal artefacts as well as receiving and passing on stolen goods which are mixed in with the legal trade. Looted antiquities can get export papers as they pass through unscrupulous jurisdictions, and thereafter their trafficking happens in the same way as regular commercial goods move across borders: as part of the global movement of container shipments, in air freight and sometimes in the personal luggage of globally mobile traders. Once in the destination markets, the objects are often sold in public and published venues such as auction houses and galleries. The price of antiquities can be very high, and the profession of dealing in these cultural goods still attracts an impression of high class and refinement. It should be no surprise then that antiquities traffickers, being participants in an international chain of supply that is to all intents and purposes a straightforward movement of desirable chattels from sources of supply to regions of demand, see their routines as a business enterprise – for that is clearly what this is.

The interpretation of the acquisition and disposal of cultural objects as simply a business enterprise provides dealers with a framework of neutralizing discourse and thought that has been observed to be one of the main characteristics of the way antiquities traders talk about their work (Mackenzie 2005b, 2007). We have already noted in various places throughout this book that traffickers deny, rationalize, justify and excuse their crimes with reference to business language and enterprise-oriented ways of thinking. In particular, we examined some of the techniques of neutralization used by human traffickers in that chapter. The application of techniques of neutralization to the analysis of trafficking is in keeping with the spectrum of enterprise approach to legal and illegal business: trafficking is normally considered a type of organized crime but the 'spectrum' approach entreats us to think of it as illegal business and therefore draw on theoretical explanations inspired by the white-collar crime literature. Among these, techniques of neutralization – while developed as a theory of delinquency rather than business crime (Sykes and Matza 1957) – have been extended and applied in relation to white-collar crime and now sit as a core part of the theoretical background to offending in business contexts (Benson 1985; Stadler and Benson 2012; Kvalnes 2019). Let us look at these techniques briefly in relation to antiquities trafficking here.

We have already seen that the idea of techniques of neutralization, as a theoretical framework in criminology with close cognate versions of the idea in psychology (Ribeaud and Eisner 2010), refers to a system of rationalizing narratives that can be drawn on to justify or excuse harmful or wrongful conduct. Antiquities dealers use techniques of neutralization to portray their deals as normal business routines, thereby distancing themselves from the taint of lawbreaking or moral turpitude by discursively severing the link between their actions in buying and selling antiquities and the harm done at source by looting.

There are many ways that business talk neutralizes the implications of harmful practice. These have been well catalogued in relation to white-collar crime (Benson 1985; Stadler and Benson 2012). Techniques include appeals to higher loyalties (for example, 'for the good of the company/firm'), and in relation to antiquities dealing this particular technique has been attributed the most significant role in framing dealers' perceptions of and professed attitudes towards looting (Mackenzie and Yates 2016). The particular higher loyalty antiquities dealers tend to hold close is the commitment to 'cultural property internationalism', which can be broadly summarized as an apparently deep-felt desire to see cultural heritage diffused around the world and made available to buyers who will appreciate, preserve and in some cases display it (Merryman 2005). Source countries are seen in this worldview as retentionist, seeking to hold on to their cultural heritage, limiting access to it and possibly not preserving it as well as rich international collectors would. This view has been criticized as neo-colonial in its orientation (Mackenzie et al 2020) but nonetheless it gives a rationalization for collecting that considers the business around marketing antiquities globally as ethically justifiable.

Another classic technique of neutralization that can be seen in use in the antiquities trade is denial of injury (for example, 'nobody got hurt'). This narrative construction is often seen in apparent 'victimless' offences and antiquities dealers use it to try to characterize their business activities as victimless. They suggest that many grave sites and other heritage sites that are ransacked by looters probably did not contain anything significant anyway, other than the objects that were removed, and these (as above) are best circulated into the market to be appreciated, studied and preserved. The work looters do is dirty and dangerous: tunnels can collapse killing people during illicit excavations and the penalties in some countries for looting if caught can be severe: corporal and, historically, capital in some countries and under some regimes such as China and Iraq (Rothfield 2009: 15–20; Soudijn and Tijhuis 2003). Rather than acknowledge these risks to individuals though, dealers use the economics of the global market to turn victims into benefactors, seeing looters and their families as benefitting economically from their illegality (Mackenzie 2005b). Business, in all its variety, is generally conceived by neoliberal entrepreneurs as rewarding to participants rather than exploitative, and antiquities dealing is no different in this.

A third technique of neutralization, the denial of responsibility, can be seen most clearly in business discourse in the much-used proposition that 'if I don't do it, someone else will'. Under this weak attempt at justification, many harmful effects are foisted on society by amoral entrepreneurs who consider their impression that the world is not a nice place as justification enough for them to fit in with that image. To resist the temptation to profit from harm would be to lose out on an opportunity and pass it along to the next trader. Antiquities dealers characterize the marketplace in cultural objects, a subset of the wider art market, as one in which many of their peers are untrustworthy (Mackenzie 2005b). Rather like the surveys of car drivers, in which a great majority of drivers report thinking they are good drivers while others are bad, the non-sequitur of each person thinking they are more trustworthy than the next subsists in antiquities trading. As well as being a self-inflating delusion, this attitude supports the general impression among market participants that there are enough dodgy dealers out there to snap up any lucrative offer of illicit antiquities, so no harm is done by taking up such an illicit offer first: 'there is always someone at the bottom of the line who is going to do a deal' (an antiquities dealer in London, reported in Mackenzie 2005b: 30).

Denial of victims and condemnation of the condemners, the last two of Sykes and Matza's techniques of neutralization, go hand in hand in the antiquities market since the predominant view among traders is that the main victims when antiquities are looted and trafficked are archaeologists and source countries, and these are also among the most vocal critics of the trade in illicit antiquities. So they are both denied as victims and condemned as condemners. In the first case, the victimhood of source countries is denied with the accusation that they bring looting on themselves: their retentionist approach stimulates a black market in these goods, since none can be exported legally (Bator 1983; Ede 1998). The victimhood of archaeologists is denied as they are portrayed in the narrative of the business of antiquities dealing as slow and self-interested, publishing only a fraction of their data and leaving much to languish in the filing drawer (Marks 1998). As such, the purported loss of knowledge to the world through looting cannot be as great as imagined, since much of it would not have made it out into the world anyway. We can see how these denials of the victims of looting are also wrapped up with condemnatory assertions, which fit the Sykes and Matza (1957) theme of the disavowal of accusers who come with dirty hands: who are they to criticize me; look at what *they* do.

Where the 'condemners' in question are not source countries or archaeologists but lawyers or regulators, the neutralizing stories in the market are of legitimate businessmen taking a wrong step and then unfairly 'being made an example of' by the criminal justice system (Mackenzie 2005b). Business is sometimes a bit 'messy', everyone makes mistakes from time to time, and where one has the misfortune to be identified making such a mistake and subsequently apprehended, is it really fair to be strung up for it when the practices involved are so widespread and normalized in the market? So goes the justificatory discourse of the dealer. Fellow traders who are caught and punished for dealing in loot were 'careless' or 'stupid' (Mackenzie 2005b), the implication being that if they had only been smarter about disguising their criminal dealing, they would have got away with it like others in the trade do. And the agencies of control are in this narrative only picking the low-hanging fruit: why are they wasting their time investigating those 'sailing close to the wind' when that kind of edgy illicit entrepreneurialism is so widespread? Surely they should target more serious, and by implication unusual, crimes than those which are so deeply normalized in the market. Such neutralizing discourse will of course seem entirely wrong-headed to scholars of white-collar crime, who are used to diagnosing the most serious criminal aspects of markets as those which are precisely so engrained as this in everyday normalized practice (McBarnet 2003, 2006).

The other approach to neutralizing the impression that the antiquities trade is, as one dealer has put it in his diagnosis, 'just a pastiche of lies, cheating and lack of integrity on all levels by most of the people involved' (Mackenzie 2005b) is to argue that crime in the market is only committed by a few 'bad apples'. This is, again, a common theme in white-collar crime studies (Bakan 2004; Whyte 2016): systemic and ingrained structural problems with a market that are over-written, or attempted to be at least, by the assertion from market participants and other vested interests that most of the trade is legitimate while a minority of criminals are giving it a bad name. This 'Othering' of the problem of crime in the market performs the trick of pulling business apart from crime, seeing the latter as a problem of infiltration of dirt into the clean world of trade. It is close to an epidemiological metaphor – the poison in the blood, the disease in the bones – in which an external evil pollutes a healthy system. In such a metaphor the solution is surely excision of the poisonous other, rather than the reorganization and rethinking of the whole world of business. There is no blurred line in this imagery between licit and illicit enterprise, when in reality that blurring is precisely the case.

These processes of denial are micro-level in that they take place in the minds of, and quite clearly influence the actions of, individual agents, but they derive from the organizational culture of the market as they are not made up on the spot by individuals. They are part of the discursive environment of the institutional and economic entrepreneurial culture and as such they are internalized by individuals as a feature of the normative structure of business life. Sutherland has explained the wider process of the internalization of group norms in the context of white-collar crime as differential association (Sutherland 1949). This is a social learning process where exposure to a particular cultural worldview becomes ingrained in the individual over time, influencing attitudes and beliefs. Aubert similarly considered white-collar crime as taking place within an ideological subculture that condoned many offences (Aubert 1952), and this conception of wrongdoing that is socially, culturally and economically normative, albeit illegal, has since then become a powerful influence on white-collar crime research and in particular on research into illicit and informal economies (Beckert and Dewey 2017). Expanding upon differential association theory, Vaughan has shown how 'toxic or criminogenic organizational cultures can explain why paradoxically, it is often *conformity* to organizational norms and goals that can explain corporate deviancy' (Vaughan 1999, my emphasis; Van Erp 2018). This is paradoxical because the conventional view of crime is of breaking rules rather than adhering to them (McBarnet 2003). Yet white-collar crime studies of organizational deviance such as Vaughan's show that the adherence to certain sets of rules can be criminogenic, when this involves internalizing normative social structures like neutralizing discourse and, as I am proposing, the compartmentalization and separation of business decision-making from moral social decision-making.

The thorough corruption of a market that can occur when business norms acquiesce in handling stolen goods can be seen in the widespread participation of 'facilitators' in the market for trafficked antiquities. We have discussed the concept of the facilitator of transnational crime in earlier chapters. In respect of antiquities, it is not only dealers and collectors who profit from the grey market in cultural objects. While these actors are doing the buying and selling, their transactions are facilitated by other business professionals who offer services that support the trade and make it possible. In studies of organized crime the presence of facilitators has been noted, often as part of analyses that call into question where we should draw the boundaries of units of analysis such as an organized crime group (von Lampe 2015). Facilitators in organized crime include professional agents like solicitors and estate agents, who can transact in the legitimate business world on behalf of professional criminals without drawing attention to the illegal sources of the funds that are being invested. In antiquities trafficking, those who facilitate crime include art historians, appraisers and conservators, who add to the value of illegal objects by restoring them, valuing them or adding elucidatory and titillating commentary to the write-ups in sales catalogues (Brodie 2017; Mackenzie et al 2019).

They also include scholars who in some cases receive government research grants to study antiquities, often without many ethical limits on what they are prepared to study, increasing the value of assessed stolen objects in the process by adding historical context and market legitimacy (Brodie 2009, 2011a, 2011b, 2016). In this way, the business of dealing in looted antiquities spreads beyond the immediate parties to the sale and purchase transactions involved, seeping like a poisonous fog out into the network of support services that has grown like a constellation around the market, fuelled by the money that filters out of the core of the illegal trade. These facilitators, like the immediate market participants, talk of their professional activities as simply normal business routines. It is easier for them to neutralize their participation in an illegal market because of the nature of that participation: working at some distance from the actual transactions themselves; able to perform their services on legal and illegal artefacts alike, with no real need for a distinction to be made between the two in terms of the effectiveness of the service they provide; likely to lose clients if they ask too many questions about the legal status of the objects; and working simply as entrepreneurs, not police officers for the market. In respect of this latter, the most common response to questions around policing is 'that's not my job', which efficiently captures the problems of the boundaries between formal and informal social control when the context is considered to be one of business and policing is perceived to be someone else's business.

The issue of facilitators, especially financial facilitators such as tax accountants, leads us to a final observation for this chapter on the tight-knit integration between the illegal world of trafficking looted antiquities and the legal world of business and taxes. In many jurisdictions, including notably some states in the US, donating a piece of art to a public museum can credit the donor with a tax deduction tied to the value of the object donated. Many scams exist around such schemes, which have been argued to be obvious loopholes that can be exploited by unscrupulous donors (Yates 2016). Trafficked antiquities can be bought for low prices and then valued-up when donated to a museum, to generate financial gains for taxpayers. Minimizing taxes paid in the course of business, and maximizing reimbursements or deductions, is a legal and smart thing to do provided it is done on the right side of the law (tax avoidance) rather than the wrong side (tax evasion). With a significant and ever-changing grey area between tax evasion and avoidance, occupied by tax lawyers and accountants always developing schemes to minimize their clients' taxes, some of which are not easily discernible as legal or illegal until they are tested in court, the idea that tax dodging is not a serious issue has become embedded in much business discourse (Braithwaite 2011). Avoidance/evasion schemes are seen as clever rather than criminal (McBarnet 1992). While the kind of money laundering we are describing here, through the misdeclaration of value and the misrepresentation of the stolen status of donated goods, is clearly and knowingly criminal and therefore substantively different from the avoidance/evasion question, it is not hard to see how it can become similarly routinized and normalized within the culture of 'business wheezes' that dealers operating in the grey areas of the antiquities market create and are influenced by. In that sense, therefore, illicit opportunity is a business asset where it is unlikely to be discovered and penalized.

In conclusion then, we can refer to the micro–meso–macro structure of explanation we have proposed for trafficking in previous chapters and observe that it stands up well in relation to what we know about antiquities trafficking. The systemic nature of the problem at the macro-level is the imbalance in access to the sources of antiquities, with the affluent art dealing and collecting world concentrated in world cities that are geographically distant from the heritage sites of developing countries. These criminogenic asymmetries exert a strain, which is resolved by trafficking in the context of the interwoven licit and illicit supply chains of the global neoliberal market. The meso-level organizational context of antiquities trafficking is constituted by a narrative discourse that, just as with other transnational criminal trades that interface with legal markets, we have seen to rationalize criminal enterprise by focusing on its apparently normal business routines and pushing moral consideration of its harmful effects outside this compartmentalized frame of reference. At the micro-level we see looters and traffickers taking advantage of market forces in order to gain in terms of short-term finance what has been denied to them in terms of long-term structural financial progression by the global economy. So they dig and take what they find, and they exploit temple structures and other historic monuments and sites for what they can sell, and a network of dealers and fixers receives these stolen goods and traffics them to meet the worldwide demand for them. That demand is in some cases for symbolic status goods, in others for financial investment goods, in others for objects to study and gain knowledge, and in many cases the desire to collect is a fusion of these different motives. As with the routines of source extraction and transit delivery, it manifests as a choice in settings that are established as ordinary business transactions, banal in their everyday unremarkable structure, little different from buying a car, or perhaps a diamond or an exotic pet.

8

Conclusion: A Social Theory of Transnational Criminal Markets

Common themes in global trafficking markets and links between them

In the course of the book we have discovered some common themes that seem to tie the trafficking markets we have studied together. Some of these themes are relatively routine, simply helping us to understand the functional commonalities across forms of trafficking. Some seem more profound and it is these that will be most helpful to reconsider in moving towards, if not definitively formulating, a social theory of trafficking. We will work through these common themes in this concluding chapter and also consider the question of practical overlaps between the transnational criminal markets we have covered.

Trafficking markets tend to be structured as networks: whether the analytical approach is production–export–import–wholesale–retail as in drug trafficking or the more straightforward source–transit–demand we have seen as a useful heuristic for all types of trafficking, the structure normally involves the linking together in a chain of supply of actors or small groups who operate only as nodes on one of the levels. We have struggled to find examples of omni-present organized crime that controls the entire chain from supply to demand. The usual structure is local producers, finders or takers who sell on to international-facing dealers or traffickers, who then sell into the lucrative retail markets abroad. There may well be more links in any given trafficking chain of supply, but there are rarely less. Such structures, composed of entrepreneurs operating at separate levels, are essentially therefore structures of 'business dealings among persons with different specialisations' (Haller 1990: 223).

Trafficking often blurs the distinction between legal and illegal business, and many traffickers exist with one foot in the conventional business world and the other in crime. Antiquities dealers knowingly fence looted artefacts; diamond traders mix conflict diamonds with their legal supply; drug dealers launder their profits through conventional 'front' business enterprises such as garages and nightclubs, which operate for most purposes like legal operations; arms dealers make legal trades while also selling off the books to unsavoury regimes; and so on. As there exists considerable consumer demand for the products of these global illicit commodities and services, markets flourish in which no participants have any reason to enquire too closely about the origins or transnational movement, legal or illegal, of the things being bought and sold. In some cases the illegality of source and/or transit is implicitly understood by the parties to a transaction; in others it may be suspected but never probed; in some there may be a background understanding by end consumers that the market in question has some problems, but that might be as far as that knowledge ever goes. As one of Tanya Wyatt's informants in her wildlife studies has put it, neatly summing up the problem of transnational illicit market deals in general:

> Illegal logging is fuelled by a global market where few actors – factory suppliers, importers, retailers, or consumers – have the incentive to ask questions. (Wyatt 2014b: 21)

The widespread forms of denial that exist on the personal level among agents who buy and sell in these illegal or grey markets run, just as Cohen (2001) has said, from those who know about the harm involved but deny its importance, or their responsibility for it, down to those who do not know much about the harm involved and have made no efforts to find out. Another aspect of the markets drawn together in this book is that while sometimes they look formal on the surface, a closer look reveals that deals are often done on a surprisingly informal basis: cash sales, minimal documents, no written contracts and generally a network of dealing that functions on trust and mutual interest rather than the usual auditable paper trails of the conventional market. These norms of informality in transaction routines generate a context in which the denials of troublesome knowledge or suspicion we have mentioned become easier to ignore.

What is the nature of the practical links between the trafficking markets discussed in this book? There are three possible types of linkages, overlap or meeting points between illicit trade that we can think about here: geographical (regions where various types of trafficking occur); transit (people or groups trafficking various commodities at once or in succession); and exchange (a barter economy in trafficked goods where one type of illicit commodity is exchanged for another).

There are clearly geographical links in that some regions of the world have been observed to be 'hot zones' for illicit trade. For example, the Caucasus has been identified as such in respect of drug trafficking, arms trafficking and human trafficking (Arasli 2007); the Golden Triangle for drug trafficking and human trafficking; and the Rif mountain region in northern Morocco for human trafficking and 'kif' (hashish) trafficking into Europe (Lehtinen 2008).

Consistent reliable evidence for examples of parallel trafficking is harder to find in the literature. This would be where, for example, a trafficking network or a single trafficker moves more than one type of commodity along the route they work. This kind of diversification makes some sense in theory, as having developed the transit method and perhaps identified and paid off the relevant malleable border and law enforcement officials along the way (the so-called 'paid corridor': South and Wyatt 2011), branching out to carry more than one type of commodity would be economically rational. The counter argument, however, would be that since the transnational criminal trades we have discussed in the book have all been shown to have their own identifiable market dynamics, the actual practical cross-overs in terms of the agents conducting the business at source, as middlemen, or in the market may not be as easily made in real life as they are in theory. While acknowledging the presence of some parallel trafficking, the weight of opinion from specialists working on analysis of each of the different types of trafficking covered in this book is that they are for the most part systems which have only minimal connections, being mostly organized by actors who specialize in trafficking one type of commodity only (van Uhm 2016: 265; Reuter and O'Regan 2017).

The evidence for parallel trafficking is somewhat circumstantial. On the one hand it comes from news reports or law enforcement press releases about seizures that have been made in which more than one commodity has been found. On the other, it is found in incidental mentions in international policy literature from observer organizations such as the UN, which are sometimes suspected of tending towards promoting a 'sky is falling' image of the transnational organized crime threat over a more fastidious approach to reporting fact.

The evidence for parallel trafficking falls into two types: first, organized crime groups and networks in the 'mafia' style (for example, in addition to the mafia, South American drug cartels, the Yakuza in Japan, and Triads and Snakeheads in China) that take part in various stages of trafficking markets and are sometimes therefore the site of commodity overlap if they operate a 'diversified portfolio of criminal activities' (Williams 1998b), and second, other evidence of trafficking commodity overlaps where there is no suggestion of organized crime involvement in that syndicated group sense of the term. On the first, Elliott reports that 'Asian crime groups are central to the trade in rhinoceros horn and tiger parts, the Cali drug cartel is thought to be trafficking drugs and wildlife together into the US, and the Neapolitan Camorra is reported to be deeply involved in the trafficking of animals' (Elliott 2009: 65). Mexican drug trafficking organizations have been said by some authors to have diversified into human trafficking (Astorga and Shirk 2010: 19; Arsovska and Janssens 2009).

In relation to the second kind of crime that is organized, as opposed to organized crime: 'Protected turtles have been found in the same shipments as marijuana. Live snakes have been found stuffed with condoms full of cocaine. Parrots and drugs have been smuggled together from Cote d'Ivoire to Israel' (Elliott 2009: 65). The sources for these observations are all secondary and often originally based in news reports of seizures. Other reports include 'anecdotal evidence' of seizures including 'elephant tusks stuffed with hashish' (Wyler and Sheikh 2013: 4) and more reports of the mixing of endangered parrots and drugs as 'American and Mexican organised crime groups are known to smuggle [them both] across the Rio Grande in addition to weapons' (South and Wyatt 2011: 554). Some authors have made general assertions of parallel trafficking based on research interviews, but often these come without further elaboration; for example, Warchol et al found such first-hand reports of parallel trafficking in their research on wildlife trafficking in Southern African countries. They say: 'those who are involved in the illegal wildlife trade also traffic in other commodities, including drugs, weapons, gems, and humans' (Warchol et al 2003: 24). So in that assessment they see ties between wildlife trafficking and all the illicit markets covered in this book other than antiquities, but evidence of the parallel wildlife–antiquities trafficking can be found elsewhere (see, for example, Mackenzie and Yates 2016), thus suggesting at least some overlaps or parallel opportunities across the board.

Different from parallel trafficking, switching from one commodity to another in a trafficking career has also been observed, such as where drug traffickers have been thought to be attracted away from drugs and towards wildlife (South and Wyatt 2011; Christy 2014) or antiquities trafficking due to the perceived lower risk relative to reward in these markets compared to drug trafficking. Criminal trafficking career development is not always rational in this sense of risk avoidance though. Criminal careers can be observed where the development is more like graduation from relatively small-time crimes and trafficking that is treated less seriously by law enforcement, moving eventually towards high level and more serious criminal trade. An example of this type of career progression can be seen in Leonid Minin, the infamous Ukrainian arms trafficker mentioned in the chapter above. Minin's early criminal activities involved drug charges, allegations of art and antiquities trafficking and a management-level role in the Odessan oil mafia, making a fortune by controlling oil and gas exports from the Ukraine in the early 1990s, after the Cold War ended. Then he moved into trafficking timber out of Liberia, and through his connections with Charles Taylor, the warlord president there, he was able to develop a highly profitable enterprise trafficking arms (Feinstein and Holden 2014).

Interestingly, Arsokova and Kostakos suggest that in the Balkans, criminal career development in the sense we have used the idea here, of switching commodities in trafficking careers, can lead to parallel trafficking because of the social network basis of Balkan enterprise crime:

> In the Balkans new criminal activities come with expansion of contacts, and old criminal activities continue to exist due to previously established networks. Due to the power of the social (criminal) network, criminals do not let down their 'old friends' for 'new friends' easily. Consequently, they often continue to operate in several markets simultaneously. (Arsovska and Kostakos 2008)

The third type of possible overlap is what we have called an exchange link. This would be where trafficking chains meet when one type of illegal commodity is traded for another. As with the transit overlap of parallel trafficking, there is some evidence of an exchange link between illegal commodities in the context of trafficking, but that evidence can be gathered from what are almost passing comments in news and policy reports, and firm assessment of the question is not possible in the present state of research knowledge. That said, as with parallel trafficking, there is some evidence of a barter trade in illegally trafficked goods:

> Protected birds have been smuggled from Australia and exchanged for heroin in Thailand. Chinese crime groups are reported to be exporting the raw ingredients

> for methamphetamine to South African drug dealers in exchange for illegally harvested abalone which can fetch up to $200 a pound in Asian retail markets. (Elliott 2009: 66)

The exchange link is on firmer empirical ground with respect to arms trafficking: it is fairly well observed and agreed that so-called 'war economies' sometimes pay for an inward supply of arms with an outward supply of natural resources and/or drugs. We have noted in the chapters on diamonds and arms that Charles Taylor paid for arms with gems, traded arms with the RUF in Sierra Leone in return for conflict diamonds, and is reputed in those transactions to have been trafficking drugs as well as arms to the RUF in these commodity exchange trades (Smillie et al 2000). Other examples of resource-for-arms deals in war economies include timber, ivory and minerals (Lock 1999: 12). The conflict in Afghanistan has been said to be fuelled by drugs and antiquities, although whether the antiquities, for example, have been traded directly for weapons or sold in order to raise finance that is then used to purchase weapons is less clear. The latter would not be a direct exchange link but still a mediated exchange link and so perhaps the distinction is somewhat academic.

Revisiting the spectrum of enterprise: business as crime and crime as business

The central argument of this book has been that criminal trafficking is just another form of morally indifferent capitalism; it is morally indifferent illegal capitalism. Capitalism is morally indifferent when it routinely causes social harm that it ignores in the pursuit of profit. Illegal capitalism is similarly indifferent, routinely causing social harm and justifying, excusing or bracketing that harm out, while it generates profit. Popular perception of trafficking and traffickers may be that these things and people are evil, and their crimes are inexplicable – they are simply wrong and the perpetrators should be caught and punished. For social scientists, whose job it is to explain rather than simply condemn, the search to understand why and how traffickers do what they do leads up the spectrum of enterprise in the search for a theory of harmful business, or, as I have put it here, morally indifferent capitalism.

The strong neoliberal view of the social responsibilities of corporations in the legitimate economy effectively not only denies that such responsibilities are constitutionally possible but considers profit an ethical goal:

> There is only one social responsibility for corporate executives: they must make as much money as possible for their shareholders. This is a moral imperative. (economist Milton Friedman, quoted in Bakan 2004: 34)

On this view, the legitimate end of the spectrum of enterprise is depressingly similar to the illegitimate end: actors engaging in trade to chase profit without concern or compassion for adverse social effects. If it is tempting to write this kind of extreme right-wing-ism off as merely ideology, and therefore existing at some distance from everyday practice, we can unfortunately easily find evidence to support the assertion that profit leads all else when it comes to corporate motivation. Here is one illustrative quote, from a lead engineer for a global oil company, which is quite representative:

> I mean, let's be real: we're here to make money; we're not here to make the world such a better place. (Räthzel and Uzzell 2017: 129)

Ruggiero suggests that 'entrepreneurs are in perpetual agitation, they possess an inherent transgressive force' (Ruggiero 2009: 127), pointing out that there seems to be an 'experimental' logic to the operation of businesses, tempting them to overstep the limits of legality 'with an eye to the social and institutional reactions that might ensue' (2009: 126). The profit motive – a moral imperative in Friedman's terms – drives enterprise in a landscape where considerations such as law and compassion are merely context. A 'necessity discourse' (Räthzel and Uzzell 2017) transforms the harmful social effects of business enterprise into background noise, ignored in the constant preoccupying mission of productivity, innovation and financial gain. Corporate ill-effects become corporate externalities: outside the moral universe of business actors, somebody else's problem (Bakan 2004).

Ultimately, the most important effect of taking a spectrum-based perspective on legal and illegal enterprise is to contextualize the contemporary global problems with trafficking. Tragic and harmful as they are, and let us not diminish that tragedy or harm, they are used all too often as a device to legitimate conventional business. By naming and casting out entrepreneurs operating most visibly at the illegal end of the spectrum, the apparatus of globalized powerful neoliberal corporate capitalism – businesses, ideologically complicit politicians and conceptually mystified police – shines the light elsewhere than on its own wrongdoing. What, though, about:

> the spread of irresponsible corporate power and, along with it, the progressive disenfranchisement of peoples, the destruction of social safety nets, the gross deterioration in the distribution of income and wealth, and rampant ecological brigandage across the world? (Naylor 2007)

To buy into the fiction that illicit business is something fundamentally different from contemporary licit business is to accept an ideological binary distinction that serves the interests of the rich and powerful masters of the business universe in drawing attention away from their crimes, which are considered merely negligent rather than deliberate. To be sure, trafficking is a pernicious scourge, but in all the ways detailed in this book, it is just business. David Harvey, in what is probably the most widely read introductory book on neoliberalism (Harvey 2005), describes that concept as the doctrine that 'market exchange is an ethic in itself, capable of acting as a guide for all human action'. This interpretation of neoliberalism describes quite accurately the core of the proposition that trafficking is 'just business'. Like conventional legal business, the neoliberal ethic that sees market exchange as what really matters explains why and how traffickers do what they do and live with the knowledge of the harm they cause.

Trafficking as illicit commodification

A consistent theme in the transnational criminal markets we have reviewed is the production or appropriation of a thing or a person and the transformation of those things and bodies into commodities. Copley cited a BBC reporter who was told by a human trafficker that the trafficked sex workers under his control were 'more like things that I own' than employees (Copley 2013: 52). She interprets this as dehumanizing, based on 'the subordination of women and a disregard for human sovereignty', and it is certainly all of those things – but we can also see commodification as core to global illicit trade when we look at the process happening alongside other types of trafficking.

Commodification is the systematic transformation of the social and economic meaning of things into items of alienable property, that is, from inalienable things to things that can be owned, bought and sold. Things that are commodified can then be commercialized, becoming objects for sale in a profit-oriented business routine. Commodification and commercialization are what happens when the natural world becomes reduced to objects to be traded, or humans become exploited as modern-day slaves. A fundamental feature of commodification and commercialization in the modern world is that as a facet of neoliberal globalization these processes are so ubiquitous and normalized as to have become unremarkable, and it takes real effort to argue that some things should not be for sale (Satz 2010; Sandel 2012).

Commodification, especially when applied to the victims of human trafficking, calls to mind the distinction made by Martin Buber between *I-It* and *I-Thou*. Buber laments that society is increasingly developing structures that limit the direct relationships between individuals in communities which are necessary for each of us to consider others as valuable beings, each in his or her own right, rather than simply means to our own self-interested rational ends. In that sense, the relationship between individuals in society becomes one that is purely instrumental, an *I-It* relation, where other people are seen merely as things: 'Is the communal life of modern man not then of necessity sunk in the world of *It*?' (Buber 1947: 33).

To the contrary, an *I-Thou* relation would require us to take the needs and desires of others seriously and respect their intrinsic worth. A similar point has been made by another famous Jewish philosopher, Emmanuel Levinas, who talks of the importance of what he calls the 'face-to-face' relationship with the Other (Levinas 1969, 1981). The two approaches are not the same, as a deeper analysis than we will go into here would show, but they share a root in their ethical requests for respect and accommodation of the intrinsic value and rights of others.

What then is the extent to which neoliberal capital markets encourage the reshaping of I-Thou relationships into I-It ones? We have observed that compartmentalization is prevalent in contemporary social and economic life, where one may 'split him(her)self into a calculating and ruthless utility- and profit-maximizer on the market, an active citizen in the public space, and a devoted friend, lover and parent in his (her) private life' (Ossewaarde-Lowtoo 2017: 439). Where *homo economicus*, the self-interested rational calculator, is the archetype in economic and (some) social theory the I-It relation is petrified *a priori*, but if one 'starts presuming the whole or authentic person, there is much to be gained in turning to Martin Buber's work' (Ossewaarde-Lowtoo 2017: 440; citing Lutz 1996). Oosewaarde-Lowtoo explains that the I-Thou relation requires a:

> turn away from the 'spirit of capitalism', which, for Buber, refers to the 'ruthless exploitation of opportunities and eventualities'(Buber 1949: 36). As a result, actions are no longer to be aimed at exploiting, either of so called 'natural

> resources' (a term that already presumes the I-It mentality) or of 'labour'. (Ossewaarde-Lowtoo 2017: 449)

The exploitation of things and people that repels Buber has been well noted as a fundamental premise of the capitalist life since Marx of course. In his studies of professional entrepreneurial criminals, Dick Hobbs (1988: 182) quotes Veblen as saying that:

> The ideal pecuniary man is like the ideal delinquent in his unscrupulous conversion of goods and persons to his own ends, and in a callous disregard for the feelings and wishes of others and of the remoter effects of his activities. (Veblen 1924: 237)

The theory of the leisure class – of forms of leisure as an economic symbol of social status – recognizes the spectrum of enterprise that runs from the high capitalist to the lowly delinquent, with similar approaches to self-interested activity and the neutralization of harm at each end. The commodification of natural and cultural resources evidenced in the chapters of this book – of drugs, diamonds, wildlife, antiquities – is the precursor to the transfer of those products into the stream of consumptive leisure pursuits that serve as markers of social and economic status. Perhaps less so with drugs, although there are clearly status inflections to certain types of drug purchase and consumption, but certainly with diamonds, antiquities and certain types of wildlife, the common understanding of the routine of acquisition and consumption, display or collection of these things is that they are indicators of a life that is rarefied, cultured and to be envied. The possession and use of the commodified symbols of certain leisure choices intersects with the business of supplying these items, forming markets in vice that apply entrepreneurialism and the enterprising spirit of capitalism to the celebration of social status and the ever-present anxiety that competitive participation in the games of status one-upmanship entail. This is classic consumer capitalism, the same for iPhones and sports cars as for the commodities that travel from source to market via grey and black market channels that we have covered here.

The globalization of neoliberal capitalism has been widely critiqued as atomizing, dehumanizing and disembedding. It is atomizing because it constructs its subjects as individual agents and pits them in competition with each other in the market, thereby prioritizing self-interest over community. It is dehumanizing because it strips away the compassion that we naturally feel for each other and requires us to be less than whole humans: there are only some parts of human rationality and emotion that are valuable to competitive capitalist enterprise, and we are to leave the rest of ourselves at the door to the office upon entry. Eventually we may become less and less able to pick it up again upon exit. And it is disembedding because it draws our working lives into the ethereal networks of globalized commerce, pulling our moral gaze away from the local communities where we live, fragmenting our existence into units of production or enterprise, in other words compartmentalizing us just as we consequently compartmentalize ourselves in response. This is merely a diagnosis, not a prescription: it is not to say that other systems of commerce are better or worse. Buber, for example, saw that both capitalism and communism – and therefore individualism or collectivism – could have similar effects in subjugating to a greater ideology the principle of fundamental self-worth in individuals (Buber 1949). The point is that in criminal business, just as in conventional business, humans are constructed and construct themselves as stripped-down versions of full beings, feeling (and saying to criminologists who interview them) things like that they just have to look out for themselves and their families; they don't have the luxury of thinking about whether other people are getting hurt by what they do; it's a harsh world and they do what they must to survive; if they didn't do it someone else would; there are people who do things that are a lot worse; it's not who they really are, it's just something they got into; it's not personal, it's just business.

Buber's philosophy crosses wires with certain lines of thought in criminology such as the 'mood of fatalism', which Matza suggested was one of the problems experienced in, and causing, some crime and delinquency (Matza 1964). The metaphor Sykes and Matza used for this mood of fatalism was that individuals felt themselves to be propelled like a billiard ball (Sykes and Matza 1957: 667) – lacking agency, unable to make life choices that seriously impact let alone govern trajectory, simply being pushed along from one thing to the next by external determining forces over which they have little control. In that situation, the mood of fatalism asks, what is the point in trying to change? Why try to do better when one is not really in control of the circumstances in life that provide the impulse or imperative to action? Buber uses a similar metaphor for what we can perhaps see as his impression of a similar mood of fatalism that prevails when I-It replaces I-Thou, where in dehumanizing systems people exist like: 'a stick stuck in a bundle moving through the water, abandoned to the current or being pushed by a pole from the bank in this or that direction' (Buber 1947: 74).

In the contemporary world, where 'the interaction with each other is mediated by impersonal, bureaucratic apparatuses', the '"most valuable of all goods – the life between man and man – gets lost" when men become cogs in a machine (Buber 1949: 132). The condition whereby men and women do not feel responsible for their actions means the death of the soul (Buber 1947: 115)' (Ossewaarde-Lowtoo 2017: 448). These sentiments can easily be read alongside the reflections of Arendt and Bauman considered in the introduction to this book, about the ethical numbing that has been a side-effect of the bureaucratic industrial and administrative processes of modernity and the routine, or banal, nature of evil that this moral anaesthesia can allow to unfold.

The systematic nature of the crimes of globalization

The economic globalization of neoliberal capitalism has created global poverty and relative inequality between countries, and continues to do so (Stiglitz 2002). Cosmopolitan theorists and writers on global justice have argued that this imbalance is so structural that it creates a responsibility for assistance of the poor, placed on the benefactors of global inequality (Pogge 2002, 2004). Criminologists have tended to focus on the strain this inequality produces, while some have also addressed the routine and systematic nature of the harm that is done by these global systems that deliver health and wealth to some, poverty and ill-health to others. For example, David Friedrichs has created a conceptual category of 'the crimes of globalisation' (Friedrichs and Friedrichs 2002; Friedrichs 2010), while I have described the crimes of globalization as 'systematic crimes' (Mackenzie 2006). This global poverty and relative inequality has been implicated at every turn in this book in the root causes of trafficking. At the macro-level it is therefore the case that the conventional routines of the world systems that govern and support global capitalist enterprise have created and sustained the conditions that produce global trafficking as we know and experience it today. On this level, as with the others noted in the spectrum of enterprise approach, business and crime are intimately related. Trafficking is the enterprise response to the opportunities for enriching trade structured by the imbalances regionally and internationally created by the neoliberal system of conventional world trade.

Of course within this very generalized critique of globalized neoliberal capitalism lie particular regional and historical specificities that provide essential background and context to the development of transnational crime and which should not be ironed out of our frame of reference lest we take an overly westernized view of the globalization process. One such recent regional reconfiguration has occurred with the end of the Cold War, and another is underway as China opens up its economy and grows as a superpower to compete with, and soon surely outclass, the US. These are very different cases of regional developments that affect opportunities for the global flows of transnational criminal markets. The swift disintegration of state control of industry as the USSR was deconstructed opened up an anomic zone of governance which was occupied by organized criminals and newly formed security 'specialists' who found their ex-military contacts and skillsets, especially the capacity to use violence, useful in exerting control over local illicit trade. The combination of the relative absence of state control with high levels of local conflict and corruption made for an ideal regional hothouse in which to propagate illicit trade. The opening up of China tells a different story, one in which opportunities have been created for legal and illegal trade alike, but in a national context where state officials are quite used to protectionist, paternalistic and clientelist forms of corruption and so it is no surprise when the state participates in, protects, or turns a blind eye to transnational illegal trade. These regional and historical features of the contemporary global economic regime, important as they are to register, are, however, constituent parts of a bigger picture in which the world has been subject to forces of trade liberalization, westernization in terms of economic ideology and growing embedded inequalities in wealth, income and life chances.

Several of the illegal markets we have studied in this book are contemporary manifestations of the legacy of colonialism. Antiquities were collected from the colonies as curios to be appreciated back home (Yates et al 2017): windows into the cultural histories and ways of life of the oppressed and stereotyped colonial 'Other', to use Edward Said's famous terminology (Said 1979). Current western attitudes towards conservation and preservation of wildlife in source countries have been criticized as inconsiderate of local interests and based on an approach that has been called 'fortress conservation', where local people are portrayed as enemies of wildlife, rather than sustainable users of it (Brockington 2002; Garland 2008). Therefore they are forcibly excluded from protected areas, which are reimagined as game parks where western science, expertise and donations can support the type of conservation and protection of endangered wildlife that local populations are thought to threaten. Comparably, in relation to diamond trafficking, for example, Sierra Leone's move from a colonial to a post-colonial state 'failed to integrate economically marginalized peasants into a functioning economy' (Montague 2002: 231), and:

> Eventually, the country became part of the international economic network of Britain, a network in which it was designed to supply cheap raw materials for British industries. With the international market as the dominant institution, what was produced in Sierra Leone was determined not on the basis of Sierra Leone's needs and capabilities but by economic competition in the world market. (Conteh-Morgan and Dixon-Fyle 1999: 3)

This post-colonial take on the resource curse of mineral-rich, cash-poor developing countries illustrates precisely the capacity of neoliberal 'free' world markets to entrench and extend global power and inequality imbalances, operating essentially as the ghost of the long arm of colonialism as that spectre continues to reach into poor countries and deplete their reserves of valued natural resources. That this takes place in the name of internationalization, free markets and global trade rather than colonial exploitation is surely of marginal interest to the struggling citizens of resource-cursed regions, who experience the effects of this as exploitation and poverty regardless. In such circumstances, trafficking naturally emerges, which exploits these resources for private ends, feeding global consumer demand that is indifferent to the legal or illegal origins of commodities that are substantively the same whatever their legal status might be. Illegal guns shoot just as well as legal ones; an illegal diamond shines as brightly; wildlife that is thought to have medicinal properties does not lose those through illegal transport; antiquities in the display case may be hermetically sealed from the elements while they are similarly figuratively sealed from their histories of illicit discovery and transit; and so on.

Trafficking as transnational crime: nothing personal, it's just business

Ultimately, having studied six forms of transnational crime and explored various parameters of the theories that are available to analyse trafficking from the perspective of a spectrum of enterprise, we come to the following propositions. Trafficking takes advantage of illicit business opportunities created by the supply and demand market dynamics of a globalized commercial world in which consumers expect and desire access to a variety of goods the legal market cannot, or is not allowed to, supply. The structural oppression and exclusion by the global economy of certain regions and communities manifests as a form of strain that invites in response the exploitation of available resources through commodification, illegal acquisition, supply and trade. In this response, traffickers are simply adhering to a norm of profit-seeking business enterprise that is at the core of the contemporary interpretation of the successful navigation of 'market forces' by individual entrepreneurs – a norm widely considered in its legitimate form to be a central and positive aspect of neoliberal life. Trafficking is normally castigated in popular discourse as a form of criminal behaviour that has little if anything to do with conventional legal business. To the contrary, it has everything to do with conventional legal business, including often interfacing with legal supply chains for the goods in question, facing similar infrastructural and trading challenges and – most important for the analysis in this book – adopting the business approach to ethical thinking about culpability and harm by bracketing these issues out of the frame. Trafficking sits on the spectrum of enterprise as a form of morally indifferent business, in which the compartmentalization of treating the activities involved as 'just business' allows the routinization of the performance of harmful acts without what one would consider to be a suitable appraisal of, and sense of guilt or shame for, the consequences. The banality of the evil of trafficking is therefore that it is a form of behaviour that in its contemporary form is made, both in thought and in action, by the normative structure of the legal business world. This illegal part of the spectrum of enterprise turns a mirror on modern society and economy that highlights some of the worst features of capitalist life, revealing a spectrum of global trade, legal and illegal, that is systematically indifferent to certain of its harmful effects. It is through this perspective that we come, in the end, to see the real meaning in the idea of trafficking as business.

References

Aas, K.F. (2007) *Globalization and Crime*. London: SAGE.

Adler, P. (1985) *Wheeling and Dealing: An Ethnography of an Upper-Level Drug Dealing and Smuggling Community*. New York: Columbia University Press.

Adler, P. (1993) *Wheeling and Dealing: An Ethnography of an Upper-Level Drug Dealing and Smuggling Community*, 2nd edn. New York: Columbia University Press.

Adler, P.A. and Adler, P. (1992) 'Relationships between Dealers: The Social Organization of Illicit Drug Transactions', *Sociology and Social Research*, 67: 261–77.

Advertising Age (1999) *Special Supplement: The Advertising Century*. Chicago: Crain Communications Inc.

Albanese, J.S. (2015) *Organized Crime: From the Mob to Transnational Organized Crime*, 7th edn. Waltham, MA: Anderson Publishing.

Albanese, J.S. and Reichel, P. (eds) (2014) *Transnational Organized Crime: An Overview from Six Continents*. London: SAGE.

Allen, B. (1996) *Rape Warfare: The Hidden Genocide in Bosnia-Herzegovina and Croatia*. Minneapolis, MN: University of Minnesota.

Amiot, C.E., de la Sablonnière, R., Terry, D.J. and Smith, J.R. (2007) 'Integration of Social Identities in the Self: Toward a Cognitive-Developmental Model', *Personality and Social Psychology Review*, 11(4): 364–88.

Andreas, P. (2000) *Border Games: Policing the US–Mexico Divide*. Ithaca, NY: Cornell University Press.

Andreas, P. (2011) 'Illicit Globalization: Myths, Misconceptions, and Historical Lessons', *Political Science Quarterly*, 126(3): 403–25.

Andrees, B. (2008) 'Forced Labour and Trafficking in Europe: How People Are Trapped In, Live Through, and Come Out', ILO Working Paper 57. Geneva: International Labour Organisation.

Antonopoulos, G.A. and Winterdyk, J.A. (2005) 'Techniques of Neutralizing the Trafficking of Women: A Case Study of an Active Trafficker in Greece', *European Journal of Crime, Criminal Law and Criminal Justice*, 13(2): 136–47.

Appadurai, A. (ed) (1986) *The Social Life of Things: Commodities in Cultural Perspective*. Cambridge: Cambridge University Press.

Arasli, J. (2007) 'The Rising Wind: Is the Caucasus Emerging as a Hub for Terrorism, Smuggling, and Trafficking?', *Connections*, 6(1): 5–26.

Arendt, H. (1958) *The Human Condition*. Chicago: University of Chicago Press.

Arendt, H. (1963) *Eichmann in Jerusalem: A Report on the Banality of Evil*. New York: Viking Press.

Aronowitz, A.A. (2009) *Human Trafficking, Human Misery: The Global Trade in Human Beings*. Westport, CT: Praeger.

Aronowitz, A.A. (2019) 'Understanding the Complexity of Trafficking in Human Beings', in M. Natarajan (ed) *International and Transnational Crime and Justice*. New York: Cambridge University Press, pp 12–17.

Arsovska, J. and Janssens, S. (2009) 'Human Trafficking & Policing: Good & Bad Practices', in C. Friesendorf (ed) *Strategies against Human Trafficking: The Role of the Security Sector*. Vienna: National Defence Academy and Austrian Ministry of Defence Sports, pp 169–212.

Arsovska, J. and Kostakos, P.A. (2008) 'Illicit Arms Trafficking and the Limits of Rational Choice Theory: The Case of the Balkans', *Trends in Organized Crime*, 11(4): 352–78.

Astorga, L. and Shirk, D. (2010) 'Drug Trafficking Organizations and Counter-Drug Strategies in the US–Mexican Context', in D. Shirk, E. Olson and A. Salee (eds) *US–Mexico Options for Confronting Organized Crime*. Washington, DC: Woodrow Wilson Center for International Scholars, pp 31–63.

Aubert, V. (1952) 'White Collar Crime and Social Structure', *American Journal of Sociology*, 58: 263–71.

Ayling, J. (2013) 'What Sustains Wildlife Crime? Rhino Horn Trading and the Resilience of Criminal Networks', *Journal of International Wildlife Law & Policy*, 16(1): 57–80.

Bakan, J. (2004) *The Corporation: The Pathological Pursuit of Profit and Power*. New York: Free Press.

Bales, K. (1999) *Disposable People*. Berkeley: University of California Press.

Bales, K. (2007) 'What Predicts Human Trafficking?', *International Journal of Comparative and Applied Criminal Justice*, 31(2): 269–79.

Bator, P.M. (1983) *The International Trade in Art*. Chicago: University of Chicago Press.

Bauman, Z. (1989) *Modernity and the Holocaust*. Cambridge: Polity.

Bauman, Z. (1995) *Life in Fragments: Essays in Postmodern Morality*. Oxford: Blackwell.

Bauman, Z. (2000) *Liquid Modernity*. Malden, MA: Polity Press.

Baumeister, R.F. (1986) *Public Self and Private Self*. New York: Springer.

Bayer, I. and Ghodse, H. (1999) 'Evolution of International Drug Control, 1945–1995', *Bulletin on Narcotics*, LI(1 and 2): 1–17.

Beare, M.E. (ed) (2003) *Critical Reflections on Transnational Organised Crime, Money Laundering and Corruption*. Toronto: Toronto University Press.

Beck, L. (2013) 'A Quarter of All Diamonds In Stores Are Blood Diamonds, and Nobody Can Tell Which Ones They Are', *Jezebel*. Available at: https://jezebel.com/a-quarter-of-all-diamonds-in-stores-are-blood-diamonds-5973648 [accessed 3 December 2019].

Beckert, J. and Dewey, M. (eds) (2017) *The Architecture of Illegal Markets*. Oxford: Oxford University Press.

Beckert, J. and Wehinger, F. (2013) 'In the Shadow: Illegal Markets and Economic Sociology', *Socio-Economic Review*, 11(1): 5–30.

Belecky, M., Singh, R. and Moreto, W. (2019) *Life on the Frontline: A Global Survey of the Working Conditions of Rangers*. Washington, DC: WWF.

Bennett, T., Holloway, K. and Farrington, D. (2008) 'The Statistical Association between Drug Misuse and Crime: A Meta-Analysis', *Aggression and Violent Behavior*, 13(2): 107–18.

Benson, M. (1985) 'Denying the Guilty Mind: Accounting for Involvement in a White-Collar Crime', *Criminology*, 23(4): 583–607.

Benson, J.S. and Decker, S.H. (2010) 'The Organizational Structure of International Drug Smuggling', *Journal of Criminal Justice*, 38: 130–8.

Bergenstock, D.J. and Maskulka, J.M. (2001) 'The de Beers story: Are Diamonds Forever?', *Business Horizons*, 44(3): 37–44.

Bilton, N. (2017) *American Kingpin: The Epic Hunt for the Criminal Mastermind behind the Silk Road*. New York: Penguin.

Black, W.K. (2005) *The Best Way to Rob a Bank Is to Own One: How Corporate Executives and Politicians Looted the S&L Industry*. Austin: University of Texas Press.

Bourdieu, P. (1984) *Distinction: a Social Critique of the Judgement of Taste*. Cambridge, MA: Harvard University Press.

Bourdieu, P. (1986) 'The Forms of Capital', in J. Richardson (ed) *Handbook of Theory and Research for the Sociology of Education*. New York: Greenwood, pp 241–58.

Bourdieu, P. (1998) *Acts of Resistance*. Oxford: Polity Press.

Bowlby, J. (1980) *Attachment and Loss, Vol. III – Loss: Sadness and Depression*. New York: Basic Books.

Braithwaite, V. (2011) 'Tax Evasion', in M. Tonry (ed) *The Oxford Handbook of Crime and Public Policy*. Oxford: Oxford University Press, 381–405.

Brauer, J. and Muggah, R. (2006) 'Completing the Circle: Building a Theory of Small Arms Demand', *Contemporary Security Policy*, 27(1): 138–54.

Brockington, D. (2002) *Fortress Conservation: The Preservation of the Mkomazi Game Reserve, Tanzania*. Bloomington: Indiana University Press.

Brodie, N. (1998) 'Pity the Poor Middlemen', *Culture Without Context*, 3(Autumn): 7–9.

Brodie, N. (2009) 'Consensual Relations? Academic Involvement in the Illegal Trade in Ancient Manuscripts', in S. Mackenzie and P. Green (eds) *Criminology and Archaeology: Studies in Looted Antiquities*. Oxford: Hart, pp 41–58.

Brodie, N. (2010) 'Archaeological Looting and Economic Justice', in P.M. Messenger and G.S. Smith (eds) *Cultural Heritage Management, Policy and Issues in Global Perspective*. Gainesville: University Press of Florida, pp 261–77.

Brodie, N. (2011a) 'Academic Involvement in the Market in Iraqi Antiquities', in S. Manacorda and D. Chappell (eds) *Crime in the Art and Antiquities World: Illegal Trafficking in Cultural Property*. New York: Springer, pp 117–33.

Brodie, N. (2011b) 'Congenial Bedfellows? The Academy and the Antiquities Trade', *Journal of Contemporary Criminal Justice*, 27(4): 408–37.

Brodie, N. (2011c) 'Academic Involvement in the Market in Iraqi Antiquities', in S. Manacorda and D. Chappell (eds) *Crime in the Art and Antiquities World: Illegal Trafficking in Cultural Property*. New York: Springer, pp. 117–33.

Brodie, N. (2015a) 'Syria and Its Regional Neighbors: A Case of Cultural Property Protection Policy Failure?', *International Journal of Cultural Property*, 22: 317–35.

Brodie, N. (2015b) 'Why Is No One Talking about Libya's Cultural Destruction?', *Near Eastern Archaeology*, 78: 212–17.

Brodie, N. (2016) 'Scholarly Engagement with Collections of Unprovenanced Ancient Texts', in K. Almqvist and L. Belfrage (eds) *Cultural Heritage at Risk*. Stockholm: Axson Johnson Foundation, pp 123–42.

Brodie, N. (2017) 'The Role of Conservators in Facilitating the Theft and Trafficking of Cultural Objects: The Case of a Seized Libyan Statue', *Libyan Studies*, 48: 117–23.

Brodie, N., Doole, J. and Watson, P. (2000) *Stealing History: the Illicit Trade in Cultural Material*. Cambridge: The McDonald Institute for Archaeological Research.

Brodie, N., Doole, J. and Renfrew, C. (eds) (2001) *Trade in Illicit Antiquities: The Destruction of the World's Archaeological Heritage*. Cambridge: McDonald Institute for Archaeological Research.

Buber, M. (1947) *Between Man and Man*, tr. R.G. Smith. London: Kegan Paul.

Buber, M. (1949) *Paths in Utopia*. London: Routledge & Kegan Paul.

Caldwell, S. (2012) 'Supply Chain Security: Container Security Programs Have Matured, but Uncertainty Persists over the Future of 100 Percent Scanning', *GAO-12-422T*. Washington, DC: US Government Accountability Office.

Cantor, N., Markus, H., Niedenthal, P. and Nurius, P. (1986) 'On Motivation and the Self-Concept', in R.M. Sorrentino and E.H. Tory (eds) *Handbook of Motivation and Cognition: Foundations of Social Behavior*, Vol. 1. New York: Guilford Press, pp 96–121.

Carrier, N. and Klantschnig, G. (2012) *Africa and the War on Drugs*. London: Zed Books.

Christy, B. (2008) *The Lizard King: The True Crimes and Passions of the World's Greatest Reptile Smugglers*. New York: Twelve.

Christy, B. (2014) 'Convicted Drug Dealer Indicted for Selling Rhino Horns. Undercover Investigation Nets Alleged Wildlife Trafficker with Ties to Former Medellín Drug Cartel', *National Geographic*, 17 April.

Christie, B. (2019) 'Drug Deaths: Record Number in Scotland Prompts Calls for urgent UK Policy Reform', *BMJ*, 366: l4731.

Clark, C. (1997) *Misery and Company: Sympathy in Everyday Life*. Chicago: University of Chicago Press.

Cock, J. (1997) 'The Cultural and Social Challenge of Demilitarisation', in G. Cawthra and B. Moller (eds) *Defensive Restructuring of the Armed Forces in Southern Africa*. Dartmouth: Macmillan, pp 117–44.

Coggins, C. (1969) 'Illicit Traffic of Pre-Columbian Antiquities', *Art Journal*, 29(1): 94–8.

Coggins, C. (2003) *The Tiger and the Pangolin: Nature, Culture, and Conservation in China*. Honolulu: University of Hawaii Press.

Cohen, S. (2001) *States of Denial: Knowing about Atrocities and Suffering*. Cambridge: Polity.

Collier, P. (2008) 'Laws and Codes for the Resource Curse', *Yale Human Rights and Development Law Journal*, 11: 9–28.

Columb, S. (2020) *Trading Life: Organ Trafficking, Illicit Networks, and Exploitation*. Stanford, CA: Stanford University Press.

Conteh-Morgan, E. and Dixon-Fyle, M. (1999) *Sierra Leone at the End of the Twentieth Century: History, Politics and Society*. New York: Peter Lang.

Cooper, N. (2006) 'What's the Point of Arms Transfer Controls?', *Contemporary Security Policy*, 27(1): 118–37.

Copley, L. (2013) 'Neutralizing Their Involvement: Sex Traffickers' Discourse Techniques', *Feminist Criminology*, 9(1): 45–58.

Cragin, K. and Hoffman, B. (2003) *Arms Trafficking and Colombia*. Washington, DC: RAND.

Csémy, L., Kubička, L. and Nociar, A. (2002) 'Drug Scene in the Czech Republic and Slovakia during the Period of Transformation', *European Addiction Research*, 8(4): 159–65.

Csete, J., Kamarulzaman, A., Kazatchkine, M., Altice, F., Balicki, M., Buxton, J., Cepeda, J., Comfort, M., Goosby, E., Goulão, J., Hart, C., Kerr, T., Lajous, A.M., Lewis, S., Martin, N., Mejía, D., Camacho, A., Mathieson, D., Obot, I., Ogunrombi, A., Sherman, S., Stone, J., Vallath, N., Vickerman, P., Zábranský, T. and Beyrer, C. (2016) 'Public Health and International Drug Policy', *The Lancet*, 387(10026): 1427–80.

Davis, T. and Mackenzie, S. (2015) 'Crime and Conflict: Temple Looting in Cambodia', in J. Kila and M. Balcells (eds) *Cultural Property Crime*. Leiden: Brill, pp 292–306.

de Carlos Sola, J. (2019) 'Blood Diamonds Keep Going through Antwerp', Universidad de Navarra, Global Affairs Strategic Studies. Available at: https://www.unav.edu/web/global-affairs/detalle/-/blogs/blood-diamonds-keep-going-through-antwerp [accessed 6 December 2019].

Decker, S.H. and Townsend Chapman, M. (2008) *Drug Smugglers on Drug Smuggling: Lessons from the Inside*. Philadelphia, PA: Temple University Press.

Desroches, F. (2005) *The Crime that Pays: Drug Trafficking and Organized Crime in Canada*. Toronto: Canadian Scholar's Press.

Desroches, F. (2007) 'Research on Upper-Level Drug Trafficking: A Review', *Journal of Drug Issues*, 37(4): 827–44.

Dewing, S., Plüddemann, A., Myers, B.J. and Parry, C.D.H. (2006) 'Review of Injection Drug Use in Six African Countries: Egypt, Kenya, Mauritius, Nigeria, South Africa and Tanzania', *Drugs: Education, Prevention and Policy*, 13(2): 121–37.

Dickson, B. (2003) 'What Is the Goal of Regulating Wildlife Trade? Is Regulation a Good Way to Achieve this Goal?', in S. Oldfield (ed) *The Trade in Wildlife. Regulation for Conservation*. London: Earthscan Publications, pp 23–33.

Dorn, N., Levi, M. and Leslie, K. (2005) *Literature Review on Upper-Level Drug Trafficking*. London: Home Office.

Dreyfus, P., Guedes, L.E., Lessing, B., Bandeira, A.R., Nascimento, M.d.S. and Rivero, P.S. (2008) *Small Arms in Rio de Janeiro: The Guns, the Buyback, and the Victims*. Geneva: Small Arms Survey, Graduate Institute of International and Development Studies.

Duffy, R. (2010) *Nature Crime: How We're Getting Conservation Wrong*. New Haven, CT: Yale University Press.

Duster, T. (1971) 'Conditions for Guilt-Free Massacre', in N. Sanford and C. Comstock (eds) *Sanctions for Evil.* San Francisco, CA: Jossey-Bass, pp 25–36.

Eastwood, N., Fox, E. and Rosmarin, A. (2016) *A Quiet Revolution: Drug Decriminalization Across the Globe*, 2nd edn. London: Release.

Eastwood, N., Shiner, M. and Bear, D. (2013) *The Numbers in Black and White: Ethnic Disparities in the Policing and Prosecution of Drug Offences in England and Wales.* London: Release.

Eck, J.E. and Gersh, J.S. (2000) 'Drug Trafficking as a Cottage Industry', in M. Natarajan and M. Hough (eds) *Illegal Drug Markets: From Research to Prevention Policy.* Monsey, NY: Criminal Justice Press, pp 241–72.

Ede, J. (1998) 'Ethics, the Antiquities Trade, and Archaeology', *International Journal of Cultural Property*, 7(1): 128–31.

Edwards, A. and Gill, P. (2002) 'Crime as Enterprise? The Case of Transnational Organised Crime', *Crime, Law and Social Change*, 37(3): 203–23.

Edwards, A. and Gill, P. (eds) (2003) *Transnational Organised Crime: Perspectives on Global Security.* London: Routledge.

Efrat, A. (2010) 'Toward Internationally Regulated Goods: Controlling the Trade in Small Arms and Light Weapons', *International Organization*, 64(Winter): 97–131.

Elliott, L. (2009) 'Combating Transnational Environmental Crime: "Joined Up" Thinking about Transnational Networks', in K. Kangaspunta and I.H. Marshall (eds) *Eco-Crime and Justice: Essays on Environmental Crime.* Turin: UNICRI, pp 58–78.

Elster, J. (ed) (1986) *The Multiple Self.* Cambridge: Cambridge University Press.

Epstein, E.J. (1982) 'Have You Ever Tried to Sell a Diamond?', *The Atlantic.* Available at: https://www.theatlantic.com/magazine/archive/1982/02/have-you-ever-tried-to-sell-a-diamond/304575/ [accessed 17 December 2019].

Evertsson, N. (2019) 'Corporate Tax Avoidance and Neutralization Techniques: A Case Study on the Panama Papers', *Critical Criminology.* Available at: https://link.springer.com/article/10.1007/s10612-019-09455-7 [accessed 29 April 2020].

Farah, D. (2013) 'Fixers, Super Fixers, and Shadow Facilitators: How Networks Connect', in M. Miklaucic and J. Brewer (eds) *Convergence: Illicit Networks and National Security in the Age of Globalization.* Washington, DC: National Defense University Press, pp 75–95.

Farah, D. and Braun, S. (2007) *Merchant of Death.* Hoboken, NJ: Wiley.

Feinstein, A. (2011) *The Shadow World: Inside the Global Arms Trade.* London: Hamish Hamilton.

Feinstein, A. and Holden, P. (2014) 'Arms Trafficking', in L. Paoli (ed) *The Oxford Handbook of Organized Crime.* Oxford: Oxford University Press, pp 444–59.

Felch, J. (2014) 'Twenty Percent ISIS Khums Tax on Archaeological Loot Fuels the Conflicts in Syria and Iraq', *Chasing Aphrodite.* Available at: https://chasingaphrodite.com/2014/08/14/twenty-percent-isis-khums-tax-on-archaeological-loot-fuels-the-conflicts-in-syria-and-iraq/ [accessed 22 December 2019].

Feldman, D.L. (2003) 'Conflict Diamonds, International Trade Regulation, and the Nature of Law', *University of Pennsylvania Journal of International Economic Law*, 24: 835–74.

Fincham, D. (2014) 'Two Ways of Policing Cultural Heritage', in S. Manacorda and A. Visconti (eds) *Protecting Cultural Heritage as a Common Good of Humanity: A Challenge for Criminal Justice.* Milan: ISPAC, p 85.

Findlay, M. (2003) *The Globalization of Crime: Understanding Transnational Relationships in Context.* Cambridge: Cambridge University Press.

Firestone, T.A. (1993) 'Mafia Memoirs: What They Tell Us about Organized Crime', *Journal of Contemporary Criminal Justice*, 9(3): 197–220.

Flores, A. and Johnson, D.G. (1983) 'Collective Responsibility and Professional Roles', *Ethics*, 93(3): 537–45.

Friedman, U. (2015) 'How an Ad Campaign Invented the Diamond Engagement Ring', *The Atlantic.* Available at: https://www.theatlantic.com/international/archive/2015/02/how-an-ad-campaign-invented-the-diamond-engagement-ring/385376/ [accessed 17 December 2019].

Friedrichs, D.O. (2007) 'Transnational Crime and Global Criminology: Definitional, Typological, and Contextual Conundrums', *Social Justice*, 34(2): 4–18.

Friedrichs, D.O. (2010) *Trusted Criminals: White Collar Crime in Contemporary Society*, 4th edn. Belmont, CA: Wadsworth.

Friedrichs, D.O. and Friedrichs, J. (2002) 'The World Bank and Crimes of Globalization: A Case Study', *Social Justice*, 29(1–2): 13–36.

Frost, N.A. (2007) 'Securing Borders & Saving Lives', *Criminology & Public Policy*, 6(2): 241–4.

Fuentes, J.R. (1998) 'Life of a Cell: Managerial Practice and Strategy in Colombian Cocaine Distribution in the United States'. PhD thesis: City University of New York.

Gabriel, Y. (2003) 'Book Reviews', *Human Relations*, 56(3): 339–48.

Galemba, R.B. (2008) 'Informal and Illicit Entrepreneurs: Fighting for a Place in the Neoliberal Economic Order', *Anthropology of Work Review*, 29(2): 19–24.

Galeotti, M. (ed) (2005) *Global Crime Today: The Changing Face of Organised Crime*. New York: Routledge.

Garland, E. (2008) 'The Elephant in the Room: Confronting the Colonial Character of Wildlife Conservation in Africa', *African Studies Review*, 51(3): 51–74.

Gerstenblith, P. (2002) 'United States v. Schultz', *Culture Without Context: The Newsletter of the Illicit Antiquities Research Centre, University of Cambridge*, 10(Spring): 27–31.

Gerstenblith, P. (2003) 'The McClain/Schultz Doctrine: Another Step against Trade in Stolen Antiquities', *Culture Without Context: The Newsletter of the Illicit Antiquities Research Centre, University of Cambridge*, 13(Autumn): 5–8.

Gerstenblith, P. (2007) 'Controlling the International Market in Antiquities: Reducing the Harm, Preserving the Past', *Chicago Journal of International Law*, 8(1): 167–95.

Gerstenblith, P. (2009) 'Schultz and Barakat: Universal Recognition of National Ownership of Antiquities', *Art, Antiquity and Law*, 14(1).

Giddens, A. (1990) *The Consequences of Modernity*. Cambridge: Polity Press.

Gilgan, E. (2001) 'Looting and the Market for Maya Objects: a Belizean Perspective', in N. Brodie, J. Doole and C. Renfrew (eds) *Trade in Illicit Antiquities: the Destruction of the World's Archaeological Heritage*. Cambridge: McDonald Institute for Archaeological Research, pp 73–87.

Gioia, D.A. (1992) 'Pinto Fires and Personal Ethics: A Script Analysis of Missed Opportunities', *Journal of Business Ethics*, 11(5/6): 379–89.

Glasser, I. (2000) 'American Drug Laws: The New Jim Crow', *Albany Law Review*, 63: 703.

Global Witness (2017) *A Game of Stones: Smuggling Diamonds in the Central African Republic*. New York: Global Witness.

Goffman, E. (1959) *The Presentation of Self in Everyday Life*. Garden City, NY: Anchor.

Goffman, E. (1974) *Frame Analysis: An Essay on the Organisation of Experience*. Boston, MA: Northeastern University Press.

Goldring, N.J. (2006) 'Two Sides of the Same Coin: Establishing Controls for SALW and Major Conventional Weapons', *Contemporary Security Policy*, 27(1): 85–99.

Gooch, C. (2011) 'Why We Are Leaving the Kimberley Process', *Global Witness*. Available at: https://www.globalwitness.org/library/why-we-are-leaving-kimberley-process-message-global-witness-founding-director-charmian-gooch [accessed 7 April 2015].

Goulding, C., Shankar, A. and Elliott, R. (2010) 'Working Weeks, Rave Weekends: Identity Fragmentation and the Emergence of New Communities', *Consumption Markets & Culture*, 5(4): 261–84.

Green, P.J. (2000) *Drugs, Trafficking and Criminal Policy*. Winchester: Waterside Press.

Gregory-Smith, D. and Manika, D. (2017) 'Consumers' Identities and Compartmentalisation Tendencies in Alcohol Consumption', *Journal of Marketing Management*, 33(11–12): 942–72.

Grover, J. (2015) 'Supply Chain Security: CBP Needs to Enhance Its Guidance and Oversight of High-Risk Maritime Cargo Shipments', *GAO-15-294*. Washington, DC: Government Accountability Office.

Guerette, R.T. (2007) 'Immigration Policy, Border Security, and Migrant Deaths: An Impact Evaluation of Life-Saving Efforts Under the Border Safety Initiative', *Criminology & Public Policy*, 6(2): 245–66.

Hagan, J. and McCarthy, B. (1998) *Mean Streets: Youth Crime and Homelessness*. New York: Cambridge University Press.

Haller, M.H. (1990) 'Illegal Enterprise: A Theoretical and Historical Interpretation', *Criminology*, 28(2): 207–36.

Harcourt, B.E. (2006) *Language of the Gun: Youth, Crime and Public Policy*. Chicago: University of Chicago Press.

Hardy, S. (2014) 'Is There Significant Evidence of Paramilitary Funding from the Illicit Antiquities Trade? Yes.', *Conflict Antiquities*. Available at: https://conflictantiquities.wordpress.com/2014/06/21/illicit-antiquities-trade-paramilitary-funding-evidence/ [accessed 22 December 2019].

Hart, K. (1985) 'The Informal Economy', *Cambridge Anthropology*, 10(2): 54–8.

Hart, M. (2003) *Diamond: The History of a Cold-Blooded Love Affair*. London: Fourth Estate.

Harvey, D. (2005) *A Brief History of Neoliberalism*. Oxford: Oxford University Press.

Hatzfeld, J. (2003) *Une Saison de Machettes*. Paris: Seuil.

Hill, S.M. (2007) 'Introduction: Future Directions in Small Arms Control', *Contemporary Security Policy*, 27(1): 1–11.

Hobbs, D. (1988) *Doing the Business: Entrepreneurship, the Working Class, and Detectives in the East End of London*. Oxford: Oxford University Press.

Hobbs, D. (2001) 'The Firm: Organisational Logic and Criminal Culture on a Shifting Terrain', *British Journal of Criminology*, 41(549–560).

Hobbs, D. (2013) *Lush Life: Constructing Organized Crime in the UK*. Oxford: Oxford University Press.

Hobbs, D. and Antonopoulos, G.A. (2013) 'Endemic to the Species: Ordering the Other via Organised Crime', *Global Crime*, 14(1): 27–51.

Holmes, G. (2007) 'Protection, Politics and Protest: Understanding Resistance to Conservation', *Conservation and Society*, 5(2): 184–201.

Hornsby, R. and Hobbs, D. (2007) 'A Zone of Ambiguity: the Political Economy of Cigarette Bootlegging', *British Journal of Criminology*, 47(4): 551–71.

Hübschle, A.M. (2016) *A Game of Horns: Transnational Flows of Rhino Horn*. Cologne: International Max Planck Research School on the Social and Political Constitution of the Economy.

Hübschle, A.M. (2017) 'The Social Economy of Rhino Poaching: Of Economic Freedom Fighters, Professional Hunters and Marginalized Local People', *Current Sociology*, 65(3): 427–47.

Human Rights Watch (2009) 'Diamonds in the Rough: Human Rights Abuses in the Marange Diamond Fields of Zimbabwe', *Human Rights Watch*. Available at: http://www.hrw.org/sites/default/files/reports/zimbabwe0609web.pdf [accessed 8 April 2015].

Hurley, R. (2019) 'How to Save Drug Users' Lives', *BMJ*, 366: l5050.

Hutton, J. and Dickson, B. (eds) (2000) *Endangered Species, Threatened Convention: The Past, Present, and Future of CITES, the Convention on International Trade in Endangered Species of Wild Fauna and Flora*. London: Earthscan.

ILO (2017) *Global Estimates of Modern Slavery: Forced Labour and Forced Marriage*. Geneva: International Labour Organization.

International Rhino Foundation (2019a) '2019 State of the Rhino Report Press Release', IRF. Available at: https://rhinos.org/2019-state-of-the-rhino-report/ [accessed 16 December 2019].

International Rhino Foundation (2019b) 'State of the Rhino Report', IRF. Available at: https://rhinos.org/2019-state-of-the-rhino/ [accessed 16 December 2019].

Jacques, S., Rosenfeld, R., Wright, R. and van Gemert, F. (2016) 'Effects of Prohibition and Decriminalization on Drug Market Conflict', *Criminology & Public Policy*, 15(3): 843–75.

Jones, C.W. (2018) 'Understanding ISIS's Destruction of Antiquities as a Rejection of Nationalism', *Journal of Eastern Mediterranean Archaeology and Heritage Studies*, 6(1): 31–58.

Kaplan, D.E. and Dubro, A. (2003) *Yakuza: Japan's Criminal Underworld*. Berkeley: University of California Press.

Kaplan, M. (2003) 'Carats and Sticks: Pursuing War and Peace through the Diamond Trade', *New York University Journal of International Law and Politics*, 35: 559–617.

Kara, S. (2017) *Sex Trafficking: Inside the Business of Modern Slavery*. New York: Columbia University Press.

Kaye, L.M. and Main, C.T. (1995) 'The Saga of the Lydian Hoard: From Ushak to New York and Back Again', in K.W. Tubb (ed) *Antiquities Trade or Betrayed: Legal, Ethical and Conservation Issues*. London: Archetype, pp 150–61.

Keller, A. (2015) 'Documenting ISIL's Antiquities Trafficking: The Looting and Destruction of Iraqi and Syrian Cultural Heritage: What We Know and What Can Be Done', US Department of State. Available at: https://2009-2017.state.gov/e/eb/rls/rm/2015/247610.htm [accessed 22 December 2019].

Kelman, H.C. and Hamilton, V.L. (1989) *Crimes of Obedience*. New Haven, CT: Yale University Press.

Kemp, L., Zolghadriha, S. and Gill, P. (2019) 'Pathways into Organized Crime: Comparing Founders and Joiners', *Trends in Organized Crime*. https://doi.org/10.1007/s12117-019-09371-w.

Kenyon, A.T. and Mackenzie, S. (2002) 'Recovering Stolen Art: Australian, English and US Law on Limitations of Action', *University of Western Australia Law Review*, 30(2): 233–50.

Kersel, M.M. (2006) 'From the Ground to the Buyer: A Market Analysis of the Trade in Illegal Antiquities', in N. Brodie, M.M. Kersel, C. Luke and K. Walker Tubb (eds) *Archaeology, Cultural Heritage and the Antiquities Trade*. Gainesville: University Press of Florida, pp 188–205.

Kleemans, E.R. and Smit, M. (2014) 'Human Smuggling, Human Trafficking, and Exploitation in the Sex Industry', in L. Paoli (ed) *The Oxford Handbook of Organized Crime*. Oxford: Oxford University Press, pp 381–401.

Klerks, P. (2003) 'The Network Paradigm Applied to Criminal Organisations: Theoretical Nitpicking or a Relevant Doctrine for Investigators? Recent Developments in the Netherlands', in A. Edwards and P. Gill (eds) *Transnational Organised Crime: Perspectives on Global Security*. London: Routledge, pp 97–113.

Klockars, C.B. (1974) *The Professional Fence*. London: Tavistock.

Koper, C.S. and Reuter, P. (1996) 'Suppressing Illegal Gun Markets: Lessons from Drug Enforcement', *Law & Contemporary Problems*, 59: 119–46.

Kurland, J. (2019) 'Wildlife Trafficking: The Problem, Patterns, and a Promising Path Toward Prevention', in M. Natarajan (ed) *International and Transnational Crime and Justice*. New York: Cambridge University Press, pp 55–60.

Kurland, J. and Pires, S.F. (2017) 'Assessing U.S. Wildlife Trafficking Patterns: How Criminology and Conservation Science Can Guide Strategies to Reduce the Illegal Wildlife Trade', *Deviant Behavior*, 38(4): 375–91.

Kurland, J., Pires, S.F., McFann, S.C. and Moreto, W.D. (2017) 'Wildlife Crime: A Conceptual Integration, Literature Review, and Methodological Critique', *Crime Science*, 6(1): 4.

Kvalnes, Ø. (2019) 'Moral Neutralization', in Ø. Kvalnes (ed) *Moral Reasoning at Work: Rethinking Ethics in Organizations*. Cham: Springer International Publishing, pp 117–31.

Landesman, P. (2003). 'Arms and the Man', *New York Times Magazine*, 17 August, Section 6, p 28.

Lavorgna, A. (2014) 'Wildlife Trafficking in the Internet Age', *Crime Science*, 3: 1–12.

Lavorgna, A., Rutherford, C., Vaglica, V., Smith, M.J. and Sajeva, M. (2018) 'CITES, Wild Plants, and Opportunities for Crime', *European Journal on Criminal Policy and Research*, 24(3): 269–88.

Lee, M. (2011) *Trafficking and Global Crime Control*. London: SAGE.

Leggett, T. (2019) 'Transnational Firearms Trafficking: Guns for Crime and Conflict', in M. Natarajan (ed) *International and Transnational Crime and Justice*. New York: Cambridge University Press, pp 37–42.

Lehtinen, T. (2008) '"At the Gates of El Dorado": Micro-dynamics in the Transnational Border Area between Northern Morocco and Europe', in F. Söderbaum and I. Taylor (eds) *Afro-Regions: The Dynamics of Cross-Border Micro-Regionalism in Africa*. Uppsala: Nordiska Afrikainstitutet, pp 121–35.

Lemieux, A.M. and Clarke, R.V. (2009) 'The International Ban on Ivory Sales and Its Effects on Elephant Poaching in Africa', *British Journal of Criminology*, 49: 451–71.

Levi, M. (2015) *Understanding the US Illicit Tobacco Market: Characteristics, Policy Context and Lessons from International Experiences*. Washington, DC: National Academies Press.

Levinas, E. (1969) *Totality and Infinity: an Essay on Exteriority*, tr. A. Lingis. Pittsburgh, PA: Duquesne University Press.

Levinas, E. (1981) *Otherwise than Being: or Beyond Essence*, tr. A. Lingis. Boston, MA: Martinus Nijhoff.

Lloyd, P. and Simmons, B.A. (2015) 'Framing for a New Transnational Legal Order', in G. Shaffer and T.C. Halliday (eds) *Transnational Legal Orders*. Cambridge: Cambridge University Press, pp 400–38.

Lock, P. (1999) 'Pervasive Illicit Small Arms Availability: A Global Threat', *HEUNI Paper No. 14*. Helsinki: HEUNI, The European Institute for Crime Prevention and Control, affiliated with the UN.

Lois, J. (2003) *Heroic Efforts: The Emotional Culture of Search and Rescue Volunteers*. New York: New York University Press.

Long, J. (2002) *The Dinosaur Dealers*. Crows Nest, New South Wales: Allen & Unwin.

Lundin, S. (2015) *Organs for Sale: An Ethnographic Examination of the International Organ Trade*. Basingstoke: Palgrave Macmillan.

Lutz, M.A. (1996) 'The Relevance of Martin Buber's Philosophical Anthropology for Economic Thought', in M. Friedman (ed) *Martin Buber and the Human Sciences*. Albany: State University of New York Press, pp 267–82.

Lynch, M.J. and Stretesky, P.B. (2014) *Exploring Green Criminology: Toward a Green Criminological Revolution*. Farnham: Ashgate.

Lyons, J.A. and Natusch, D.J.D. (2011) 'Wildlife Laundering through Breeding Farms: Illegal Harvest, Population Declines and a Means of Regulating the Trade of Green Pythons (*Morelia viridis*) from Indonesia', *Biological Conservation*, 144(12): 3073–81.

MacCoun, R.J. and Reuter, P. (2011) 'Assessing Drug Prohibition and Its Alternatives: A Guide for Agnostics', *Annual Review of Law and Social Science*, 7(1): 61–78.

MacIntyre, A. (1999) 'Social Structures and Their Threats to Moral Agency', *Philosophy*, 74(289): 311–29.

Mackenzie, S. (2005a) 'Dig a Bit Deeper: Law, Regulation and the Illicit Antiquities Market', *British Journal of Criminology*, 45: 249–68.

Mackenzie, S. (2005b) *Going, Going, Gone: Regulating the Market in Illicit Antiquities*. Leicester: Institute of Art and Law.

Mackenzie, S. (2006) 'Systematic Crimes of the Powerful: Criminal Aspects of the Global Economy', *Social Justice*, 33(1): 162–82.

Mackenzie, S. (2007) 'Transnational Crime, Local Denial', *Social Justice*, 34(2): 111–24.

Mackenzie, S. (2010a) 'Counterfeiting as Corporate Externality: Intellectual Property Crime and Global Insecurity', *Crime, Law and Social Change*, 54(1): 21–38.

Mackenzie, S. (2010b) 'Scams', in F. Brookman, M. Maguire, H. Pierpoint and T. Bennett (eds) *Handbook on Crime*. Cullompton: Willan, pp 137–52.

Mackenzie, S. (2013) 'Conditions for Guilt-Free Consumption in a Transnational Criminal Market', *European Journal on Criminal Policy and Research*, 20(4): 503–15.

Mackenzie, S. (2015) 'Do We Need a Kimberley Process for the Illicit Antiquities Trade? Some Lessons to Learn from a Comparative Review of Transnational Criminal Markets and their Regulation', in F. Desmarais (ed) *Countering Illicit Traffic in Cultural Goods: The Global Challenge of Protecting the World's Heritage*. Paris: International Council of Museums, pp 151–62.

Mackenzie, S., Brodie, N., Yates, D. and Tsirogiannis, C. (2019) *Trafficking Culture: New Directions in Researching the Global Market in Illicit Antiquities*. London: Routledge.

Mackenzie, S. and Davis, T. (2014) 'Temple Looting in Cambodia: Anatomy of a Statue Trafficking Network', *British Journal of Criminology*, 54(5): 722–40.

Mackenzie, S., Hübschle, A. and Yates, D. (2020) 'Global Trade in Stolen Culture and Nature as Neo-Colonial Hegemony', in J. Blaustein, K. Fitz Gibbon, N.W. Pino and R. White (eds) *Emerald Handbook of Crime, Justice and Sustainable Development*. Bingley: Emerald, pp 419–38.

Mackenzie, S. and Yates, D. (2016) 'Collectors on Illicit Collecting: Higher Loyalties and Other Techniques of Neutralization in the Unlawful Collecting of Rare and Precious Orchids and Antiquities', *Theoretical Criminology*, 20(3): 340-57.

Mackenzie, S. and Yates, D. (2017a) 'Trafficking Cultural Objects and Human Rights', in L. Weber, E. Fishwick and M. Marmo (eds) *The Routledge International Handbook of Criminology and Human Rights*. New York: Routledge, pp 220–30.

Mackenzie, S. and Yates, D. (2017b) 'What is Grey about the "Grey Market" in Antiquities?', in J. Beckert and M. Dewey (eds) *The Architecture of Illegal Markets*. Oxford: Oxford University Press, pp 70–86.

Malamut, S.A. (2005) 'A Band-Aid on a Machete Wound: The Failures of the Kimberley Process and Diamond-Caused Bloodshed in the Democratic Republic of the Congo', *Suffolk Transnational Law Review*, 29(1): 25–52.

Marks, J. (1990). 'The Paradox of Prohibition', in J. Hando and J. Carless (eds) *Controlled Availability: Wisdom or Disaster?* Sydney: National Drug and Alcohol Research Centre Monograph No. 10.

Marks, P. (1998) 'The Ethics of Art Dealing', *International Journal of Cultural Property*, 7(1): 116–27.

Marmo, M. and Chazal, N. (2016) *Transnational Crime and Justice*. London: SAGE.

Marsh, K., Wilson, L. and Kenehan, R. (2012) 'The Impact of Globalization on the UK Market for Illicit Drugs Evidence from Interviews with Convicted Drug Traffickers', in C.C. Storti and P. De Grauwe (eds) *Illicit Trade and the Global Economy*. Cambridge, MA: MIT Press, pp 159–78.

Maruna, S. and Copes, H. (2005) 'Excuses, Excuses: What Have We Learned from Five Decades of Neutralization Research?', *Crime and Justice*, 32: 221–320.

Matrix Knowledge Group (2007) 'The Illicit Drug Trade in the United Kingdom', *Home Office Online Report 20/07*. London: Home Office.

Matza, D. (1964) *Delinquency and Drift*. New York: John Wiley.

Matza, D. (1969) *Becoming Deviant*. Englewood Cliffs, NJ: Prentice-Hall.

McBarnet, D. (1992) 'Legitimate Rackets: Tax Evasion, Tax Avoidance, and the Boundaries of Legality', *The Journal of Human Justice*, 3: 56–74.

McBarnet, D. (2003) 'When Compliance Is Not the Solution but the Problem: From Changes in Law to Changes in Attitude', in V. Braithwaite (ed) *Taxing Democracy: Understanding Tax Avoidance and Evasion*. Aldershot: Ashgate, pp 229–44.

McBarnet, D. (2006) 'After Enron will "Whiter than White Collar Crime" Still Wash?', *British Journal of Criminology*, 46(6): 1091–1109.

McDougal, T.L., Shirk, D.A., Muggah, R. and Patterson, J.H. (2014) 'The Way of the Gun: Estimating Firearms Trafficking across the US–Mexico Border', *Journal of Economic Geography*, 15(2): 297–327.

Merryman, J.H. (2005) 'Cultural Property Internationalism', *International Journal of Cultural Property*, 12: 11–39.

Merton, R.K. (1968) *Social Theory and Social Structure*. Glencoe, IL: Free Press.

Messner, S.F. and Rosenfeld, R. (1994) *Crime and the American Dream*. Belmont, CA: Wadsworth.

Michalowski, R.J. and Kramer, R.C. (1987) 'The Space between the Laws: The Problem of Corporate Crime in a Transnational Context', *Social Problems*, 34: 34–53.

Middleton, J., McGrail, S. and Stringer, K. (2016) 'Drug-Related Deaths in England and Wales', *BMJ*, 355: i5259.

Miklian, J. (2013a) '"Let's Deal": A Conversation with a Diamond Smuggler', *Words Without Borders*. Available at: https://www.wordswithoutborders.org/article/lets-deal-a-conversation-with-a-diamond-smuggler [accessed 3 December 2019].

Miklian, J. (2013b) 'Rough Cut: Nearly all the World's Diamonds – Legal or Not – Pass Through this One Indian City', *Foreign Policy*. Available at: https://foreignpolicy.com/2013/01/02/rough-cut/ [accessed 3 December 2019].

Minor, W.W. (1981) 'Techniques of Neutralization: A Reconceptualization and Empirical Examination', *Journal of Research in Crime and Delinquency*, 18(2): 295–318.

Molland, S. (2010) 'The Value of Bodies: Deception, Helping and Profiteering in Human Trafficking Along the Thai–Lao Border', *Asian Studies Review*, 34(2): 211–29.

Montague, D. (2002) 'The Business of War and the Prospects for Peace in Sierra Leone', *The Brown Journal of World Affairs*, 9(1): 229–37.

Morselli, C. (2001) 'Structuring Mr Nice: Entrepreneurial Opportunities and Brokerage Positioning in the Cannabis Trade', *Crime, Law and Social Change*, 35: 203–44.

Morselli, C. (2002) 'The Relational Dynamics of Illegal Firearm Transaction', *Canadian Journal of Criminology*, 44: 255–76.

Morselli, C. (2009) *Inside Criminal Networks*. New York: Springer.

Morselli, C. (2012) 'Assessing Network Patterns in Illegal Firearms Markets', *Crime, Law and Social Change*, 57: 129–49.

Morselli, C., Giguère, C. and Petit, K. (2007) 'The Efficiency/Security Trade-Off in Criminal Networks', *Social Networks*, 29(1): 143–53.

Murphy, J.D. (1995) *Plunder and Preservation: Cultural Property Law and Practice in the People's Republic of China*. Hong Kong: Oxford University Press.

Myrdal, A. (1977) *The Game of Disarmament*. Manchester: Manchester University Press.

Naim, M. (2009) 'Wasted: The American Prohibition on Thinking Smart in the Drug War', *Foreign Policy*, 172: 168.

Natarajan, M. (2011) 'Drug Trafficking', in M. Natarajan (ed) *International Crime and Justice*. New York: Cambridge University Press, pp 5–11.

Natarajan, M. (2019a) 'Drug Trafficking', in M. Natarajan (ed) *International and Transnational Crime and Justice*, 2nd edn. Cambridge: Cambridge University Press, pp 5–11.

Natarajan, M. (ed) (2019b) *International and Transnational Crime and Justice*. Cambridge: Cambridge University Press.

Natarajan, M. (2019c) 'Introduction' *International and Transnational Crime and Justice*. Cambridge: Cambridge University Press, pp xxxiii–xlv.

Natarajan, M., Zanella, M. and Yu, C. (2015) 'Classifying the Variety of Drug Trafficking Organizations', *Journal of Drug Issues*, 45(4): 409–30.

Naylor, R.T. (2004) *Wages of Crime: Black Markets, Illegal Finance and the Underworld Economy*. Ithaca, NY: Cornell University Press and Montreal: McGill-Queen's University Press.
Naylor, R.T. (2007) 'Marlboro Men. [Review of the book *Illicit: How Smugglers, Traffickers and Copycats are Hijacking the Global Economy*]', *London Review of Books*, 29(6): 37–9.
Ngoc, A.C. and Wyatt, T. (2013) 'A Green Criminological Exploration of Illegal Wildlife Trade in Vietnam', *Asian Criminology*, 8: 129–42.
Nordstrom, C. (2007) *Global Outlaws: Crime, Money and Power in the Contemporary World*. Berkeley: University of California Press.
Nørskov, V. (2002) *Greek Vases in New Contexts: the Collecting and Trading of Greek Vases – an Aspect of the Modern Reception of Antiquity*. Aarhus: Aarhus University Press.
Nurse, A. (2015) *Policing Wildlife. Perspectives on the Enforcement of Wildlife Legislation*. Basingstoke: Palgrave Macmillan.
Nurse, A. and Wyatt, T. (2020) *Wildlife Criminology*. Bristol: Bristol University Press.
Nuwer, R.L. (2018a) 'The Pangolin Poacher', *Hakai Magazine*. Available at: https://www.hakaimagazine.com/features/the-pangolin-hunter/ [accessed 5 December 2019].
Nuwer, R.L. (2018b) *Poached: Inside the Dark World of Wildlife Trafficking*. New York: Da Capo Press.
O'Hear, M.M. (2004) 'Sentencing the Green-Collar Offender: Punishment, Culpability, and Environmental Crime', *Journal of Criminal Law and Criminology*, 95(1): 133–276.
O'Keefe, P.J. (1997) *Trade in Antiquities: Reducing Destruction and Theft*. London: Archetype.
Oram, S., Stöckl, H., Busza, J., Howard, L.M. and Zimmerman, C. (2012) 'Prevalence and Risk of Violence and the Physical, Mental, and Sexual Health Problems Associated with Human Trafficking: Systematic Review', *PLOS Medicine*, 9(5): e1001224.
Orlean, S. (1998) *The Orchid Thief: A True Story of Beauty and Obsession*. New York: Random House.
Ossewaarde-Lowtoo, R. (2017) 'The Humanization of Economic Life: The Legacy of Martin Buber', *CrossCurrents*, 67(2): 439–57.
Ottisova, L., Hemmings, S., Howard, L.M., Zimmerman, C. and Oram, S. (2016) 'Prevalence and Risk of Violence and the Mental, Physical and Sexual Health Problems Associated with Human Trafficking: An Updated Systematic Review', *Epidemiology and Psychiatric Sciences*, 25(4): 317–41.
Pantel, S. and Anak, N.W. (2010) *A Preliminary Assessment of Sunda Pangolin Trade in Sabah*. Petaling Jaya: Traffic South East Asia.

Paoli, L., Greenfield, V. and Reuter, P. (2009) *The World Heroin Market: Can Supply Be Cut?* New York: Oxford University Press.

Paoli, L. and Reuter, P. (2008) 'Drug Trafficking and Ethnic Minorities in Western Europe', *European Journal of Criminology*, 5(1): 13–37.

Parker, C. (2013) 'The War on Cartels and the Social Meaning of Deterrence', *Regulation & Governance*, 7: 174–94.

Passas, N. (1999) 'Globalization, Criminogenic Asymmetries and Economic Crime', *European Journal of Law Reform*, 1(4): 399–423.

Passas, N. (ed) (2013) *Transnational Financial Crime*. London: Routledge.

Passas, N. and Goodwin, N.R. (eds) (2004) *It's Legal but it Ain't Right: Harmful Social Consequences of Legal Industries*. Ann Arbor: University of Michigan Press.

Paul, K.A. (2016) 'How Daesh Turns Illicit Digs into Dollars', *The Antiquities Coalition*. Available at: https://theantiquitiescoalition.org/how-daesh-turns-illicit-digs-into-dollars/ [accessed 22 December 2019].

Pearlstein, W.G. (1996) 'Claims for the Repatriation of Cultural Property: Prospects for a Managed Antiquities Market', *Georgetown Journal of Law and Policy in International Business*, 28(1): 123–50.

Pearson, G. and Hobbs, D. (2001) 'Middle Market Drug Distribution', *Home Office Research Study 227*. London: Home Office.

Pearson, G. and Hobbs, D. (2003) 'King Pin? A Case Study of a Middle Market Drug Broker', *The Howard Journal of Criminal Justice*, 42(4): 335–47.

Peters, G. (2010), 'Crime and Insurgency in the Tribal Areas of Afghanistan and Pakistan' *Harmony Program*, New York: Combatting Terrorism Center at West Point.

Peterson, M.N., von Essen, E., Hansen, H.P. and Peterson, T.R. (2016) 'Illegal Fishing and Hunting as Resistance to Neoliberal Colonialism', *Crime, Law and Social Change*, 67(4): 401–13.

Pickles, S. (2018) 'Diamond Industry Fails to Clean Up Its Act', *Global Witness*. Available at: https://www.globalwitness.org/en/press-releases/diamond-industry-fails-clean-its-act/ [accessed 23 September 2019].

Pires, S. and Clarke, R.V. (2011a) 'Are Parrots CRAVED? An Analysis of Parrot Poaching in Mexico', *Journal of Research in Crime and Delinquency*, 49(1): 122–46.

Pires, S.F. and Clarke, R.V. (2011b) 'Sequential Foraging, Itinerant Fences and Parrot Poaching in Bolivia', *British Journal of Criminology*, 51: 314–35.

Pires, S.F. and Moreto, W.D. (2011) 'Preventing Wildlife Crimes: Solutions that Can Overcome the "Tragedy of the Commons"', *European Journal on Criminal Policy and Research*, 17: 101–23.

Pires, S.F., Schneider, J.L. and Herrera, M. (2016) 'Organized Crime or Crime that is Organized? The Parrot Trade in the Neotropics', *Trends in Organized Crime*, 19: 4–20.

Pogge, T.W. (2002) *World Poverty and Human Rights: Cosmopolitan Responsibilities and Reforms*. Cambridge: Polity Press.

Pogge, T.W. (2004) 'Assisting the Global Poor', in D.K. Chatterjee (ed) *The Ethics of Assistance: Morality and the Distant Needy*. Cambridge: Cambridge University Press, pp 260–88.

Polk, K. (2000) 'The Antiquities Trade Viewed as a Criminal Market', *Hong Kong Lawyer*, September: 82–92.

Pollack, H.A. and Reuter, P. (2014) 'Does Tougher Enforcement Make Drugs More Expensive?', *Addiction*, 109(12): 1959–66.

Portes, A., Castells, M. and Benton, L. (1989) *The Informal Economy*. Baltimore, MD: Johns Hopkins University Press.

Presser, L. (2013) *Why We Harm*. New Brunswick, NJ: Rutgers University Press.

Prott, L.V. and O'Keefe, P.J. (1984) *Law and the Cultural Heritage, Volume 1: Discovery and Excavation*. Abingdon: Professional Books.

Prott, L.V. and O'Keefe, P.J. (1989) *Law and the Cultural Heritage, Volume 3: Movement*. London: Butterworths.

Rademeyer, J. (2012) *Killing for Profit: Exposing the Illegal Rhino Horn Trade*. Cape Town: Random House Struik.

Räthzel, N. and Uzzell, D. (2017) 'Environmental Policies and The Reproduction of Business as Usual: How Does It Work?', *Capitalism Nature Socialism*, 30(1): 120–38.

Redmond-Cooper, R. (1997) 'Good Faith Acquisition of Stolen Art', *Art, Antiquity and Law*, II: 55.

Redmond-Cooper, R. (2000) 'Limitation of Actions in Art and Antiquity Claims: Part II', *Art Antiquity and Law*, 5(2): 185–206.

Reichel, P. and Albanese, J.S. (eds) (2016) *Handbook of Transnational Crime and Justice*. London: SAGE.

Renfrew, C. (1999) *Loot, Legitimacy and Ownership: The Ethical Crisis in Archaeology*. Amsterdam: Joh. Enschede.

Reuter, P. (2009) 'Systemic Violence in Drug Markets', *Crime, Law and Social Change*, 52: 275–84.

Reuter, P. (2014) 'Drug Markets and Organised Crime', in L. Paoli (ed) *The Oxford Handbook of Organised Crime*. Oxford: Oxford University Press, pp 359–80.

Reuter, P. and Haaga, J. (1989) *The Organisation of High-Level Drug Markets: An Exploratory Study*. Santa Monica, CA: RAND.

Reuter, P. and O'Regan, D. (2017) 'Smuggling Wildlife in the Americas: Scale, Methods, and Links to Other Organised Crimes', *Global Crime*, 18: 77–99.

Ribeaud, D. and Eisner, M. (2010) 'Are Moral Disengagement, Neutralization Techniques, and Self-Serving Cognitive Distortions the Same? Developing a Unified Scale of Moral Neutralization of Aggression', *International Journal of Conflict and Violence*, 4(2): 298–315.

Richter, K.P. and Levy, S. (2014) 'Big Marijuana — Lessons from Big Tobacco', *New England Journal of Medicine*, 371(5): 399–401.

Rosenfeld, R. and Messner, S.F. (2013) *Crime and the Economy*. London: SAGE.

Roth, M.P. (2017) *Global Organized Crime: A 21st-Century Approach*. Abingdon: Routledge.

Rothfield, L. (2009) *The Rape of Mesopotamia: Behind the Looting of the Iraq Museum*. Chicago: University of Chicago Press.

Rozuel, C. (2011) 'The Moral Threat of Compartmentalization: Self, Roles and Responsibility', *Journal of Business Ethics*, 102(4): 685–97.

Ruggiero, V. (2001) *Crime and Markets: Essays in Anti-Criminology*. Oxford: Oxford University Press.

Ruggiero, V. (2009) 'Transnational Crime and Global Illicit Economies', in E. Wilson and T. Lindsey (eds) *Government of the Shadows*. London: Pluto Press, pp 117–29.

Ruggiero, V. and South, N. (2010) 'Green Criminology and Dirty Collar Crime', *Critical Criminology*, 18(4): 251–62.

Saffron, I. (2002) *Caviar: The Strange History and Uncertain Future of the World's Most Coveted Delicacy*. New York: Broadway Books.

Said, E. (1979) *Orientalism*. New York: Vintage.

Salzman, T.A. (1998) 'Rape Camps as a Means of Ethnic Cleansing: Religious, Cultural, and Ethical Responses to Rape Victims in the Former Yugoslavia', *Human Rights Quarterly*, 20(2): 348–78.

Samboma, J.L. (2019) 'Sierra Leone: Local Population Doesn't Benefit from Diamond Industry Due to Corruption & Smuggling, Says Analyst', *African Business Magazine*, 7 May.

Sampson, A. (1977) *The Arms Bazaar*. New York: Viking.

Sampson, A. (2002). 'No Stone Unturned', *The Guardian*, 2 February.

Sandel, M.J. (2012) *What Money Can't Buy: the Moral Limits of Markets*. London: Penguin.

Sartre, J.-P. (1956 [1943]) *Being and Nothingness*, tr. H.E. Barnes. New York: Philosophical Library.

Satz, D. (2010) *Why Some Things Should Not Be For Sale: The Moral Limits of Markets*. New York: Oxford University Press.
Scheper-Hughes, N. (2001) 'Commodity Fetishism in Organs Trafficking', *Body & Society*, 7(2–3): 31–62.
Schick, J. (1997) *The Gods Are Leaving the Country: Art Theft from Nepal*. Bangkok: White Orchid Books.
Schneider, J.L. (2008) 'Reducing the Illicit Trade in Endangered Wildlife: The Market Reduction Approach', *Journal of Contemporary Criminal Justice*, 24(3): 274–95.
Schouten, P. (2013) 'Keith Hart on the Informal Economy, the Great Transformation, and the Humanity of Corporations', *Theory Talks*. Available at: https://www.files.ethz.ch/isn/165155/Theory%20Talk56_Hart.pdf [accessed 17 December 2019].
Schroeder, M. (2016) 'Dribs and Drabs: The Mechanics of Small Arms Trafficking from the United States', Issue Brief Number 17. Geneva: Small Arms Survey.
Scott, M. and Lyman, S. (1968) 'Accounts', *American Sociological Review*, 33: 46–62.
Seddon, T. (2019) 'Markets, Regulation and Drug Law Reform: Towards a Constitutive Approach', *Social & Legal Studies*: https://doi.org/10.1177/0964663919868756 .
Shearing, C.D. (1993) 'A Constitutive Conception of Regulation', in P.N. Grabosky and J. Braithwaite (eds) *Business Regulation and Australia's Future*. Canberra: Australian Institute of Criminology, pp 67–80.
Shelley, L. (2010) *Human Trafficking: A Global Perspective*. New York: Cambridge University Press.
Shelley, L. (2019) 'The Globalization of Crime', in M. Natarajan (ed) *International and Transnational Crime and Justice*, 2nd edn. Cambridge: Cambridge University Press, pp 223–8.
Sheptycki, J.W.E. and Wardak, A. (eds) (2005) *Transnational and Comparative Criminology*. London: Glasshouse Press.
Shiner, M., Carre, Z., Delsol, R. and Eastwood, N. (2018) *The Colour of Injustice: 'Race', Drugs and Law Enforcement in England and Wales*. London: StopWatch & Release.
Shover, N., Coffey, G.S. and Hobbs, D. (2003) 'Crime on the Line: Telemarketing and the Changing Nature of Professional Crime', *British Journal of Criminology*, 43: 489–505.
Shover, N., Coffey, G.S. and Sanders, C.R. (2004) 'Dialling for Dollars: Opportunities, Justifications, and Telemarketing Fraud', *Qualitative Sociology*, 27(1): 59–75.

Showers, C. (1992) 'Compartmentalization of Positive and Negative Self-Knowledge: Keeping Bad Apples Out of the Bunch', *Journal of Personality and Social Psychology*, 62(6): 1036–49.

Siegel, D. (2008) 'Diamonds and Organized Crime: The Case of Antwerp', in D. Siegel and H. Nelen (eds) *Organized Crime: Culture, Markets and Policies*. New York: Springer, pp 85–96.

Siegel, D. (2009) *The Mazzel Ritual: Culture, Customs and Crime in the Diamond Trade*. Dordrecht: Springer.

Siegel, D. (2011) 'Trafficking of Conflict Diamonds', in R. Barberet, S. Zhang and C.J. Smith (eds) *Routledge Handbook of International Criminology*. Abingdon: Routledge, pp 220–30.

Simon, H.A. (1982) *Models of Bounded Rationality*. Cambridge, MA: MIT Press.

Smillie, I., Gberie, L. and Hazleton, R. (2000) *The Heart of the Matter: Sierra Leone, Diamonds and Human Security*. Ottawa: Partnership Africa Canada.

Smith Jr, D.C. (1980) 'Paragons, Pariahs and Pirates: A Spectrum-based Theory of Enterprise', *Crime and Delinquency*, 26(3): 358–86.

Smith, K.F., Behrens, M., Schloegel, L.M., Marano, N., Burgiel, S. and Daszak, P. (2009) 'Reducing the Risks of the Wildlife Trade', *Science*, 324(5927): 594.

Soudijn, M.R.J. and Tijhuis, E.A.J.G. (2003) 'Some Perspectives on the Illicit Antiquities Trade in China', *Art, Antiquity and Law*, 8(2): 149–65.

South, N. and Wyatt, T. (2011) 'Comparing Illicit Trades in Wildlife and Drugs: An Exploratory Study', *Deviant Behavior*, 32(6): 538–61.

Stadler, W.A. and Benson, M.L. (2012) 'Revisiting the Guilty Mind: The Neutralization of White-Collar Crime', *Criminal Justice Review*, 37(4): 494–511.

Stein, H.F. (2001) *Nothing Personal, Just Business: A Guided Journey Into Organizational Darkness*. Westport, CT: Quorum Books.

Stiglitz, J.E. (2002) *Globalization and Its Discontents*. New York: W.W. Norton.

Sutherland, E., Cressey, D.R. and Luckenbill, D. (1995) 'The Theory of Differential Association', in N.J. Herman (ed) *Deviance: A Symbolic Interactionist Approach*. Lanham, MD: General Hall, pp 64–8.

Sutherland, E.H. (1949) *White Collar Crime*. New York: Dryden Press.

Sutton, M. (1998) 'Handling Stolen Goods & Theft: A Market Reduction Approach', Home Office Research Study 178. London: Home Office.

Sykes, G.M. and Matza, D. (1957) 'Techniques of Neutralisation: A Theory of Delinquency', *American Sociological Review*, 22: 664–70.

Tamm, I. (2002) 'Diamonds in Peace and War: Severing the Conflict–Diamond Connection', WPF Report 30. Cambridge, MA: World Peace Foundation.

Tanaka, Y. (2003) *Japan's Comfort Women: Sexual Slavery and Prostitution during World War II and the US Occupation*. New York: Routledge.

Tanner, S. (2011) 'Towards a Pattern in Mass Violence Participation? An Analysis of Rwandan Perpetrators' Accounts from the 1994 Genocide', *Global Crime*, 12(4): 266–89.

Tanner, S. (2012) 'Some Thoughts on the Banality of Evil, Inspired by Conversation with Jean-Paul Brodeur', *Hommages à J-P. Brodeur*', *Champ Pénal*, IX (Hommages à J-P. Brodeur: Actes de Colloque).

Thosarat, R. (2001) 'The Destruction of the Cultural Heritage of Thailand and Cambodia', in N. Brodie, J. Doole and C. Renfrew (eds) *Trade in Illicit Antiquities: the Destruction of the World's Archaeological Heritage*. Cambridge: McDonald Institute for Archaeological Research, pp 7–18.

Thoumi, F.E. (2003) *Illegal Drugs, Economy and Society in the Andes*. Washington, DC: Woodrow Wilson Center Press.

TRACE (2016) 'Trace-ing Human Trafficking: Handbook for Policy Makers, Law Enforcement Agencies and Civil Society Organisations', *TRACE project consortium*. Available at: https://www.cbss.org/wp-content/uploads/2013/01/TRACE-report.pdf [accessed 29 May 2020].

Tsirogiannis, C. (2013a) 'Something Is Confidential in the State of Christie's', *Journal of Art Crime Research*, 9: 3–20.

Tsirogiannis, C. (2013b) 'Unravelling the Hidden Market of Illicit Antiquities: The Robin Symes–Christos Michaelides Network and its International Implications'. Unpublished PhD thesis: University of Cambridge.

UNESCO (1970) *Convention on the Means of Prohibiting and Preventing the Illicit Import, Export and Transfer of Ownership of Cultural Property*. Paris: UNESCO.

UNIDROIT (1995) *Convention on Stolen or Illegally Exported Cultural Objects*. Rome: UNIDROIT.

United Nations (2000) *Convention Against Transnational Organized Crime*. Palermo: UN.

UNODC (2010) *The Globalization of Crime: A Transnational Organized Crime Threat Assessment*. Vienna: United Nations Office on Drugs and Crime.

UNODC (2012) *World Drug Report 2012*. Vienna: United Nations.

UNODC (2016) *World Wildlife Crime Report: Trafficking in Protected Species*. Vienna: United Nations Office on Drugs and Crime.

UNODC (2017a) *Research Brief: Wildlife Crime Status Update 2017*. Vienna: United Nations Office on Drugs and Crime.
UNODC (2017b) *World Drug Report 2017*. Vienna: United Nations.
UNODC (2019) *World Drug Report 2019*. Vienna: United Nations.
Van Erp, J. (2018) 'The Organization of Corporate Crime: Introduction to Special Issue of Administrative Sciences', *Administrative Sciences*, 8(3): 36.
van Schendel, W. and Abraham, I. (eds) (2005) *Illicit Flows and Criminal Things: States, Borders and the Other Side of Globalization*. Bloomington, IN: Indiana University Press.
van Uhm, D. (2016) *The Illegal Wildlife Trade: Inside the World of Poachers, Smugglers and Traders*. Cham: Springer.
van Uhm, D. and Moreto, W.D. (2018) 'Corruption within the Illegal Wildlife Trade: A Symbiotic and Antithetical Enterprise', *British Journal of Criminology*, 58: 864–85.
Vaughan, D. (1999) 'The Dark Side of Organizations: Mistake, Misconduct, and Disaster', *Annual Review of Sociology*, 25: 271–305.
Veblen, T.B. (1924) *The Theory of the Leisure Class*, new edn. London: Allen & Unwin.
Veblen, T.B. (1994 [1899]) *The Theory of the Leisure Class*. New York: Dover Publications.
Vetlesen, A.J. (2005) *Evil and Human Agency: Understanding Collective Evildoing*. Cambridge: Cambridge University Press.
Viuhko, M. and Jokinen, A. (2009) *Human Trafficking for Sexual Exploitation and Organised Procuring in Finland*. Helsinki: HEUNI.
Von Lampe, K. (2015) *Organized Crime: Analyzing Illegal Activities, Criminal Structures, and Extra-Legal Governance*. London: SAGE.
Wallace, T. and Mesko, F. (2013) *The Odessa Network: Mapping Facilitators of Russian and Ukrainian Arms Transfers*. Washington, DC: C4ADS.
Walsh, L. (1997) *Firewall: The Iran-Contra Conspiracy and Cover-up*. New York: Norton.
Warchol, G.L. and Harrington, M. (2016) 'Exploring the Dynamics of South Africa's Illegal Abalone Trade via Routine Activities Theory', *Trends in Organized Crime*, 19: 21–41.
Warchol, G.L., Zupan, L.L. and Clack, W. (2003) 'Transnational Criminality: An Analysis of the Illegal Wildlife Market in Southern Africa', *International Criminal Justice Review*, 13: 1–27.
Watson, P. and Todeschini, C. (2007) *The Medici Conspiracy: The Illicit Journey of Looted Antiquities – From Italy's Tomb Raiders to the World's Greatest Museums*, rev. edn. New York: Public Affairs.

Wellsmith, M. (2011) 'Wildlife Crime: The Problems of Enforcement', *European Journal on Criminal Policy and Research*, 17: 125–48.

Werb, D., Rowell, G., Guyatt, G., Kerr, T., Montaner, J. and Wood, E. (2011) 'Effect of Drug Law Enforcement on Drug Market Violence: A Systematic Review', *International Journal of Drug Policy*, 22(2): 87–94.

Wexler, L. (2010) 'Regulating Resource Curses: Institutional Design and Evolution of the Blood Diamond Regime', *Cardozo Law Review*, 31(5): 1717–80.

Weyzig, F. (2004) *The Kimberley Process Certification Scheme One Year Ahead: State of Affairs in the European Union*. Amsterdam: Netherlands Institute for Southern Africa.

Whyte, D. (2016) 'It's Common Sense, Stupid! Corporate Crime and Techniques of Neutralization in the Automobile Industry', *Crime, Law and Social Change*, 66(2): 165–81.

Williams, P. (1998a) 'The Nature of Drug Trafficking Networks', *Current History*, 97: 154–9.

Williams, P. (1998b) 'Organizing Transnational Crime: Networks, Markets and Hierarchies', *Transnational Organized Crime*, 4: 57–87.

Wilson, M. and O'Brien, E. (2016) 'Constructing the Ideal Victim in the United States of America's Annual Trafficking in Persons Reports', *Crime, Law and Social Change*, 65: 29–45.

Wong, R. and Krishnasamy, K. (2019) *Skin and Bones Unresolved: An Analysis of Tiger Seizures from 2000–2018*. Petaling Jaya: TRAFFIC Southeast Asia Regional Office.

Woodiwiss, M. and Hobbs, D. (2009) 'Organized Evil and the Atlantic Alliance: Moral Panics and the Rhetoric of Organized Crime Policing in America and Britain', *British Journal of Criminology*, 49: 106–28.

Wright, J. and Rossi, P. (1986) *Armed and Considered Dangerous: A Survey of Felons and Their Firearms*. Hawthorne, NY: Aldine de Gruyter.

WWF (2016) 'WWF Response to Statement of Concern by Tiger Biologists', World Wildlife Fund. Available at: http://tigers.panda.org/wp-content/uploads/WWF-Response-to-Statement-of-Concern-by-Tiger-Biologists-22-April-2016.pdf [accessed 16 December 2019].

Wyatt, T. (2009) 'Exploring the Organization of Russia Far East's Illegal Wildlife Trade: Two Case Studies of the Illegal Fur and Illegal Falcon Trades', *Global Crime*, 10(1–2): 144–54.

Wyatt, T. (2013) *Wildlife Trafficking: A Deconstruction of the Crime, the Victims and the Offenders*. London: Palgrave Macmillan.

Wyatt, T. (2014a) 'Non-Human Animal Abuse and Wildlife Trade: Harm in the Fur and Falcon Trades', *Society & Animals*, 22: 194–210.

Wyatt, T. (2014b) 'The Russian Far East's Illegal Timber Trade: An Organized Crime?', *Crime, Law and Social Change*, 61: 15–35.

Wyler, L.S. and Sheikh, P.A. (2013) *International Illegal Trade in Wildlife: Threats and US Policy*. Washington, DC: Congressional Research Service.

Yates, D. (2016) 'Museums, Collectors and Value Manipulation: Tax Fraud through Donation of Antiquities', *Journal of Financial Crime*, 23(1): 173–86.

Yates, D., Mackenzie, S. and Smith, E. (2017) 'The Cultural Capitalists: Notes on the Ongoing Reconfiguration of Trafficking Culture in Asia', *Crime, Media, Culture*, 13(2): 245–54.

Zaitch, D. (2002) 'From Cali to Rotterdam: Perceptions of Colombian Cocaine Traffickers on the Dutch Port', *Crime, Law and Social Change*, 38(3): 239–66.

Zhang, L., Messner, S.F., Liu, J. and Zhuo, Y.A. (2009) 'Guanxi and Fear of Crime in Contemporary Urban China', *The British Journal of Criminology*, 49(4): 472–90.

Zhang, S.X. and Chin, K.-L. (2011) 'Ants Moving Houses: Cross-Border Drug Trafficking in the Golden Triangle', in C.J. Smith, S. Zhang and R. Barberet (eds) *The Routledge Handbook of International Criminology*. Abingdon: Routledge, pp 237–47.

Zimbardo, P.G. (1970) 'The Human Choice: Individuation, Reason, and Order Versus Deindividuation, Impulse and Chaos', in W. Arnold and D. Levine (eds) *Nebraska Symposium on Motivation 1969*. Lincoln: University of Nebraska Press, pp 237–307.

Index

A
addiction, drugs 22
advertising 32, 41, 82–3
Afghanistan 23, 113, 126
Africa 21, 24, 26, 41, 72, 77, 96
  South 59, 68, 72, 102, 124
airline personnel 61
airlines 94
Albania 23
alien conspiracy theory 6
America 21, 24, 27, 41, 107
Angola 71, 72, 95
animals 56, 57, 62, 63, 65, 66, 69
anti-personnel landmines 98–9
anti-poaching 56
antiquities 90, 105–20, 126, 130, 133
antiquities dealers 16, 59, 114, 115, 116, 121
'ants' 100
Antwerp 73, 74, 77
anxiety 38, 130
appraisers 118
archaeologists 105, 116
archaeology 105, 107
Arizona 102
Armenian dealers 74
arms 76, 89–104, 123, 126
The Arms Bazaar 89
arms dealers 76, 91, 122
arms embargoes 92, 97
Arms Export Controls Act 1976 (US) 96–7
arms-for-diamonds deals 72
art crime database 112
art historians 118
art history 107
artisanal miners 80
Art Loss Register 112
Asia 24, 41, 57, 77, 107
Assad regime 92
auction houses 108–9, 111, 114
auctions 82, 109
auditing 81, 122
Australia 24, 58, 72
authoritarianism 89, 97
autocratic despotism 72
awareness raising 44–5

B
baggage handlers 61
Balkans 41, 102, 125
banality of evil 14–16, 17, 47, 132, 135
banking secrecy 3
bans, on trade from particular regions 110, 111
Barbary macaque traders 61
barter trade 125–6
BDB (Bharat Diamond Bourse) 77
Belgium 24
birds 58, 59–61
black market 76, 91, 98, 116
blood diamonds 71, 82, 86
  see also conflict diamonds
Bolivia 23, 60–1
border lockdown approaches 46–7
Botswana 72
Bout, Viktor 95, 97, 103–4
Branch Energy Limited 77
bribery 46, 59, 79, 90
British Virgin Islands 101
brokers, criminal 90
burden of proof 110–11
burglary 22
burner phones 33, 45
business, illicit 32–6, 69–70, 84–7, 134–5
business decision-making 118
business enterprise 99–104, 113–20
business ethics 11
business metaphors 8
business tool 102–3

C

Cali cartels 24
Cambodia 107
Cameroon 81
Canada 93
cannabis 23, 31
cartelitos 24
cartels 29
Caucasus 123
caviar 59, 61, 62, 65
Cayman Islands 101
Central Africa 21
Central African Republic (CAR) 80, 81
Central America 24, 107
Central Europe 24
certification system, diamonds 78–82
chattels, title claims 111–12
cheap labour 37, 42, 72
child labour 82, 83
children
  and consent 39
  and sex trafficking 37
China 24, 61, 96, 107, 111, 133
Chinese medicine 61
CITES (Convention on International Trade of Endangered Species of Wild Flora and Fauna) 62–3
Ciudad Juárez 24
civil wars 73
client confidentiality 108
'cloned' phones 33
cocaine 21, 23
'cog in the machine' arguments 10, 48
Cold War 91, 92, 95, 133
collectors
  antiquities 107, 110, 112, 115, 118
  firearms 102
  wildlife trafficking 57, 65, 66, 70
Colombia 23, 24, 27
colonialism 133–4
'the colonialism of weapons' 100
commodification 38, 49, 51, 53, 128–32, 135
communications technology 45
compartmentalization 8–15, 16, 17, 18, 86, 118, 129, 131
  and drug traffickers 35–6
  and human traffickers 47–8, 49–50
  and 'just business' 135
conflict 43, 67, 74, 77, 85, 90, 92
  and mixed export scheme 76
conflict diamond fence 16
conflict diamonds 71, 75, 80, 81, 84, 95, 121
  and arms trafficking 90, 126
  definition 73
  and human rights 72
  and Kimberley Process 78, 79
conservation 62, 67, 68, 133
conservators 118
conspicuous consumption 65, 66
consumer capitalism 130
consumer countries 22, 23
consumer desire 66, 67, 70, 85–6
control 28–30, 31, 44–6, 78–82, 96–9, 109–13
Convention on Stolen or Illegally Exported Cultural Objects 109, 110
Convention on the Means of Prohibiting and Preventing the Illicit Import, Export and Transfer of Ownership of Cultural Property 109, 110
corporate–military complex 77
corruption 23, 67, 72, 79, 82, 109
  and arms trafficking 90
  and human trafficking 46
corrupt officials 76
couriers 24, 94
crack 21, 22
crime control 2
  see also control
crimes of globalization 132–4
crimes of obedience 10
criminal brokers 90
criminal justice 22, 99, 100
cultural artefacts 102–3, 118
cultural capital 50, 51
cultural heritage 105, 107, 115
cultural property internationalism 115

customs forms 95
cut diamonds 74

D
Daesh 113
damage, artefacts 105–6
darknet 33
dealers 107, 110–11, 117, 120
deaths
 drugs 21, 22
 human trafficking 46–7
De Beers 73, 77, 82
debt bondage 40
decriminalization 31
demand-end interventions 21, 30, 99
Democratic Republic of the Congo (DRC) 71, 72
denial narratives 12, 85, 115, 116, 117, 122
depression 38
deprivation 42, 62
deregulation 2
desire, consumer 66, 67, 70, 85–6
destination countries 41–2, 44, 45–6, 51, 109
developed countries 57–8
developing countries 57, 63, 67, 68, 92, 107, 134
diamantairs 83–4
diamond lung 72
diamond pipeline 73
diamonds 71–87, 95, 121, 133–4
diamonds laundry 74
diamond smuggling 74, 76
Diamond: The History of a Cold-Blooded Love Affair 86
Diamond Trading Company 73
diamond trading exchanges 74
dictatorship 89, 97
differential association 6, 8–9, 17, 118
dirty collar crimes 60
disposable SIM cards, 33
distribution, drugs 22
domestic work 40, 42
donations, art 119, 120
drug dealers 31–2, 121–2
drug smugglers 25, 34
Drug Smugglers on Drug Smuggling 35
drug traffickers 24, 26, 33–4, 35, 41, 124
drug trafficking 21–36, 90, 93, 102, 123, 124, 126
Dubai 77

E
East Asia 24
Eastern Europe 41
economic capital 50, 51, 66
economic globalization 17, 51, 52, 132
economic inequality 85
economic migrants 19
economic status 130
economic wellbeing 106
ecosystems 55–6, 67
ecstasy 24
education campaigns 112–13
Egypt 107
Eichmann, Adolf 14, 15
electronic financial transfers 33
elephant ivory 61
encryption, file 33
endangered species 62
enforcement *see* law enforcement
environmental damage 55–6, 82
ethical accounting 49–50
ethic of care 11, 18
ethnic minorities 27–8
EU 41, 97
Europe 23, 24, 41, 57, 107
Europol 29
evil, banality of 14–16, 17, 47, 132, 135
exchange links 122, 125–6
Executive Outcomes 77
exotic birds 59–60
exotic game hunting 67
exploitation 38, 39, 50–1, 67, 134, 135
export certificates 78
export/import system 61, 69, 78, 79
export restrictions 109
exports, illicit 76, 110
extinction 62

F
facilitators 95, 118–19
fake paperwork 61, 79, 85, 94, 95
falcons 58
fauna 55, 57, 61, 62
fentanyl 21
file encryption 33
financial facilitators 119
financial investment goods 120
financial system, global 101–2
financial transfers 33
firearms 62, 90, 102
'the Firearms Protocol' 96
fixers 75, 95, 120
flora 55, 57, 61, 62
forced labour 37, 40, 82
formal economy 102
fortress conservation 133
front companies 95

G
galleries 114
game hunting 67
game parks 133
gecko 57
gender bias 51
girls, and sex trafficking 37, 38
global crime, compared with transnational 1
global financial system 101–2
global illicit market enterprise 6
global inequality 51, 132
globalization 1, 2, 3, 4, 5, 129, 130–1
  crimes of 132–4
  and drug trafficking 27, 32–3
  of indifference 17
  and travel 43
  and vulnerability 51–3
Global Witness 81
Golden Triangle 24, 41, 123
Greater Mekong 24
Greece 107
green criminology 55, 60
grey market 91, 106, 112, 118
guanxi 61
Guatemala 107
gun parts 93–4
gun runners 100

H
handguns 93
harm 10, 13, 14, 15, 17, 122, 135
  antiquities 105–7, 114–15
  arms 89–90, 103
  diamonds 71–2
  drugs 21–2, 31, 35–6
  human trafficking 37–8, 52
  wildlife 55–7
'harm agents' 3
hashish 123
heritage sites 105, 115
heroin 23
historical cultural heritage 105
historical knowledge 105, 106
HIV infections 22
Hồ, Tám 69
Hobbs, Dick 26
holiday travellers 26
holocaust 14
homo economicus 129
Hong Kong 77, 111
hot zones 41, 123
human rights 10, 44, 72, 81, 82, 99
human trafficker 16
human trafficking 37–53, 90, 123, 124
hunting 59, 68
Hutus 15

I
I-It 129, 131
illicit business 32–6, 69–70, 84–7, 121–2, 134–5
illicit diamonds 74
illicit economies 4
illicit exports 76, 110
illicit market 6, 71, 75, 76–7, 122
import–export system 61, 69, 78, 79
income inequality 5
India 26, 72, 74, 77, 82, 84, 107
Indian Directorate of Revenue Intelligence 82
indifference to suffering 17, 51

industrial nations 92
inequality 51, 62, 85, 132, 134
informal business 86, 93, 101, 122
informal economies 3–4, 38
insects 58
insecurity 68, 92
insider knowledge 108
instability 43, 77, 85, 89
institutional anomie theory 13
internalization, of group norms 117–18
international bans 110–11
international crimes 1, 8, 10
International Labour Organization 40
International Traffic in Arms Regulations 97
internet 44
Interpol 29, 112
Iran 92
Iraq 90, 107, 110, 113
ISIS 90, 113
Italy 107
I-Thou 129–30, 131
ivory 61

J
Jamaica 23
Japan 3
jewellery shops 72
Jewish families 74
Johannesburg 73
Jordan 107
'just business' 12, 16, 19, 86, 128, 135
  and human traffickers 47, 48, 50

K
khums taxes 113
'kif' 123
Kimberley Process Certification Scheme 78–82, 84–5
kingpins 24, 68
knock-on crime events 22

L
labour, forced 37, 38, 40
land evictions 68, 72
landmines 98–9
Laos 24
Laroche, John 66
Latin America 24, 27, 41, 107
laundering 79, 85, 101, 111, 112, 120, 121–2
  wildlife 60, 63
law enforcement 7, 45–6, 64, 95, 97, 123, 125
  drugs 23, 28–30
Lebanese dealers 74
ledger metaphor 49–50
legal business 2, 8, 27, 60, 121–2, 128, 135
legal international trade 2
legalization, drugs 31
legitimate labour 85
leisure class 130
leisure travel 26
Liberia 71, 72, 95
Libya 107
licences 59, 109
licensed/unlicensed diamond mines 74–5
limitation periods 111–12
lobbying 98, 110
local cultures of consumption 61
looters 105, 106, 120
looting 90, 106, 107–8, 113, 114, 115, 121
  denials of the victims of 116
loyalties, appeal to higher 49, 114–15

M
Machete Season 15
macro-level 9, 52, 120, 132
mafia 6–7, 24, 26, 29, 123–4
manufacturing 40
marginalization 68
market countries 109, 110
market-oriented crimes 1–2
market reduction approach 64–5
mass murder 14
means 39
Medellín cartels 24
medicines 57, 61

merchants of death 94
meso-level 9, 52, 85, 120, 132
metaphors of business 8
methamphetamine 23–4
Mexico 23–4, 41, 93, 107, 124
micro-level 9, 52–3, 85, 117, 120
Middle East 57, 58, 77, 107
middle-market 22
migrants 19, 42
military generals 80
military-grade weapons 93
Minin, Leonid 125
mining, diamond 72, 73, 74–5, 77, 80, 81
modern day slavery 40–1
money-in/diamonds-out processes 76
money laundering 32, 33, 42, 101, 120
morality 7, 12, 49–50, 69, 135
Morocco 23, 61, 123
Mugabe regime 81
mules 24, 29, 69, 84
multi-jurisdictional trade flows 2
multinational corporations 101
Mumbai 77, 84
Myanmar 23, 24

N

Namibia 72
narco-states 23
national parks 68
natural resources 67, 72, 75, 85, 105, 126, 134
  see also antiquities; diamonds; wildlife
neighbourhood crime 23
'neighbourhood dissembling' 80, 81
neo-colonial interventionism 100
Nepal 107
nepotism 34–5
Netherlands 24
networks 25, 121
neutralization 48, 49, 114–15, 119
New Psychoactive Substances (NPS) 34
New York 73
New Zealand 57–8
NGOs 78, 80–1
Nicaraguan Contras 93
Nigeria 26
North Africa 21, 24
North America 21, 24

O

Oceania region 24
office cleaning firms 42
office criminals 14, 15
offshore financial centres 101
opioid overdose deaths 21
opium 23
opportunistic trafficking 26, 59, 61, 85, 93
opportunity poaching 64
opportunity structure 28, 31
opportunity theorists 63–4
orchidelerium 66
organizational deviance 118
organized crime 1, 6, 9, 10, 24, 32, 118
  and wildlife trafficking 56, 60
organized crime groups 1, 74, 123–4
organized criminal 7
osprey 58
the Other 129, 133
'Othering' 117
Ottawa Convention 98–9
overdose deaths 21

P

Pakistan 107
Panama Papers 101
pangolin 69
parallel trafficking 123–4, 125
parrots 61
permit laundering 59
Peru 23, 60–1, 107
pets 57, 61
plants 56, 62, 63, 66
poachers 60–1
poaching 56, 58–9, 62, 64, 68, 90
police negligence 23
policing 64, 119

polishing, diamonds 72, 73, 77
polishing factories 74
political destabilization 43, 72, 85, 89
post-colonialism 134
post-traumatic stress disorder 38
poverty 62, 69, 74, 132, 134
prevention, drugs 21
private collectors 57
producer countries 22, 23, 24, 30
profit 16, 68, 126–7
'Program of Action to Prevent, Combat and Eradicate the Illicit Trade in Small Arms and Light Weapons in All its Aspects' 96
'pro-return' provisions 110
Protocol against the Illicit Manufacturing of and Trafficking in Firearms, their Parts and Components and Ammunition 96–7
The Protocol to Prevent, Suppress and Punish Trafficking in Persons, Especially Women and Children 39, 45
provenance 108–9, 111
pseudo-diamantairs 83–4
public relations 82–3
pull factors, trafficking 43, 98
push factors, trafficking 43–4

Q

Al Qaeda 113

R

racial injustice 21–2
railway personnel 61
rapes 72
rarity 70, 85–6
Reagan administration 92
recreational drugs 31
recruitment 42–3, 44
recycling and reuse 92
regulation 28–31, 62–4, 78–82, 96–9, 109–13
reptiles 57, 69
resource curse 67, 134
'respectable' world 91
responsibility, denial of 115–16
rhinos 56, 58–9, 64, 65, 68
Rif mountain region 123
Rio de Janeiro 102–3
risk, of detection 23, 24, 25, 29, 33, 124
  wildlife 60, 64, 69
robbery 22
rough diamonds 72, 73, 74, 77, 78, 81
routine activities theory 64
RUF (Revolutionary United Front) 71, 72, 77, 126
Russia 41, 58, 61, 72, 92, 97
Rwandan genocide 15

S

schizophrenia 8
security, heritage sites 113
seizures, wildlife 57
self-regulation system 81
self-stratification 13
sentencing dispositions 21–2
service industries 42
sex trafficking 37, 38, 46, 47, 50–1
sex work 41, 42
shadow economies 4–5
shadow facilitators 75, 95
'shadow world' 91
shipping 3, 61, 94, 95
Sierra Leone 71, 72, 76, 77, 80, 95, 126
  from a colonial to a post-colonial state 133–4
sightholders 73
SIM cards, disposable 45
situational crime prevention approach 63–4
slavery 40–1
small arms and light weapons (SALW) 96, 99
smugglers, drug 25
smuggling 39, 74, 76
  see also trafficking
social exclusion 62
social harm 35–6
  see also harm

social media 44
social responsibilities 126–7
social status 65, 130
see also status
soft power 100
source countries 72, 73, 106, 107, 110, 115, 116
South Africa 24, 59, 68, 72, 102
South America 24, 27, 41, 107
Southeast Asia 24, 107
Southern Africa 124
Soviet Union 95
specialist policing 64
spectrum of enterprise 6, 7, 8, 9, 19, 114, 127–8
and morally indifferent business 135
and recreational drugs 31
state negligence 23
state theft 109
statutes of limitation 111–12
stockpiles, weapons 91, 92, 95, 97, 98
stolen goods, mixed in with legal trade 113
stolen objects' databases 112
straw purchasers 93
street dealers 24
Strictly Reptiles 69
super fixers 75, 95
supply and demand 34, 40
supply-chain intervention approach 21
supply chain security 94
supply-side controls 30, 98, 99
Surat 72, 77, 84
sustainability 62, 67, 106
symbolic capital 66
symbolic status goods 102, 120
symbolic value 61–2, 66, 70, 82, 85, 103
synthetic drugs 21, 23–4, 33–4
Syria 90, 92, 107, 110, 113

T
Tajikistan 28–9
Taliban 113
tax avoidance 119–20
taxes 101, 113, 119–20
tax evasion 119–20
tax havens 101
tax lawyers 119–20
Taylor, Charles 72, 75, 76, 95, 125, 126
teenage labour 72
Tel Aviv 73, 74, 77
Thailand 24, 107
Thai-Lao border 50–1
thefts, diamonds 72–3
tigers 56, 65
timber 76
time–space distanciation 2
title claims 111–12
tour firm employees 61
tourism 42, 56, 67, 68
tracking mechanisms 98
traditional medicines 57, 61
trafficking 2, 7, 9
antiquities 90, 105–20, 126
arms 76, 89–104, 123, 126
diamonds 71–87, 95, 121, 133–4
drugs 21–36, 90, 93, 102, 123, 124, 126
human 37–53, 90, 123, 124
wildlife 55–70, 90, 113, 124
tramadol 21
transit countries 26, 30
transit links 122, 123–5
transit ports 111
translucent lie 50
transport companies 42, 61
trapping 69
treatment, drugs 21
trust 24, 33, 35, 61, 108, 122
tuatara 57
tuberculosis 72
Turkey 107
Tutsi 15

U
UK 26, 58, 107
Ukraine 92, 95
underbelly 4
underworld 4, 60
unemployment 43, 62

UNESCO *Convention on the Means of Prohibiting and Preventing the Illicit Import, Export and Transfer of Ownership of Cultural Property* 109, 110
UNIDROIT *Convention on Stolen or Illegally Exported Cultural Objects* 109, 110
UNITA 95
United Nations (UN) 34, 56–7, 79, 97
  General Assembly resolution 81
  International Drug Control Programme 29
  Program of Action/PoA 96
  security resolutions 110
UNODC (United Nations Office on Drugs and Crime) 22, 29, 34, 57
UNTOC (*United Nations Convention against Transnational Organised Crime*) 39, 45, 96–7
US
  antiquities 107
  and arms trafficking 92–3, 94, 96–7
  drugs 21, 24
  mafia investigations 6–7
  and Mexican border 41
  and wildlife trafficking 57
USSR 133

V
Van Nostrand, Mike 69
victimhood 116
victimization 45–6
victimless offences 115
violence 22, 33, 38, 53, 62, 68
  and diamonds 72, 81
vision impairment 72
vulnerability 38, 51–2

W
'the wandering weapons' 92
war economies 126
warranties, diamonds 81
wars 37, 73, 77, 81
wealth 3, 5, 67, 82, 105, 133
weapons 62, 76, 80, 90
West Africa 21
Western Europe 24
western interventionism 63
white-collar crime 6, 9, 10, 114, 117, 118
  and green crimes 55, 60
white-collar criminal 7
white rhino 68
wholesalers 22, 23, 73
Wildlife Crime Report 57
wildlife trafficking 55–70, 90, 113, 124
women
  commodification of 48–9, 51
  and sex trafficking 37, 38
working conditions, dangerous 38, 72, 83, 115
World Customs Organization (WCO) 29
World Diamond Council (WDC) 78, 79
World Drug Report 21
World Peace Foundation 71
World Wildlife Fund 56
WorldWISE 57

Y
Yemen 107

Z
Zimbabwe 81